CREATE ABUNDANT POSSIBILITIES

SEVEN STEPS TO MANIFEST YOUR DREAMS

WENDY MCARA

Copyright © 2024 by Wendy McAra

All rights reserved.

No part of this book may be reproduced in any form or by any electronic or mechanical means, including information storage and retrieval systems, without written permission from the author, except for the use of brief quotations in a book review.

The material in this book is intended for education. No expressed or implied guarantee of the effects of the use of the recommendations can be given nor liability taken. Most names have been changed to protect the privacy of individuals.

Text design and editing by *Meri France Publishing*.

Book cover design by Georgia Wilson, *The Drawing Room*.

Learn more at: https://www.wendymcara.com.au/

All rights reserved.

ISBN: 978-1-7638007-0-0

CONTENTS

Introduction   xiii

PART I

1. The 'How & Wow' of ScriptWriting   3
2. My First Script Changed My Life   9
3. How Does ScriptWriting Work?   15
4. How to Make Your Dreams Crystal-Clear   27
5. Scripting Success Stories   45
6. How to Become a Master of Scripting   63
7. What If Your Script Doesn't Materialise?   83
8. Together, We Can Create a Better World   93

PART II

Preface to Part Two   103
9. Free Yourself from Old Stories   107
10. Get to Know your Inner Child   131
11. Keeping Love Alive   149
12. Confidence   161
13. Unhook from Anxiety   183
14. Shift Depression   219

Epilogue   239

Resources   241
Acknowledgements   245

With gratitude for the support and encouragement of my husband, Peter, and my beloved children, Gina, Geoff and Michael, who are my inspiration and joy.

∽

PRAISE FOR CREATE ABUNDANT POSSIBILITIES

"*Create Abundant Possibilities* is like having a wise friend guide you through a process of transforming your life in the simplest way possible - by writing it into reality!

As a life coach and relationship expert, Wendy introduces the concept of ScriptWriting, a powerful and easy way to get clear on what you really want and bring it to life. Through captivating storytelling, you'll be taken on a journey as Wendy shares how, by committing her own dreams to paper, she was able to double her income and attract her dream partner. Alongside her story, you'll read about her clients' successes.

The book is filled with relatable examples and very practical tips to overcome limiting beliefs and habits that may be holding you back. Wendy makes it feel like you're getting advice from a good friend who really 'gets' you. The book is an inspiring, easy-to-follow roadmap for those ready to create a life filled with love, abundance and joy through the art of ScriptWriting.

Wendy provides a toolkit to build the life you dream of. She also explains the science behind why this works and how your brain is wired to make changes, no matter where you are in life. So, grab a pen and get ready to start scripting your dreams - because this book will show you that they really can come true!"

- **Paula Fenwick**, Keynote Speaker, and Author of *Bounce Back Fast* and *More LOVE at Work*

"Wendy's book is a treasure trove of experience and warmth. It's not just delightful and easy to read – it's a true page-turner. In her own words, '*The hero of the book is scripting. Script yourself not just a good future. Script yourself a GREAT future. If that is the possibility you imagine, you dramatically increase the odds that possibility becomes a probability.*'

But beyond the empowering nature of scripting, the book offers even more clear strategies to transform how you live. It's filled with compelling examples and practical exercises that guide you towards a deeply meaningful life, fostering contentment and nurturing fulfilling relationships. I recommend this book to everyone."

- **Julie-Anne Geddes**, Principal Psychologist, The Psychology Space

"In the words of Wendy McAra, *'What we focus on exerts a powerful influence on what we experience. There is no such thing as a thought, an expectation, a belief which doesn't matter, which doesn't have some influence on your life and on your world.'*

In her book, Wendy reveals how to focus your energy to fulfil your dreams through the gentle art of Scriptwriting. She is a soothing presence, respectfully engages, challenges and guides you to uncover your deep and hidden longings, and transform them into reality.

I loved this book. Through her transparency, life's experiences and professional training, Wendy walks beside you on your journey, creating a climate for your unique growth. The process unfolds clearly, logically, providing simple practical steps, enriched by warmth, real life examples and wisdom from researchers and leading thinkers.

The integrity of a person's philosophy is measured by how well it's demonstrated. Wendy is a beautiful embodiment of all she believes. You will not read her book and remain unchanged".

- **David Kerr**, Relationship and Family Therapist, Author *Wall of Tears* and *Out of Latvia*

"Wendy McAra's book, *Create Abundant Possibilities*, is just wonderful! Written with wisdom and love, it provides practical guidance as to how we might better manifest our lives. Her experience in a lifetime spent helping others in a professional capacity is evident in the heart-centred and caring way in which she takes us on a journey to a better life. Readers will not just come to an understanding of ScriptWriting, but, magically, will be introduced to many life changing concepts and practices. It will change people's understanding of their life story for the better and give them the tools to assist their growth. I can 'see' many 'Aha' moments from readers and the ripple effect of this teaching. I follow Wendy's guidance with much delight."

- **Tim Carter**, Author of *Journey To The Light*

"Wendy has written an inspirational and encouraging self-help book. She pulls together many years of study and experience of what has worked to transform the lives of clients in her psychology and life coaching practice. Her writing is engaging, and the stories she includes are fascinating. These moving and very convincing examples of successful outcomes provide 'how to' guidelines and give substance to the power of techniques she describes, such as ScriptWriting and deprograming of core identity blocks. The book exudes confidence that the insights and toolkit can help people overcome problems and change their lives. I am confident many readers will agree."

- **Lena Nordholm**, Senior Professor of Psychology, University of Boras, Sweden

"Wendy's book is truly sensational. It encapsulates what we've covered on my therapeutic journey with her. I was stuck in fear-based, crippling beliefs and thoughts of who I was and feelings of despair. With Wendy's help I have evolved and been able to embrace what I am. I have come into a greater sense of being. I've become more resilient and confident. I feel like I'm stepping into living more fully in my true nature, gifts and abilities. It's a daily practice of mind mastery and a higher self-awareness. I'd recommend this book to anyone wanting to experience more pleasure and fulfilment in life."

- **Leisa McMahon**, Teacher

"With a lifetime of personal experience and a long career as a psychologist and coach, Wendy has written a wonderful book that will change the life of anyone who follows the wisdom and guidance within. She has pulled together processes and exercises from a wide range of experts to create a unique approach to help the reader improve whatever aspect of their life they might want to change. The stories she relates offer compelling evidence that this approach works. As a therapist myself I am inspired by her methods and her clients' success in using them to overcome anxiety, depression, loneliness and relationship problems. Wendy's warmth, generosity and compassion in sharing her knowledge and skills with her readers shines through on every page."

- **Jan Hatch,** Gestalt Therapist and Somatic Experiencing Practitioner

"This is a fabulous book. I wholeheartedly recommend it. Coming from a deep love of her work, Wendy shares her extensive knowledge and experience as a psychologist. The book takes you on the touching and inspirational journeys she and her clients took as they learnt how to create and live their dreams.

Wendy speaks to and understands what holds people back from living what they long for. She provides answers and step-by-step guidance to show you how you too can overcome self-defeating thinking and behaviours to manifest your dreams. In her words, *'Having the choice to change is one of the greatest gifts of being alive.'*"

- **Jann Walsh,** Group Empowerment Trainer

"Wendy's book proves how helpful script writing can be to those seeking a way to improve a situation in their lives, whether it be a career path, a relationship or finding a better outcome in managing everyday life. Encouraging people to sit down and think about themselves, then considering & physically noting down positive outcomes which they'd love to achieve, is an incredible practice.

It's something we all should consider doing regularly to recalibrate our life's direction in a way that makes it possible for our dreams to come true."

- **Wanda Magill,** Teacher and Workshop Participant

"Wendy's book is a powerful and inspiring guide to creating a life filled with opportunity and fulfilment. Drawing from her extensive experience as a psychologist and life coach, she introduces readers to practical strategies like scripting and overcoming deep-seated mental blocks. What makes this book stand out is its warmth and accessibility- it's easy to follow yet profoundly insightful. Wendy offers readers a clear roadmap to personal transformation, a toolkit for change. Highly recommended for anyone looking to elevate their life."

- **Jane Monica-Jones,** Financial Therapist-SEP and Author *The Billionaire Buddha: Financial therapy for your bank balance*

"If you want MORE in your life - more connection, more joy, more physical, mental, emotional, financial or spiritual wellbeing - this book is for YOU.

In sharing powerful stories and practical tips from her own life and from the lives of those with whom she has worked, Wendy INSPIRES you, the reader, to 'go for it!' Her book provides you with the tools for getting MORE of what you WANT, and LESS of what you Don't Want in your life. Wendy believes in creating a better world, and is playing a significant role in creating one. Doing a workshop with her is a life-changing and heart-warming experience."

- **Carol Davis**, Workshop participant and life-long friend

"This is more than a book—it's a sophisticated yet remarkably accessible form of manifestation 'technology'. Its practical magic began working in my life even before I finished editing the manuscript. This transformative guidebook offers a unique approach to create the life that you've not only dreamed of, but maybe even beyond your wildest dreams!

Grounded in best-practice psychology and embedded in everyday experience, the book offers a powerful key to unlocking your infinite potential. Its writing is refreshingly clear and easy to follow, making personal transformation feel both achievable and enjoyable. Beyond mere theory, it provides a genuine blueprint for meaningful change. I will enthusiastically recommend *Create Abundant Possibilities* to all my friends—it's a truly remarkable read that can genuinely transform lives."

- **Meri France Harli**, Editor and Publisher

INTRODUCTION
CREATE THE LIFE YOU DREAM OF

Like you, I read and heard hundreds of stories as a child, most of which I never thought of again. Yet some stories stuck, especially this one: I was enchanted with the idea that fun, imagination and creativity can take us beyond ordinary reality.

In primary school, we were told the story of a radio weatherman who was always right. As the story goes, if he predicted a sunny morning, followed by rain in the afternoon, it would be sunny in the morning, followed by rain in the afternoon. If he predicted an overcast day with intermittent showers, clearing in the early evening, it was an overcast day with intermittent showers, clearing in the early evening.

The trouble was the weatherman was bored with always being right! Where was the fun in that?

One day, for a joke, he predicted it would rain jellybeans and chocolates. The people knew that was impossible and laughed when they read the prediction.

Imagine their (and the weatherman's) surprise when it rained jellybeans and chocolates. As children do, when they read fantasy books or see films like *'The Chronicles of Narnia: The Lion, the Witch and the Wardrobe'* or *'Charlie and the Chocolate Factory'*, I knew it hadn't really rained jellybeans and chocolates, but I felt the excitement and joy of

Introduction

creativity and possibility. Little did I realise what would open for me on this front as my life unfolded.

Years passed. My life went on from my school and university days, through teenage romances, career choices, marriage, and three beautiful children. Then came divorce.

Some people may be relieved to escape a miserable, desperately unhappy or even abusive marriage. Mine was neither disastrous nor miserable, but it wasn't sufficiently loving, happy or emotionally intimate for me to want to stay for life.

Nonetheless, I found divorce to be one of the most distressing experiences of my life. The consequences, for me, were unexpected and profound.

Being thrown into survival mode, questioning everything I had believed in and expected, catapulted me into the unknown, into exploring new options and possibilities. My new life started with attending a workshop that taught me how to make my dreams come true! While there I learned what I now call **ScriptWriting** – the solid gold foundation of this book.

Anyone can learn how to write a script which gives them what they long for. This book can take you by the hand and lead you along the path to a life of love, abundance and wellbeing.

I say this with confidence because I am living proof. I used what I teach in the book to manifest my own dreams. Dreams like 'scripting' husband number two into my life; like doubling my income in the space of one year.

As a relationship psychologist and life coach, I also have had the privilege of teaching clients - men and women from all walks of life - to manifest their dreams, whether it be finding their ideal partner, a great job, their dream home, whatever they long for. Teaching this has become my life's mission.

You may be like I was when I was introduced to ScriptWriting:

- Longing for a loving relationship where you feel appreciated, seen, respected, understood, loved by a partner you can love in return

Introduction

Or maybe you:

- Desire more from your career – more enjoyment, more satisfaction, more recognition, more success, more money
- Want to improve your health and wellbeing
- Have unfulfilled dreams and goals, like a home and lifestyle you'd love, better family relationships or great friendships
- Have short-term dreams for a new hobby or creative project
- Want to treat yourself to an adventurous, fun, or relaxing holiday
- Be at a transition in your life, taking exams, or exploring a new career, or course or training you'd love to do
- Be looking for more meaning and direction in your life
- Want to step up and fulfil your potential.

ScriptWriting expanded my vision beyond the horizons of what I believed was possible. It empowered me to go for a future I deeply desired! It can transform yours too, whatever **you are seeking.** This book can teach you how to harness possibilities, how to ask for, and manifest, dreams that seem unattainable from where you now stand. Example scripts in the book are rich in idea starters for possibilities you may not even have dreamt of.

The act of writing their script, following the simple directions in Chapter One, has been enough to help most of my clients manifest most of their dreams. That's what I love about ScriptWriting: it's simple, it's quick. Just do it, and your life is likely to change in ways you may have only dreamt of in your wildest dreams.

Once you've received what you scripted – having brought a romantic partner into your life, having manifested the job you longed for - you may well stop there. Or this could be the start of a journey of you falling in love, as I did, with infinite possibility, continuing to unlock your hidden potentials, year after year.

When my first script bore fruit, that ignited my desire for self-actualization. It gave me more mastery of my thinking, of my actions, of my power to create in my world. As you turn the pages, this book invites you to allow your hidden potentials to naturally emerge. It shares tips and strategies to help you overcome limitations you may have unintentionally soaked up through the role modelling of your family-of-origin, as well as through experiences in your childhood and beyond.

Part One teaches you the ins and outs of ScriptWriting, and how to make it work for you. Example scripts from real clients bring the theory to life. Their scripts may act as idea starters for you. They provide a range of scenarios, for example, what joyful, loving relationships, or rewarding, satisfying jobs look like for different people. These examples can literally seed ideas for inspirational changes and levels of happiness you may not yet have the insight or courage to imagine yourself living.

Part Two, the toolkit, shares the techniques, tips and the how-to of releasing limiting beliefs and bad habits that hold people back and sabotage them. It also provides touching vignettes of extraordinary changes made by my clients as they did the work to identify and shift limiting beliefs and core identity blocks which had been standing in the way of their fulfilment in the past.

I needed to do some of that work myself to maximise and maintain the success of the changes I brought into my life. For example, I learned how to manage issues which arise in intimate relationships better than I had done in my first marriage.

Exciting new research into the neuroplasticity of the brain confirms our brains are malleable and can change. Even as we get older, we can make significant changes for the better to our personalities, our relationships, and our lives. If I can make changes, if my clients can, so can you!

Having the choice to change is one of the greatest gifts of being alive. Will you take it?

The Law of Attraction and quantum physics, outlined briefly in this book, explain how the magic of ScriptWriting works.

Learn how to let what you dream of be inspired by your highest and most noble intentions and potentials. Your most heart-centred intentions will align with and guide you to live consciously from love, generosity and optimism, rather than living unconsciously, reacting from fear, lack and pessimism. Living from your highest potentials will literally change your personality, your life and your impact in our shared world.

Introduction

Possibilities become unlimited when we step past our limiting beliefs. There are mysteries to be explored and magic to be discovered as we do so. It was this that William Shakespeare alluded to when he put these words into Hamlet's mouth all those centuries ago:

> *'There are more things in Heaven and Earth, Horatio*
> *Than are dreamt of in your philosophy.'*

Shakespeare was suggesting human imagination is limited. There are things we don't know, things that haven't been discovered, things we haven't even dreamt of.

In the pages which follow, together we will investigate some of these *'mysterious things'*, so that your life can expand in mind-blowing and miraculous ways. We will find empowering opportunities and solutions to what have previously seemed insoluble problems.

Thank you, dear clients, for letting me use your stories. Thank you for your honesty, for your vulnerability, and for applying the techniques, tips and guidance in your own lives, to manifest your dreams. I've changed names and key characteristics to protect privacy, but the words are those which these clients spoke as they battled demons like those many of us face during difficult times. The words which express their delight when their dreams come true are theirs too.

I hope you'll love these people as much as I do, and that their stories touch and inspire you. I hope you, too, will create the happiness you not only deserve, but which is patiently waiting for you to claim it.

Wendy

PART I

BEGIN YOUR JOURNEY
OF POSSIBILITY

1

THE 'HOW & WOW' OF SCRIPTWRITING
THE SEVEN STEPS

A certain December day is burned into my brain.

My first marriage was over. I was a worried single mum. I felt insecure, I doubted myself. I felt like I was revisiting my teens. I feared I'd never be happy again. It was day three of a four-day personal development workshop called *'Future Pace'* presented by life coach Mahni Dugan. I was one of twenty participants. All I was interested in was how I'd find the man of my dreams. A dear friend had encouraged me to take the course. "Just do it," she said. I trusted her. And I needed help. So, I enrolled.

On days one and two each of us told our stories, did exercises to identify our inner critic, our strengths, our dreams, our fears. We laughed, we cried, we bonded. Then we learnt ScriptWriting. The reason it's burned into my brain is that what I learned that day transformed my life.

What do I mean when I say transformed my life? In that first script I wrote that I was living with the man of my dreams, and we were deeply in love. I also wrote that I'd doubled my billings. Within a year, both had come true. And that was just the beginning. Years of being committed to creating yearly scripts for the many changes I desired has delivered me dream after dream.

What I find even more encouraging is that as a workshop presenter, psychologist and life coach, I have watched with joy as many people have used ScriptWriting to meet their dream partner, get the promotion or job they love, dramatically increase their income, find inner peace. Their successes confirmed that I was onto something important: it's simple to learn, it's easy to use, and it **works**.

There are many examples in the book of dreams clients have scripted, and manifested. I invite you to use these stories to inspire more expansive ideas for your own scripts and bring you what you dream of.

Walk with me on my journey and learn how to take your own journey of transformation. The tools I share are hugely powerful. The empowerment they bring is invaluable.

What is it that you long for? Where are the greatest gaps in your life? Helping people like you move past their limitations, learn better ways of getting their needs met and fulfilling their dreams, is my business. This book is the culmination of my desire to share this gift with as many life adventurers as possible.

What is a Script?

A script is your opportunity to let your imagination flow, express what you long for, then claim it **as if it has already happened**.

Write a date up to a year ahead at the top of Page 1; write the year ahead in the past tense, as if it has already happened; make it so positive it exceeds your dreams of what's possible, and cover **every area** of your life - relationships, health and fitness, career, finances, family, friendships, and so on.

This is how the first paragraph of my first script looked:

31 December 1996

In October, I met the man of my dreams. He was tall and lean and into exercise. He was nice looking and well dressed. Divorced, with two children. We got on like a house on fire. We just liked each other from the first moment.

He was confident, friendly, with a good sense of humour – well educated, in a good professional job, financially independent. He had done his share of personal development work. He was emotionally mature, easy-going, well balanced, with good social and communication skills and good mental health.

We're both committed to a growth-oriented relationship, and open to listening and responding to each other's wants and needs in a mature, adult way. We found each other very attractive, and our relationship soon blossomed into one of great love, affection, sexual compatibility, respect, mutual care, trust, support, fun, laughter and joy.

We started dating the week we met, and he moved in with me two months later. They were the happiest months of my life. From the moment he met my children, he and they clicked. My relationship with his children has been equally good.

My script then went on to detail how fabulous the other parts of my life had been. The results I got that year were so rewarding, I've written a script every year of my life since then.

Scripts can cover not only the year ahead, but they can also focus on short-term projects or events. Anything and everything can be the subject of a short-term script: applying for a new job, an important interview coming up, going on a date, planning a holiday, arranging a party, building, buying or selling a house.

An example:

'The advertising campaign for our house was pitched exactly right. It drew the viewers who were really interested in and cashed up to buy a house like ours. It sold within weeks. Two parties fell in love with it. They kept outbidding each other, to the point that we received a figure in the multi-millions. We were thrilled with the outcome. We have moved into our new house. It's just perfect for us.'

The date at the top of a short-term script might be a week or month or two after what you're planning, to allow you to write in the past tense about how it went, and some of the outcomes that followed on.

For example, if the party is to be held on June 30, 2025, you might head the page July 31, 2025. The principle is the same for short and long-term scripts: Describe the experiences as though they **exceeded your wildest dreams**.

I recommend you write a script for the year ahead, and add short-term supplementary scripts, as the need arises. It's worth writing a script every year, as I still do.

Some people are not used to expecting good things to happen. I've even heard clients say that they don't let themselves imagine good things because they are superstitious this could jinx them.

If you feel doubtful about claiming love, or earning a lot of money, or being happy, you'll find chapters in Part Two help you shift such doubts. They show you how you can reframe any limiting beliefs, and how to transform your inner child, your inner critic, your core identity blocks that place a glass ceiling on what you think is possible.

In addition to teaching you the skills of ScriptWriting, this book provides psychological guidance and life coaching to help you break old self-sabotage patterns and dispel the fear that nothing will change. It coaches you to live with an openness to possibility.

The Seven Steps of ScriptWriting

Your script is your written blueprint for the year to come. There are a few simple rules. The next chapters show you how you can infuse your script with life and positive intentions.

WRITING YOUR SCRIPT

- **Step One:** Hand-write a date up to a year ahead at the top of the page. (Later I'll explain why you use hand writing instead of typing on a keyboard.)
- **Step Two:** Write the year as if it has **already happened**, in other words, in the past tense.
- **Step Three:** Be specific where possible. Don't write '*I earned more this year.*' That could be only a dollar more! Instead write, '*I am now on an annual package of $xxx,xxx.*'
- **Step Four:** Be highly positive. In my first workshop, I scripted that I doubled my billings that year. Ridiculously ambitious? Maybe, but we were told to make our scripts highly positive. I doubled my billings that year! Shoot for the stars. This is the kind of possibility that the most satisfying dreams are made of.
- **Step Five:** Cover every area of your life. Career, intimate

relationships, your health, your fitness, your family life, your spirituality, etc.
- **Step Six:** Clarify your dream by identifying what's really important to you as described in Chapter Four.
- **Step Seven:** At the end of your script, add, *'I choose this, or something even better, for the greatest good of all concerned.'* Coming from an open and generous heart opens more doors and is aligned with a win-win mindset. Then sign your script, and date it with the date you're writing it.

Tips for Manifesting Your Dreams

- **Ask yourself this question:** "What if the first step I can take to make my dreams a reality?" Just let the answer come to you. Maybe something like, 'Say "hello" to that guy in the coffee shop.' Or, 'Join the debating society.' Or, 'Apply for that job.' THEN TAKE THAT STEP. In the words of German poet and philosopher, Goethe, *'Whatever you do or dream you can do, begin it. Boldness has genius, power and magic in it.'*
- **Practice gratitude:** You are like a tuning fork. If you let yourself dwell on emotions like anger, resentment, guilt, sadness, regrettably you'll attract people and experiences vibrating at that level. To maximize the likelihood that your dreams become your reality, **cultivate a mindset of gratitude and graciousness. Every morning, think of three things for which you are grateful.** It could be a kind friend, a beautiful coffee, blossoms on a tree. This is an essential baseline for masterful dream manifestation. In the words of Deepak Chopra, *'Gratitude isn't just a feeling. It's a frequency. A portal. A quiet 'Yes' unlocks the power, creativity and wisdom of the universe.'*
- Insofar as this is possible for you, write your script with a **lightness of being and an openness to possibility**. Write it not from your head and your logic, but from your heart, with an energy of allowing and freedom. I write my scripts

almost with the innocence of a child, **asking, allowing, and letting go**.

Now, put it away in a drawer, and look at it at the end of the year.

If you're writing a short-term script, the same rules apply, though the date will be in the short-term future, and you'll probably restrict what you're scripting to only one or two areas of your life.

It's that simple.

It doesn't matter if you're wordy, using descriptive phrases and writing whole paragraphs, or you use bullet points.

Be aware, you can't choose for someone else. You can't script your daughter or son into a loving relationship or a great job. You can't script your husband into doing things he dislikes. That's interfering in the life path of another. All you can do is script the quality of your relationship with others – like being cooperative, loving, trusting, respectful.

2

MY FIRST SCRIPT CHANGED MY LIFE
MY FIRST (FABULOUS!) SCRIPT

My first script changed my life.

When I was hurting and single again, I was frightened I'd never meet anyone worthwhile, let alone the love of my life.

I knew the script I wanted to write would focus on my love life. But the ScriptWriting instructions advised we include **every area of our lives**. There clearly was more to my dreams than being in a loving relationship.

At the time I was a partner in a successful boutique marketing research consultancy firm. I was also a doting single mother of a daughter and two sons whom I loved dearly – still do. I valued my friends and social life; I played tennis and went to the gym. Health and family were important to me.

The headlines of that script were:

December 1996 (a year after the date I wrote the script)
 1. In October, I met the man of my dreams (see page 4).
 2. Business went amazingly well for me. I attracted new clients and doubled my billings this year.
 3. Future Pace opened a door for me. I did three other workshops under the Future Pace umbrella. My confidence, my self-esteem, my happiness, improved dramatically. I have learned so much about my

thinking, my communication style, my old fears and self-sabotage patterns and behaviours. I've reframed limiting beliefs, and I've made significant changes for the better. My wisdom and inner peace have expanded exponentially. I feel like my spiritual journey is progressing even better than I could have hoped for.

4. I have stuck conscientiously to a program of three visits a week to the gym, and I'm in good shape and great health. My body is trim and strong, and I'm looking good. My new partner really loves my look and pays me lots of compliments, which I lap up.

5. I made a couple of lovely new friends through these workshops, people on the same page as I am, and my social life has been enjoyable and rewarding.

6. The kids have been doing well, happy at school and at home. They have been spending every second weekend with their dad. They went on a great holiday with him last school holidays. They seem to be handling the co-parenting arrangements pretty well. They get on well with his new partner. Both their dad and I have been very careful to say only positive, respectful things about each other, and we've been co-operative about the logistics of co-parenting and finances.

And of course, I ended with *"I choose this, or something even better, for the greatest good of all concerned.'*

21 December 1995 Wendy Bloom

*Note: I specified meeting my new partner in October, even though I wrote the script in the previous December. I did this because I thought I would need most of the year to identify and release my baggage, improve my relationship communication skills, learn how to set better boundaries and re-build the self-confidence and self-esteem damaged by my divorce. I hoped that by October, I'd be a wiser, more self-loving, empowered me. It was the wiser me that I wanted to take into my dream relationship.

How my First Script Changed my Life:

I met the man of my dreams

In February 1996, I attended a follow-up meeting of past attendees of Future Pace programs. At the end of the meeting a man sought me out and started chatting. He asked for my phone number. As we said our goodbyes, he said *'Don't expect to hear from me for several months. I'll be working overseas.'* In October, the phone rang. Two months later, he moved in with me. A year later, we married. He was tall and lean and into exercise. Nice looking and well dressed. Divorced, with two children, etc. etc. – just like the script specified. We've been happily married ever since.

Like everyone else, we've had our ups and downs, because that's what happens when work and other stresses impact intimate relationships. When we've hit a down patch, we've seen a couples counsellor and embraced change to make our marriage even better.

I doubled my billings
In June I was invited to speak at the Pan-Pacific Marketing Congress in Sydney. My topic was advertising campaigns I had tested: *How to Choose Greyhounds, Not Lame Dogs.* I picked up two of Australia's biggest pharmaceutical companies as new clients – **and doubled my billings that year.** I'd have to say I was knocked out by the success of this particular script. It seemed like a miracle!

I was so impressed that since then, I've written a script every year of my life. I have also written short-term scripts when a special project was in the pipeline. I'm both grateful and delighted to say that I keep getting just about everything I ask for in my scripts.

The icing on the cake
The crowning glory for me happened in 1998 when I scripted that we sold our market research company.

My husband Peter and I were holidaying in Africa, staying at Chobe Lodge in Botswana. The lodges were beautiful Moorish Adobe architecture in a game reserve on the beautiful Chobe River.

Ours was the suite where Elizabeth Taylor and Richard Burton had stayed when they celebrated their re-marriage.

Every dawn and dusk, we'd climb into Land Rovers and be driven around the game park, enchanted by chattering monkeys, elephants, herds of springboks, and prides of lions.

Since the recent death of one of my business partners, I had flirted with the idea of selling the company and working less.

As we lounged in deck chairs sipping our cocktails on our last evening in Africa, I said to Peter, "Let's write a script for the year ahead."

We had an agreement to roughly align our scripts to ensure that one wasn't working hard at home while the other holidayed overseas.

"I'm going to script that we sell the company," I said. "I want two bidders."

The only company I knew of which had a similar mix of consumer and pharmaceutical business is Taylor Nelson in the UK. (I'd heard of them because one of my pharmaceutical clients in Australia had shared a Taylor Nelson report for their UK parent company).

"I guess if no one's approached us by the end of the year, I might get in touch with Taylor Nelson." We flew home to Australia the next day, January 26, 1996.

I duly wrote the script, including the dollar value I wanted for my share of the company, and of course, I also scripted every other area of my life for the year to come – health, fun, social life, etc.

This may seem hard to believe, but two weeks later, as I sat at my office desk, the phone rang.

"You don't know me. My name is Tony Cowling. I'm the managing director of Taylor Nelson in the UK. I've heard about you. I'm in Australia for a week and I'd like to meet you."

As he was on his way across the Sydney Harbour Bridge in a cab, I scribbled a quick script: *'Love at first bite. He offered to buy the company.'*

That meeting was truly amazing. This phlegmatic Englishman lit up like a Christmas tree. He explained that they wanted to buy a company in Australia. It was early evening, but Tim Lenehan, one of my business partners, was still around, so I invited him to join us. We were all on the same page and agreed to start exchanging documentation, with a view to a sale.

A week later I was on an industry function boat cruise where I met a man who had just sold his company.

I asked him, "What are the pros and cons? We've just had a nibble."

The next day the company that had bought his business phoned. "We believe you're on the market. We want to buy you."

Remember, I had scripted there were two bidders? We didn't wait for Taylor Nelson to touch base with us. We sold to the second company. And I received exactly the amount of money I had asked for in my script.

Later, when I reviewed that script, the one I'd scribbled on the day of Tony Cowling's visit, it said *'offered to buy the company'*, not *'**bought the company'**.* And that's exactly what happened. Taylor Nelson offered, but didn't buy.

Be careful about the words you use in your scripts. Words are powerful. This is a very important distinction, discussed more fully in Chapter Nine where we explore how to free yourself from old, self-limiting stories.

Aligning Your Script with Your Partner's

If you're married or living with a partner, or you have someone in your life you see on a regular basis, it makes sense to give each other a bit of a heads-up about your key intentions for the upcoming year. As I see it, this doesn't need to be in fine detail, nor cover every aspect of your life.

When I told my husband of my intention to put the company on the market, I felt it was important that he be aware of my plans. I anticipated that if the company did change hands, it would probably lead to longer hours at work during the buy-out period of the contract. I wouldn't be available for extended holidays during that time, which wouldn't have sat well with him if he was hoping to take the year off and travel! It's a matter of taking each other's needs and plans into account.

Imagine if one of you is, say, contemplating enrolling for a university degree. This would mean a major time commitment, significant ramifications for your joint activities and responsibilities, including your social life, child-minding and household chores.

If you're planning on something which could affect your home life and shared responsibilities, like further education, a change in career, or taking up a new hobby, it could be beneficial to talk it through with your partner. If you don't see eye to eye on a big life decision like that, you may need to negotiate a reasonable way forward – a compromise.

Even if it means agreeing to disagree, communicating respectfully, and understanding each other's views, values, and what is non-negotiable for each of you, will increase trust, harmony and cooperation. And it could save you an acrimonious falling out down the track.

Taking time to talk with your partner about your goals and dreams makes your relationship flow better. It helps you both maintain connection. You don't want to end up years down the track, having drifted apart, going your own way, not really considering each other, feeling alone in your relationship. Sharing and talking about things important to both of you breeds a healthier, closer, more emotionally intimate relationship.

That said, your partner may or may not be interested in writing a script and may or may not be interested in and supportive of your ScriptWriting. Be open-hearted and open-minded to their choice and respond accordingly. Don't let their non-interest in ScriptWriting deter you from writing yours. It is still worth talking about your goals and intentions in a general way, given that more communication and connection between you is better than less.

Earlier, I pointed out a sacred rule of ScriptWriting: **you cannot choose for another**, whether it be your partner, your child, your parents, or your boss. That is interfering in the life path of another soul, which is a spiritual no-no. You cannot write a script for someone else.

However, you can suggest to them what you would like - provided you do so respectfully, without an intention to control or force them to do or see things your way. Here, we're entering the complex territory of relationship skills, good communication, and setting healthy boundaries.

As a 'second-time-arounder', I've traversed this path myself as I sought help to learn and change whatever had contributed to the break-up of my first marriage. I then went all the way and became a couples counsellor. You'll learn more about relationship communication in Chapter Eleven where we explore how to develop better relationship skills, which contribute to greater harmony and happiness all round.

∽

3

HOW DOES SCRIPTWRITING WORK?
THE MECHANICS OF MANIFESTATION

Writing the year ahead as if you're already living your dream, and then having that come true seems pretty magical and mysterious, doesn't it? What could possibly explain how that works?

I have always been a results-oriented, proof-of-the-pudding type of person. By that I mean that if something works, I do more of it, even if I don't understand how it's working. Conversely, if something creates problems, or gives me results I don't like, I stop doing it.

I certainly took great notice of the fact that my first script delivered my new husband and a huge increase in my earnings directly into my lap.

ScriptWriting's track record of delivering my dreams on cue, as scripted, and then delivering dreams for so many of the people I've taught scripting to, was more than enough to convince me I was onto something big!

It made me a convert. I didn't know how the magic happened. That didn't matter to me, as long as scripting kept on delivering. However, for those who want to understand how this could possibly work, there is a growing body of evidence which explains the mechanics of tools like scripting and visualising your ideal future.

The Law of Attraction

The Law of Attraction is a major underpinning of teachings of the billion-dollar personal development industry. And for good reason because it accounts for the effectiveness and power of ScriptWriting.

The essence of the Law of Attraction is the principle that **like attracts like**—as championed in the phenomenally successful book and film, *'The Secret'* by Rhonda Byrne. Whatever you focus on, and appreciate, is what you get more of. This means that if you focus on:

- The good stuff, like love, or kindness, or generosity, or happiness, or care and connection with others,
- Or the unhappy stuff, like resentment, or lack, or loneliness, or sadness,

...then that's what you'll get more of.

How does this look in your day-to-day life?

Take Tess. She's somebody who goes around feeling lonely, regretting she doesn't have a partner, feeling envious and resentful of friends and colleagues who seem to be happily married while she's alone.

The confronting news is that she's unconsciously holding in place the very thing she most wants to change. It's as though she's telegraphing the universe on a daily basis that she's lonely, miserable and lacks love. So that is what keeps showing up for her. Just the opposite of what she says she wants!

> **The solution is to start focusing on what you DO want, instead of dwelling on what's missing – which is what you <u>don't</u> want.**

According to the Law of Attraction, when you focus on any love and happiness that already exists in your life, more love and happiness start showing up.

If you decide to work on changing your inner world of thoughts and feelings, then your outer world – what you experience day-to-day — changes accordingly.

Create Abundant Possibilities

When you're stuck in your story (in this case, **'I'm alone, I'm lonely, I'm unlucky in love'**) you are viewing your life from the **past** rather than from the **future**.

You are focusing on what's missing in your life, reinforcing problems and the misery of your current situation, and in so doing, creating more of the same.

What you're not doing is making room for some different, **new possibility** to show up. This is why, even if your current reality is that you are lonely, resentful, frightened you'll never find love, I strongly recommend that you start imagining yourself in a happy relationship and being happy for people in loving relationships.

At the same time, focus on, and be grateful for whatever is good in your life. This could be a secure job, good health, a close relationship with your mother or your sister, a beloved dog or cat, the beauty and magic of nature.

Perhaps you can set an intention to be kind, encouraging and helpful to others, volunteering, joining an interest group and expanding your connections with others. The more you radiate love and light in your world, the more you will draw this to yourself.

Your Thoughts Act like a Tuning Fork

The universe doesn't recognise the words when you say or think what you desire and need. What it responds to is your energy, the frequency of your vibration, your **vibe**.

If you are vibrating at a frequency of love, generosity, self-respect, happiness, you will attract experiences and people that support that frequency.

Conversely, if you're vibrating at a frequency of fear, anger, resentment, jealousy, shame, sadness or scarcity, the experiences and people you'll draw to you will be at that frequency.

Just as you need to be careful to choose the radio station which offers the programs and music you like, you need to be careful to transmit the energy or frequency you would like in your life.

Because it's invisible, energy, 'frequency' or 'rate of vibration' may not be easy to believe in. Think of this as being similar to the invisibility of electricity. Even though we don't see electricity we know it's running because we see the results when we plug into it. Similarly, we don't see the air we breathe, but we're breathing it and it's keeping us alive.

Allow yourself the gift of being open to **abundant possibilities**.

When your inner knowledge is awakened, you can unlock yourself from the matrix of limitation you may have placed around yourself. By harnessing possibility – the possibility you can script joy and fulfilment into your life - the energy you carry can shift from shut down and doubtful to open and hopeful, drawing positive energy, positive experiences to you.

Please be clear, I'm not suggesting you sweep your problems under the rug, pretending they don't exist - that's known as 'spiritual bypassing' and can result in the situation coming back even bigger or more dramatic than before. Instead, write your script for what you **want** and take the very real and grounded **actions** that can support you in moving forward.

The next chapter, Chapter Four introduces you to your **values**. It will help you identify what you long for in your life, like love or companionship, or a new career opportunity.

Say you're working on relationship:

- You'll be led to clarify your requirements for an ideal relationship.
- You'll identify and confirm what is truly important to you – e.g., kindness, fun, good communication skills, understanding, admiration, adventure etc. to **give you clarity on your ideas** of what would make you happy in a relationship.
- Next step, you'll imagine yourself in a relationship where all that is present.
- Then you'll 'install a picture' in your mind's eye of you in that relationship – your future self, waiting for you in your future.
- This will lay down a new pathway in your neurology. It will become your tuning fork, a higher emotional frequency, signalling the universe what to deliver.

What we experience in our lives is the out-picturing (mirroring on the outside the ideas and pictures we make on the inside) of the 'stories' we tell ourselves, our beliefs of what is likely or possible.

I fervently believe that doing this relationship values exercise in my between-marriages phase is one of the ways I made my relationship dream come true. The landscape looked bleak in terms of desirable, available men.

Nevertheless, every night I imagined myself being happy with the sort of man who appeals to me. Mine might be tall and lean, yours might be medium height and muscular.

According to the Law of Attraction, imagining myself being loved and happy, as though I already was loved and happy, was what worked to draw love to me. My script that I had met Mr Right and was in a loving relationship, in tandem with visualising myself happily married, proved a winning combination.

Just as it has worked for many of the people I've taught this to, it allowed each of us to script a new future, a new story, a new destiny for ourselves.

The World of Quantum Physics

Understanding the Law of Attraction and how your script could deliver the life you long for taps into the realm of **quantum physics**.

Quantum physics is a highly reputable branch of science, developed by famous scientists like Albert Einstein, Niels Bohr, Werner Heisenberg and Max Planck. It explores and explains the very nature of matter and energy at the atomic and subatomic level.

If you want a glimpse into the field of quantum physics, I found this plain English explanation from Alex Chen in https://www.weeklywisdomblog.com/:

> *'The observer effect shows that when an observer focuses attention on any one location of the energy cloud, the electron will appear there. If there is no observer, then the electron returns to being non-physical energy spread across the whole energy cloud. The conclusion is that our focused thought*

> *causes wave energy to condense there and become matter. This is the link between thought and matter.*
>
> *Just as an atom's nucleus is surrounded by a non-physical electron cloud, all of us are surrounded by a non-physical field of infinite energy. Quantum physics calls it the **quantum field**. And just like an electron manifests out of that energy cloud, all of your physical universe manifests out of the quantum field.'*

The quantum physics of manifestation has discovered that our thoughts are **electric**, and our emotions are **magnetic**.

Together they represent an electromagnetic field around our bodies. Our electromagnetic field is always communicating with the quantum field. Heady stuff, isn't it? Our thoughts and emotions are **right now** manifesting our current reality – yours and mine.

The Law of Attraction explains that if we change our electromagnetic field (by changing our thoughts and emotions) then we will attract a new reality from the quantum field.

The story we tell ourselves about life, about ourselves, our expectations and beliefs, the very words we use, directly influences what we experience and what shows up in our lives.

Dr Joe Dispenza is a best-selling author and teacher of possibility made famous by the film, *'What the Bleep Do we Know?'*

He has amassed a decade of scientific evidence for all kinds of life changes, including the healing of several physical conditions experienced by many of his followers. Transformations in their health have correlated with measurements of changes in their cellular metabolism, gene expression and immune regulation.

In his words, '*A cornerstone of this work is (that) your personality creates your personal reality. Therefore, when you change, or your personality changes, your life changes. To create something new in our lives – or arrive at a new future – we must first change ourselves- mastering ourselves to create a new reality from unlimited possibilities... The healing journey begins when we overcome our limitations, open our hearts, and experience a new future as if it is already ours... We learn to intentionally create states of being that unlock hidden potentials.*'

ScriptWriting and visualising a desirable, happy future are simple-to-use tools to unlock such hidden potentials, to access new and unlimited possibilities.

Depending on your philosophy and openness to spirituality, you could view your script as a kind of prayer. The Bible says, *'Ask, and it will be given to you; seek, and you will find; knock, and it will be opened to you.'*

Many powerful teachers and presenters currently strutting the world stage are emphatic that **igniting the magic to manifest dreams involves quantum physics** - teachers like Dr Jean Houston, Eckhardt Tolle, Neale Donald Walsch, Sai Maa, Dr Deepak Chopra, Dr Claire Zammit, Marci Shimoff, and Marianne Williamson.

In the world of manifesting, this entails turning towards and co-creating with your higher power.

Whether you call it the Quantum Field, Source, Universal Flow, Spirit, Divine Intelligence, Your Higher Self, God, The Beloved, Buddha, Allah, or something else is up to you.

What Thoughts and Possibilities Are You Choosing?

As we move through the different stages of our lives, there are many possible options, and we are faced with an infinite number of decisions and choices.

At every stage, there are many scenarios which could materialise. In our innocence and naivety, we often fail to realise, at a conscious level, that every choice will lead us along a certain path, opening and shutting different doors.

- Should I be a good kid, or a rebel?
- Should I be friendly with this kid at school, or that one?
- Should I study hard and get the best grades I can, or goof around?
- Should I sleep all day and party all night, or join the early rising 5am club?
- Should I choose these subjects or those, this career path or that?

- Should I go for a more responsible, better paid job or stay put?
- Should I ignore the red flag when my boyfriend yells and swears at me, or break up with him now?
- Should I give in to my impatience and anger and scream at my children, or my partner, or should I take a deep breath and be compassionate and respectful? Should I choose connection or separation?

We have free will to choose any of the above, and other possible options. We have the ability to do any of these things, live any of many possible stories, follow many possible paths – and infinitely more.

The critical thing to realise is that by choosing to do one thing, we are effectively choosing **not to do another**. In each and every moment, we are making a choice. A sobering thought! In economic terms it's known as 'opportunity cost'. When you invest your energy or resources in one direction, they are not available for something else.

Dr Joe Dispenza explains '*Your past shortfalls can be traced, at their root, to one major oversight: you haven't committed yourself to living by the truth that your thoughts have consequences so great that they create your reality.*'

This is a book about creating abundant possibilities.

It aims to:

- Help you become conscious that there are many possibilities, including possibilities you haven't dared dream of, and,
- More especially, to help you choose the most empowered thoughts and options possible for yourself.
- (Part Two shows you how to reverse limiting beliefs and core identity blocks like *'I'm alone'* or *'I don't deserve good things'*, or *'I'm not good enough to do really well in life.'* But we'll come to that later.)

Fight-or-Flight Hardwiring Undermines Relationship Harmony

It is critically important to be aware that, left alone, the unconscious mind is primed to fire off the fight-or-flight response. This response is rooted in fear and anxiety, hard-wired into us. We inherited this response from our early hunter-gatherer caveman ancestors, fending for themselves in a dangerous environment.

In those days, this was very useful. It determined whether they fought the woolly mammoth, ran away, or huddled down and froze. Unfortunately, this can be more of a liability than an asset in our current life circumstances.

Thankfully, we are rarely faced with the danger of the size and shape of woolly mammoths. But the fight-flight-freeze-fawn response to protect us can easily kick in when we're triggered by upsetting day-to-day situations in our current lives, for instance, when we are criticised, rejected, yelled at, or ignored.

These are not life threatening in the way triggers were for our ancestors. Yet by kicking in, they still unleash fight-or-flight responses, which undermine our ability to respond in thoughtful, resourceful ways which nurture ourselves and our relationships.

Stresses activate our **limbic brain**, where our emotions reside. Unless we are emotionally mature and secure in our self- love and our relationships with others, we bypass the prefrontal cortex; the **executive brain** which allows us to manage our feelings and make wise adult decisions.

Because we turn that rush of adrenaline inwards (rather than using it physically to fight or flee from a woolly mammoth) anxiety and depression can reach their all-time high in today's world.

Human history (or should I say *inhuman* history?) carries much trauma. Think of wars, genocides, the negativity of our daily news, corruption, dysfunctional family structures, high divorce rates, poor role modelling, racism, huge inequalities in the distribution of wealth, natural disasters, the COVID pandemic, gender inequality, homophobia, and so on.

These traumas have bred a human race which is on high alert to defend, attack, grab what we can, plunder and abuse the planet and each other.

At the same time, these responses run in tandem with magnificent behaviour, stirring courage, love, sacrifice, kindness, generosity, art, music, magnificent achievements, the sublime in the natural world.

This is the duality, the light and dark of our planet. Worrying about something over which we have no control is totally counterproductive. It neither stops problems from occurring nor solves them. It simply makes you anxious and depressed. (Part Two of this book outlines ways to better manage anxiety and depression.)

The question—and the opportunity—offered by positive psychology, is: What do you focus your attention on? Do you spend the majority of your time and energy on the mud or the stars, the darkness in human life, or the wonders and stirring achievements? Do you see the glass as half empty or half full?

When you write a script and identify and visualise yourself living what is desirable and important to you in life, you are:

- Scanning a sea of possible (and abundant!) futures
- Consciously choosing the best possible year ahead
- Focusing with laser-beam intensity on that possibility as the one you heart-fully choose
- Shifting away from unconscious ambivalence or dread to which your mind could lead you when left to its own inclinations and habits.

Who knows what will happen to others, to their loved ones, to their community, to their world today, let alone tomorrow? A sea of possibility swirls around us. In the words of the popular song of yesteryear, Que Sera Sera: '*Will I be famous? Will I be rich? Whatever will be, will be.*'

The meaning of that famous song is that the future is up in the air, and whatever is going to happen will happen. When you adopt the life-stance of scripting your best possible future, you are not adopting a passive *'Whatever is going to happen is going to happen. I'm OK taking a lying down approach to how I live my life.'*

Instead, you are saying:

'Yes, the future is up in the air, but my thoughts and intentions will create my future—and I choose a great one!'

To write a script where you visualise yourself in a brilliant future, is to dramatically increase the probability that what you script will materialise.

At this stage, you may see it as ridiculously unrealistic to set your sights on a life of happiness and fulfilment. You may be thinking, *'Who me? You've got to be kidding. Look at my life circumstances! I'm so far from a dream life it's not funny!'*

You may hear a voice in your head saying *'That's all very well for her, she was born privileged. But look at me! What chance have I got?'*

I want to reassure you that scripting works for people of all cultures, all ethnicities, and all socio-economic levels of society.

If you struggle with low self-esteem and can't imagine yourself being happy or having what you want, Part Two of the book has been designed to gently coach you into discovering a new you. You will learn how to heal limiting beliefs and dysfunctional thinking and behaviour. You will acquire optimistic, expansive, soulful ways of thinking and being, and compassion and respect for others. You will learn how you can repair dysfunctional and self-sabotaging habits. You will learn new skills for living a fulfilling, joyful life – the life we all deserve.

Chapter Ten will start you on a journey of recovering your true self. In this chapter you'll meet your **inner child**. This is your playful, innocent, spontaneous, intuitive self. Your inner child is an enthusiastic creator of possibilities. This is your **true self**, the self you were before disappointments and perhaps even serious traumas caused your true self to go into hiding in your unconscious mind.

The good news is you can reconnect with that wonder, that playfulness and that creativity of your inner child. They are just waiting for you!

And once you meet them, it is this part which can give you free reign to be audacious, to dare to dream - big, beautiful, intriguing dreams to shape your new life.

4

HOW TO MAKE YOUR DREAMS CRYSTAL-CLEAR
MAKE YOUR VALUES EXPLICIT

One of the critical keys for scripts that give you the future you dream of is to include the qualities that matter to you.

Taking the time to remind yourself of what's really important to you is great preparation for writing your script. It will help you avoid disappointment down the track when what you've scripted actually manifests.

So, for example, if building the house of your dreams and having a permaculture garden would give you joy, be sure to describe your ideal partner as having a similar love.

If spiritual development and the spiritual journey are important to you, make sure to write that your new partner has a commitment to their own personal growth and a spiritual journey similar to yours.

You don't want to wish you'd added another paragraph when you wrote the script that brought your new partner into your life. You don't want to find yourself lamenting, "He's lovely, but he's not willing to talk about issues in our relationship. How I wish I'd asked for that too!"

That's the reason to do the following exercise before you write your script.

This chapter will lead you through the steps to uncover what's important to **you**. However, I recommend you read the book from start to finish and then come back to this chapter. That's when to do the process of identifying your values and visualising your future self, living a life where your values are being fulfilled.

This process can be done in relation to any part of your life.

I've included examples of areas as diverse as intimate relationship, career, friendship and travel. You can work on those or anything else you'd love to include in your dream life. While I hope it's helpful for you to see examples of other people's responses when they get in touch with their values, your values are unique to you.

Visualising myself fulfilled and in a happy relationship, I released my doubt that I could be really fulfilled and happy in a long-term partnership; a doubt which could have blocked my script from becoming reality. (In case you're worrying that you don't know how to ditch doubts you may have, there's a process in Chapter Nine to help you do that.)

Another reason the process described in this chapter is so valuable is that it lays down **new neurological pathways** of success and happiness, rather than digging deeper the grooves of old pathways of failure and unhappiness.

What follows is a step-by-step outline to help you identify your values, then place the vision of yourself living your dream into your future.

Using similar instructions, participants in my workshops pair off and alternate in leading each other through this process. I encourage you to give it a go. Simply follow the steps outlined, one at a time, and you will get the benefit.

If you have a friend or partner who is willing to do this process with you, have them ask the questions while you respond. If you don't have someone to do this for you, you might want to record yourself reading the questions. Read them slowly, then play the recording when you're ready, and do the process that way.

Exercise: How to Identify Your Relationship Values

Choose one area of your life to focus on at a time and apply these two simple steps for uncovering your values. This example considers your values in intimate relationships.

Step One: Make a list – just words and phrases – of what's important to you in a relationship. These are the qualities that must be there for you to be really happy, the bare bones of your values.

Step Two: Go back and flesh out each value, recording what they mean to you. Below is a list of values that my client Jonathan listed in Step One, in answer to the question: *'What's important to you in an intimate relationship?'*

- Love
- Affection
- Security
- Trust
- Honesty
- Being positive, learning to be a better person
- Sex
- Support
- Being there
- Someone willing to try new things

Once he'd exhausted his list of what is important to him, starting with his first value I asked, *'What does ... (love) mean to you? What else?'*

Then I moved onto the second: *'What does...(affection) mean to you? How does it look to you?'*

And so on, for every one of his values.

This is what these values meant to Jonathan:

- **Love**: Feelings towards a particular person that you don't have for anybody else. You really want to be part of that person's life, and you care about them and everything about them is important to you.
- **Affection**: It's a whole lot of things – holding hands, touching, and feeling; touching each other on the backside; showing the person you love that you love them.
- **Security**: Knowing if you have an argument that you're not going to be out the door; knowing that if you have an argument, you'll resolve things without conflict. Security is about your partner's love for you; you're secure that you are

loved, you don't doubt it, because they show you affection, honesty; all of the above values.
- **Trust**: Believing that your partner means what they say: security, nothing hidden, knowing everything about your partner. It means good communication.
- **Honesty**: Being able to express your feelings; having trust; it's important to know how your partner feels, how you both feel, because you care.
- **Being positive, learning to be a better person:** That comes back to the emotional bank account model; you're happy; it's about moving forward and looking ahead and looking for a better future; you're all about improving.
- **Sex**: Sex is togetherness; touching, loving, nurturing; and it's good fun!
- **Support**: Because I'm away on fly in - fly out, supporting me in my career and the situation we're in; also supporting each other, from something that's happening with the children to something that's happening at work; being there for each other.
- **Being there**: It's like support - always being there for each other even if you don't want to visit the hardware shop or the boat shop or the football, you come along anyway; it's being reliable.
- **Someone willing to try new things**: Someone who likes to try new things and have new experiences; someone who likes to travel with me; someone who's funny, who can make me laugh.

Exercise: Visualisation to Create Your Dreams

This next exercise brings your values into the light. It then uses them to guide your creation of a compelling future.

If it's a relationship you're working on, this will significantly improve your chances of avoiding the frog and choosing the prince or princess instead.

If it's a career you're working on, it will help you attract a career and

Create Abundant Possibilities

a working environment and conditions you desire, rather than one you dislike.

Having defined your values in **Steps One** and **Two**, the next step is to imagine yourself actually **living your dream**.

In **Step Three**, you'll explore where you store your past and future memories.

The visualisation process which follows is a step-by-step process. It's designed to help you install a picture of your dream (relationship, job etc.) into your future.

To maximise the power of that visualisation, start by discovering in which direction you store your past and your future memories. This is called your **timeline**.

For most people, either,

- Their past lies **behind** them and their future lies in **front** of them, or,
- Their past lies to **one side** of them, and their future to the other,
- And for a minority it's some mix of the above.

Follow the directions below to find yours. Again, if you have a partner or friend who is happy to help you do this process, she/he can lead you through these instructions.

If you're doing this solo, you could record the italicised instructions below, then play them back to guide yourself through.

- *Close your eyes and take a deep breath. If you knew where your past lies, in which direction would you point? Raise your hand and point in that direction. Don't think about it much, it's just a feeling or sense of where it is.*
- *And if you knew where your future lies, in which direction would that be? Point in that direction.*
- *Now when I ask you to put the 'picture' of you in your ideal relationship/job etc. into your future, you will do that in the direction in which your future lies.*

- *Keeping your eyes closed, give yourself the experience of floating above your timeline so that you are looking down on yourself sitting here now. As you float up there, imagine that you are turning and looking in the direction of your past.*
- *Imagine the top of your head opening and the infinite source of light and love and healing flowing through it, filling your entire body with light and love and healing – filling you so full that the light and love now flow through your heart, all the way into your past, filling your entire past with light and love and healing.*
- *Now, as you float up there, turn and look to your future. Allow that infinite source of light and love and healing to continue to flow through you. Let it flow out of your heart all the way into your future, so that your entire future now is filled with light and love and healing.*

Step Four: Installing the picture of you living your dream into your future.

- *Imagine yourself in a (relationship/ job etc.) where your values are met...* (This is the point where your support person, helping you do this process, or yourself, having recorded this, reads back to you everything you spelt out in Step One.)

- To use Jonathan's example, I read, '*Now imagine yourself in a relationship where the **love** is there, feelings towards a particular person that you don't have for anybody else. You really want to be part of that person's life, and you care about them, and everything about them is important to you. There's **affection**: it's a whole lot of things—holding hands, touching and feeling; touching each other on the backside; showing the person that you love them, etc.*'

I continued reading his words back to him, until we reached the end of his list.

- *Create a picture of yourself in that moment in time, where you know all of that is there. Or if you're unable to visualise, just get a sense of it. Imagine what you'd be seeing, feeling, thinking, hearing. What your future self would be feeling is very important. Feel right now what you'd be feeling in your future if you had already experienced having this the way you dream it could be. Make sure you are in your body in that picture, in that experience.*

Note: Allow time to imagine this, and likewise, allow time for each part of the process which follows, rather than rushing through.

- *Take a snapshot of yourself in that situation. Holding that snapshot in your hands, float above your timeline to the moment in your future where it feels just right for you to be in that experience, the way you dream it can be.*
- *Float down onto your timeline, placing the picture in your future. Fine-tune it one last time to make it as real and compelling as you can.*
- *Leaving the picture there in your future, float way above it, looking down on yourself in that experience.*
- *Take a deep breath and blow vitality into that picture.*
- *Turn back and look towards 'now'. Get a sense of the changes that will happen between now and then that will make that experience of yourself in that (relationship/job etc.) absolutely inevitable.*
- *Turn and look in the direction of your distant future. Get a sense of how you will surprise and delight yourself with all the changes which flow through to you as a result of your being in this (relationship/job etc.) the way you dream it can be.*
- *Float back slightly ahead of now. Drop down onto your timeline, looking at yourself waiting for yourself in your future. Know that the neurological pathway has been laid down in your brain, and you are being drawn inevitably towards it.*
- *Float back up again, remembering how good that feels, and*

> *know that you can revisit that experience in your mind's eye – and it's a good thing to daydream.*
> - *Finally, become aware of your fingers and toes, the temperature of the air, the sounds around you, and when you're ready, open your eyes.*

A Few Tips on Making Your Values Work

How many values are enough?

Values, and the number of them, differ for different people. While there's no correct number, I suggest you go for at least **six** before accepting that's all you're able to come up with.

If you dry up pretty soon, ask yourself, '*Is there something else I'd miss if it wasn't there in my relationship?*'

The real-life responses that clients have shared in the pages which follow may prompt you to realise there are things that are important to you, that you mightn't have come up with yourself.

You might not even have dared to entertain the idea they could be possible for you!

If you'd love to experience them, I invite you to have the courage to include them in your list of what you long for. This, of course, needs to be practical within reason. For example, you wouldn't list being an astronaut on the next space mission if you've had no training in this area.

Imagine solutions, not problems

I've already alluded to the fact that, for many of us, left unchecked, our unconscious mind tends to be hard-wired to fear things going wrong, rather than to expect great things to happen automatically.

As you describe what is important to you, you need to take out **insurance against pessimism**. You don't want to drag fears, doubts and past failures into your future!

If you witnessed, contributed to, or bore the brunt of aggression in your family of origin, or in previous relationships, you will have amassed some pretty negative behaviours and attitudes towards resolving problems. You will most likely have developed trust issues.

Create Abundant Possibilities

If you're depressed, if you have a punitive inner critic, if you suffer from anxiety, if you've been betrayed or a victim of abuse, if your dad cheated on your mum, if your partner cheated on you, if you cheated on your partner, if there was domestic violence in your family of origin... There are many reasons people think of relationships and think of tomorrow with dread rather than hope.

For example, if your last partner was controlling and bossy, and didn't bother consulting you on important decisions, you probably fear getting into another relationship with someone like that. If so, it is important that you do some work on your self-esteem, and learn assertive communication skills, as outlined in Chapter Twelve. It is essential to set boundaries such as, *'No thank you, I don't want to go to your ex's party this weekend.'*

Be very **direct** about what you ask for, rather than alluding to it in a vague way, hoping they'll read between the lines and understand what you mean. Express your needs clearly, in an empowered and respectful manner.

Without doing self-help processes or seeking therapy or life coaching to break old patterns, you may well choose another controlling, bossy partner, even if they don't look like that on the surface. You don't want to put up with behaviour that makes you unhappy because you fail to ask for what you want and re-create the same problems all over again.

When you list your values, the same instructions apply as when you write a script: **make sure there are no negative words or fears!** What do I mean by this? Consider the example of Louise, who had come out of a relationship with a man who would disappear for days at a time after an argument. Security was an important value for her.

'Security means I feel confident he won't leave; our relationship won't end. I'll feel this is my family, this is where I'm going to be for the rest of my life. The feeling that if you have a fight, it's not the end of the relationship.'

Her notion of security was fear-based, predicated on a limited belief in lack (her fear that this would be a problem). This is how Louise reframed security as a positive, not a negative value:

'Security is feeling confident he's fully committed to me; this is our house, this is our family, this is where we're going to be for the rest of our lives. It's knowing that if we have a fight, we repair; we talk it through.

That leaves us feeling we can trust, believe in and rely on each other. We work through issues respectfully for the good of the relationship.'

Similarly, you wouldn't say: *'Loyalty means my partner won't cheat on me and leave me'*. Instead, you'd say *'Loyalty means my partner is faithful; he's in the relationship for the long haul and so am I.'*

Identifying your negative expectations, your fears, your doubts, allows you to transcend your past and transform your present and your future. You want to avoid dragging your past into your future or letting it define your future. Allow yourself to dream of wonderful new possibilities.

This is an opportunity to challenge your expectations, your story of who you are, your story of how life is and will be. This is an opportunity to create a different, happier outcome than you created in the past. You can choose again. You can choose different values to those exhibited in your family of origin, your past relationships, your old jobs etc. There are no 'shoulds' when it comes to values. You can make a better, more informed choice at any time, based on what you've learned from the past or what you see in the world that you desire.

Becoming a fully conscious human

Don't limit this practice of becoming aware of, and changing, your limited beliefs to just this values identification exercise. This is a life changing practice I recommend you apply every moment.

Make it a conscious choice to be on the alert to catch yourself whenever you slip into negative, shut-down feelings. This includes the whole gamut of negativity, like anger, judgement, anxiety, sadness, guilt, denial, being fake, hiding, withdrawal, self-criticism and shame.

Whenever you become aware that you're retracting your energy in these ways, imagine taking that feeling into your hands, and place your hands on your heart. Ask your loving heart to transmute and deprogram that feeling. Surround that feeling with light. Allow yourself to believe this is happening. You don't have to do it perfectly. Just do it. Just doing it and having the intention that your shut-down, negative feeling is being transmuted is enough.

. . .

Re-run your visualisation often

After you've written your script, repeat your visualisation often. Every night, every morning, imagine yourself being happy in your new relationship, your new job, your new hobby – whatever it is you visualised in Step Four, above.

This will reinforce and deepen your '**future memory**.' It will strengthen the neurological pathway of you living your dream.

Remember, you write your script (once) for the year, then put it in a drawer, and allow what shows up to show up. In the meantime, your visualisation will be working hand-in-hand with your script. They support and augment each other.

Super-charge your visualisation practice

I have used visualisation as a daily practice ever since I learned how to visualise my future.

Every morning, with very rare exceptions, I briefly imagine my day going very well. If I have something specific planned for the day, like a meeting, client sessions, a party, I briefly imagine it being enjoyable and rewarding.

And I imagine myself feeling great, and grateful at the end of the day. I seem to be lucky in that I have a very happy life. Or maybe visualising each day going well is the secret to a joyful, blessed life? I recommend you do it too.

Feelings and passion are an important part of your visualisation

As you follow the instructions in Step Four of the visualisation process, 'seeing' or 'imagining' your future self in the dream situation, **feel the feelings** associated with having the things you dream of, feeling how you'd feel as that person. These aren't just passive words and thoughts. They are the **seeds** of your new reality. They have wings and creative power.

Therefore, to the extent you are able, invest feeling and passion as you imagine yourself having what you dream of. Smell it, taste it, revel in it **as though you already have it!**

At a visceral level, know the delight of being your future self, that new you, living this new experience. Embodying your 'future' experience like this also regulates your nervous system, giving your body a sense of safety when this experience actually turns up.

Getting it right

Having encouraged you to be mindful of what you can do to maximise the success of the creation of your dream scenario, I want to reassure you that **however you do this process, you'll be laying down new neurological pathways for optimism and change**.

You may be like me – one of the 20% or so of people who aren't 'visual', in that it's hard to see in your mind's eye; when I close my eyes I see no pictures, no colour. I see nothing.

Don't be concerned if this is you too. The process has worked well for me even though I couldn't really 'see' myself in my dream relationship. I had to make do with a sense or feeling that I had it all.

Doing the process was invaluable to me. It really helped me clarify what I longed for in a relationship, and then having imagined the 'picture' of me in such a relationship, I was blessed to meet the man with whom I could create that. Intention and emotional energy is what counts, with or without 'pictures.'

Discovering your values in other areas of your life

Obviously, in addition to relationships, career/work is another biggie. It's well worth putting in the time to explore what's really important for you in your work, and to visualise yourself in the job you'd love following the process spelt out above.

This process can also be helpful in areas such as:
- Family/being a parent/a friend
- Health and fitness
- Upcoming holiday/travel
- Your dream wedding.

Below, I've included more examples from clients I've worked with.

An Example of Career Values

This is what he came up with when I asked Michael what was important to him in his job and career:

- **Having fun**: I enjoy what I do; you don't take your work too seriously even though it is serious; you laugh about it. I want to go to work wanting to be with the people I work with, looking forward to working with them; understanding everyone's uniqueness and working towards a common end that gives us all satisfaction.
- **Being appreciated for what I do**: I have a unique skill set. It's important to me that anything I do has to be good down the road, with things being able to be added on instead of needing to be re-engineered. The business outcomes need to be leveraged from the work you do, to provide the return on investment. What I want to hear is *'Thanks, great job!'* or, *'That's better than expected, far less pain involved than anticipated, so thank you.'*
- **Work that is technically challenging**: By nature, I'm a problem-solver; I'm at my happiest when I've got something challenging technologically, and I'm able to work around it – whether it's a piece of software, or electronics or electrical, it doesn't matter to me. I'm an enabler, and if other people are involved, that's even better. I enjoy people being happy.
- **Having an open relationship with the people I work with**: I value being a mentor as well as being mentored; no hidden agendas; the ability to sit down and have a discussion, and have disagreements, then coming to a resolution everyone is happy with, taking account of certain deadlines, and accepting that not everyone was right, whether that be me or someone else; it's great just to talk to people and say, *'How do you solve this problem?'*, asking with goodwill and a willingness to learn, like we do at our morning tea discussions.
- **Trusting and respecting the people I work with and being trusted and respected by them:** If I'm responsible

for something, and there has been consensus on the way to go forward, I am open to change, on the proviso that the change is discussed and agreed upon in a respectful way.
- **Being paid well and putting money into superannuation**: That's important, for when I'm no longer working; it's awesome that 14% of my salary goes into superannuation. I'm extremely grateful for that.
- **Flexibility**: I'm happy with the flexibility I have in my job; being able to take four days as flexi days, so I can go on my six-day bike rides – I love that about my job.

An Example of Travel Values

Monique was a university student planning her first trip overseas. After she shared her trepidation about travelling on her own as a young woman, and what she feared could go wrong, I considered it worthwhile to spend some time helping her imagine what the trip would be like if it went incredibly well.

We then installed the picture of this dream trip in her future. This would be the vision she would focus on and anticipate rather than letting her mind obsess about the problems she dreaded. I also encouraged her to write a script for her upcoming trip. I was delighted when, on her return, she acknowledged she had a wonderful time.

I started by asking Monique, "What's important to you about travel, about this trip? What will it be like if it turns out to be beyond your wildest dreams?" For each value/attribute she came up with, I then asked, "And what does (e.g. being different) mean to you?"

- **Being different**: Seeing how different other countries are; the people I'm going to meet; it will feel amazing, meeting new people, travelling with them. You're having an experience with them that you're not having with anyone else; like a unique experience. The only people that will know what it feels like are the people there at the time.

- **Exciting**: It's new; it's not expected, and that is exciting; being in a different place is exciting.
- **Experience**: Having the opportunity to go and see different things, meet different people, create different memories. I'm very lucky because a lot of people don't get these opportunities.
- **Knowledge**: I'm going to come back with so much information on so many different places that I don't know. That will be exciting, knowing this information and having a broader mind; I'll be more open-minded.
- **Other cultures**: That comes under experience and knowledge because I'll be learning so much about other cultures. I'll be able to appreciate them more.
- **A lot of great memories**: I'll think back, I'll remember when this great thing happened, great times; it will always be a pick-me-up. I can be grateful for those memories and experiences, like a bank account of good memories in the storage unit of my mind.
- **Positivity**: It will be a positive change for myself; little things are going to change my mind, and I'll appreciate things in a different way.
- **Friendship**: I'll be meeting new people, and it will create a bond; we can be friends with each other and hopefully friends for a long time because we've done things together and dealt with hiccups together that other people haven't had the opportunity to do together. I'll feel a bit more whole. I'll find someone genuine there, someone to communicate with.
- **Love**: Love is a broad word – I'm going to love the people, love the countries, love the food I'm going to eat. I love the image of everything.
- **Happiness**: I'm happy that I'm in a new place with new people, seeing new things and being in a different atmosphere. I'm going on a holiday, and I'm happy about that.
- **Safety**: I'll be with other people, have other people around me. I'll be resilient and aware. When I get home, I'll be

relieved, grateful, relaxed, because it all went well, it was great, it was a great holiday.
- **Relaxed and easy, not thinking about anything**: I'll find comfort and pleasure in that; being mindful. I'll feel relaxed and I'll feel more energy; everything will go well. It will be easy.
- **The Group**: We don't know each other yet, don't know anything about each other yet, we're just starting, but you never know, I want to get along with them, really feeling part of the group, and love being part of the group. It's going to be easy, easy going. You support each other, it's fun.

Reframe any fear-driven values

Earlier, I quoted Louise's fears that her partner might leave her, and the relationship might end. A classic and not uncommon case of focusing on past problems, rather than future possibilities.

Before you start eliciting your own, or someone else's values, remember that if negatives do come up (also called '*away-froms,*' as in, '*what is this person wanting to get away from*') in response to the question, '*What's important to you?*', **don't write down the negative**.

You don't want to install a negative or a problem in the picture of the future. Instead, aim to reframe that fear-based thinking by asking, ***'What would you like instead of that?'***

This is an example of reframing fear-based thinking into a positive script:

Libby: '*My partner won't be unfaithful to me.*'
Wendy: '*What would he be like instead?*'
Libby: '*He'll be trustworthy and faithful.*'

In a similar way, in describing what was important to her in her upcoming trip, Monique initially mentioned that it was important: '*Not to be attacked or robbed when on tour.*'

Alert to the negativity of such thinking, and not wanting to install this idea into her vision of her trip, I asked her '*What will happen instead?*'

And that's when she came up with:

- ***Safety**: I'll be with other people, have other people around me. I'll be resilient and aware; when I get home, I'll be relieved, grateful, relaxed, because it all went well, it was all great, it was a great holiday.*

Similarly, when Monique initially came up with: '*I won't be lonely, not feeling like part of the group,*' I challenged that by asking, '*So what would you prefer? What will it be like instead?*'

Monique was able to imagine this:

- ***Friendship**: I'll be meeting new people, and it will create a bond. We can be friends with each other and hopefully friends for a long time because we've done things together and dealt with hiccups together that other people haven't had the opportunity to do together. I'll feel a bit more whole. I'll find someone genuine there to communicate with.*

Focusing on the **positive**, rather than what she feared, delivered her dreams. Rather than run into the problems she feared might spoil her trip, when Monique returned, she reported that she'd had a wonderful time, and she'd experienced the dream trip of her visualisation.

Let's do this! Place Your Dream in Your Future

Now's the time to start creating your compelling future. Choose which area of your life you want to work on, then follow **Steps One** to **Four** on the previous pages of this chapter.

Good luck with getting up close and personal to your values. This is very powerful, and I wish you well. I wish you a future you love living. That's what we are here to experience — the power of our thoughts and choices to create abundant and infinite possibilities.

5

SCRIPTING SUCCESS STORIES
SUCCESSES - MANY AND VARIED

Are you feeling excited to write your script? You may find the following scripting successes inspirational, or you may use them as a launching pad for even bigger, brighter and bolder choices.

Romance Scripts

A few years ago, my good friend Carol brought her sister and niece, visiting from the US, for a taste of the country at our semi-rural rainforest property in Australia.

Her sister, attractive, in her early sixties, was separated from her husband and single again. Her niece, in her early thirties, was in a defacto relationship from which she wanted out. Carol of course suggested that I teach them ScriptWriting, which I did. Both their scripts took them to the stars!

A year later her sister met a man who had been widowed a couple of years earlier. True to her script, like her,

- He was a spiritual person who had done a great deal of personal development work
- He was financially secure
- They were physically attracted to each other

45

- He had independent adult children with whom she developed good relationships.

The wedding took place a year after they met, and by all accounts, they are enjoying a fulfilling and happy life together.

Carol's niece went home, completed her degree, broke up with her boyfriend, and took a long holiday in Italy.

It was in Rome that a handsome Italian came into her life. It was love at first sight. As per her script, they now live in the US, both have excellent professional jobs in their chosen fields, and last I heard, she was on maternity leave.

Another romance-come-true I want to share with you concerns a woman single again after two failed marriages. She was relocating to another state. Her script included finding a beautiful five-acre property on the outskirts of a small country town and falling in love with the man of her dreams.

The good news was that both came to pass. The not-so-good news was that he was married.

Since she reported that, I have recommended that clients scripting to meet a partner specify that person be single, and ready for a committed relationship. Reiterating what I suggested earlier, take the trouble to specify/ask for whatever is important to you.

Before leaving the romance area of your script, check if there's anything you haven't asked for which you'd miss if it wasn't there. It might be a passion for music, or bush walking, or a partner who happily picks up their share of housework and childminding.

Examples of qualities many people may desire in a mate include: appreciation of differences, faithfulness, trustworthiness, honesty, good communication skills, sense of humour, fun, creativity, an easy-going temperament, maturity, empathy, similar interests, similar goals and family values, affection, kindness, caring, good mental and physical health, financial stability, physical attraction and sexual compatibility.

This chapter includes example scripts which may seed ideas for you. That said, don't bother with things that may be important to someone else but not important to you.

For example, if you're scripting a new job, consider including things like a good relationship with management and workmates, flexible hours, challenge, opportunity for promotion, excellent remuneration, and so on, if that's important to you.

On the other hand, if a low key, low-responsibility, under-the-radar position is what you're seeking, ask for it. Or, if qualities like adventurousness, quirkiness, etc. are important to you in a partner, make sure you include them in your script.

The majority of clients to whom I teach ScriptWriting are people who have experienced a relationship or marriage breakdown and are longing to meet a new partner. And most of them – male and female, looking for a heterosexual or same sex relationship - have been thrilled by how close their new partner turns out to be to the one they described in their script.

Matt is in real estate. He is 40+, tall, dark and handsome, with an easy manner, oozing friendliness. He wrote his script at the workshop he attended with me in November 2022. Nine months later he arrived for an individual session, clutching his script and all but dancing for joy.

Matt was overjoyed that he'd met the girl of his dreams. He was amazed that she was the woman he asked for in his script.

He was happy for me to include it word for word in this chapter. I've copied it faithfully. His script is very much his creation. He followed some of the rules and didn't bother with others. And in that form, it delivered his dream. I like the way his personality is writ large in his script, as I hope yours will be in your script.

The energy of scripting is that of vitality, being present in the moment, being in touch with your feelings, your preferences, your longings. I hope that seeing the uniqueness of Matt's script encourages you to have the courage to let your script be your own thing.

Let it be an expression of your unique creativity and authenticity, your heart, your love, your longing, your glorious potential to live a life you love.

My Girl, My Woman, My Dream November 2022

- *Smart, witty and funny — Understands my humour.*
- *Challenges me to be better every day in every way.*

- *Beautiful inside, & heart of gold, giving, generous, open to love, being loved and giving love.*
- *Loves herself and proud of who she is.*
- *Solid values, aligned with mine — trust, loyalty, honesty, gentle yet firm.*
- *Driven yet content.*
- *Adventurous, daring and fun.*
- *Sexually — on my level — anywhere, curious, magical.*
- *Health — Fit, sporty & loves food.*
- *Does not mind a party, festival, or dinner.*
- *Maybe has kids who I will help her with, or,*
- *Wants more — I would love to be a dad, and I'd make a wonderful father.*
- *Ideally, a woman who is 28-37 who has not had kids yet, not because of any reason.*
- *Financial/career success does not matter to me.*
- *Cute 5'2 to 5'9, brunette, girl next door.*
- *Great body. Healthy skin, nice smile, healthy eyes.*
- *Someone who I fall in love with (1 second-1 month).*
- *Strong, does not put up with any BS.*
- *Understanding and open to others' opinions.*

His note at the end of the copy he gave me read:
'I met my beautiful girl, woman and dream on 16 July 2023. And we began courting and falling in love on Friday 25 August 2023
Thank you Wendy'

Matt is not alone in being surprised at the close match between the partner who shows up and the partner scripted. I hear comments like, *'It's ridiculous how much she is like my script!'*

Looking After Your New Relationship

Scripting is ideally suited to 'designing' the relationship/partner you dream of, and then writing out the next year as if you are already in a close, loving relationship. Once your new partner shows up, this is merely the start of the journey.

Bear in mind that the qualities you value in a partner need to provide a compass for your actions too. If you want kindness and empathy, a sweet temper and patience, respect, a good listener, someone who is fair and pulls their weight, you need to bring those qualities to the relationship yourself. Live your values, don't flout them. Relationships are a two-way street.

You're putting your hand up for a loving relationship. You now need to be a person who will sustain and nurture this new relationship, avoiding relationship sabotage/curdling behaviours that may have contributed to the failure of your previous relationships.

That's why, after I wrote my script to meet the man of my dreams, I enrolled in workshops which teach skills in relationship management. If you've had a troubled relationship history, I suggest you start reading self-help books and perhaps get guidance from a couple counsellor. (I introduce some Do's and Don'ts for loving respectful relationships in Chapter Eleven.)

What if you're in a relationship where you are thinking *'Should I go or should I stay?'* You can certainly script how much better you have been getting along, as a couple, and specify what the rebuilt relationship looks like. But make sure you don't use negative words like, *'no longer angry, controlling, or nasty'*.

Instead, use words like, *'both of us have been understanding and reasonable, accepting, forgiving, flexible and kind.'*

What if your beautiful new relationship slips out of the honeymoon phase and starts running into trouble? I recommend you see a relationship counsellor right away, as well as read state-of-the-art books like Terence Real's *'The New Rules of Marriage' and 'US'*.

I also recommend John Gottman's *'Seven Principles for Making Marriage Work.'*

Even if only one of you sees a counsellor (if the other is resistant to couple therapy), you can bring about significant improvements.

Remember, if you keep doing what you've been doing, you'll keep getting what you're already getting. To get a different outcome you have to do something different.

How much fun and adventure can you have by changing your thinking and your behaviour so your relationship can turn around?

Career Scripts

Scripting opens doors to reach the goals you dream of in your academic pursuits, your occupation, and your professional life.

I have encouraged many university students to script that they handle their projects and exams exceptionally well and achieve excellent grades.

The duration of therapy means I don't necessarily get feedback on their exams many months away. However, where I've had feedback, it has been gratitude for their success.

It's a good idea to unpack your job/career values as described in Chapter Four before writing your script.

Make sure to specify what matters to you. It could be things like flexible hours; in-office, or work-from-home; a friendly supportive workplace; understanding and respectful managers; fulfilment and stimulation; a sense of achievement; competence; recognition and acknowledgement of your contribution; a good or brilliant salary package; opportunities for advancement; the promotion you aim for; or, a pay rise of $x amount (specify how much).

Whatever it is, write the past year as if these things **have already happened**.

In doing so, it pays to aim high. Recapping the rules of ScriptWriting, be **extremely positive**. And when opportunities present themselves, take them.

I remind you of my super-ambitious script where I wrote that I doubled my billings that year. Who would believe that could happen? It did.

And each year I wrote a script stating that they stayed at that level and they did, for the remaining years of my market research career. I had no idea how that would come to pass when I wrote the script.

However, I took opportunities when they arose.

When I was invited to be a speaker at the conference where I ended picking up two large companies as clients, I said yes.

When I changed careers and retrained to work as a psychologist, I scripted that I got a great job. I joined the *'Celebrity Relationship Psychologist'* practice in Sydney's Neutral Bay and never looked back!

So, I advise you to go for it. That said, while I encourage you to aim high, this does need to be pragmatically achievable.

Scripting that you are a pilot working for a leading airline is not likely to happen in the space of a year if you haven't yet started flying lessons.

If the economy has just taken a nosedive, that's possibly not a year to script a large increase in earnings.

The dream of the young client whose story I share in Chapter Thirteen was to become a professional in the field of Martial Arts competition. When I last heard from him, he was practising up to three hours a day.

If winning an award, or getting your article accepted by a prestigious journal is within your sights, script that it happened and then do whatever it takes to open the doors of possibility.

This reminds me of a client who was a university lecturer. He scripted winning the departmental prize for the best developmental project. He didn't win first prize, but he was awarded second prize. I'd still consider that a script success.

A script does not guarantee results, but when you allow and embrace what's possible, you'll be surprised how often the possible becomes the tangible, real experience.

If there is a big gap between the workplace in which you'd be happy, and your current workplace, this could be a sign it's time to look for a new job. Make sure you script the conditions that you'd love in your new job.

Allen was a case in point. He refused the 'promotion' to CEO offered him by the multi-national company he worked for, because it required him to uproot his family yet again, to yet another country.

Instead, he had his eye on an executive position in a large, successful Australian-owned company. Having got in touch with his career values, and visualised himself living his dream job, he wrote his script, applied, got to the top of the short list, and was overjoyed to land the job.

House and Home Scripts

Looking for a new home absolutely asks for a script. I've had clients write a script describing the house they would love, then finding themselves buying or renting something very like what they had described in their script.

Likewise, script when you're building or renovating - the process will be so much smoother!

When we built our new house, I scripted the following:

'The house turned out even better than I ever imagined. It is the best house I've ever lived in, and I love it with a passion. The architect and builder got on incredibly well, and we had an excellent relationship with both of them. On its completion, we gave a dinner party for them and their partners. It was a great celebration and a great night. They were highly professional, dedicated to top quality workmanship, and we couldn't have been more delighted with their work.

I was somehow led to the most beautiful materials and products for the building. We're surrounded by beauty, and my heart sings whenever I stroll from room to room.

The house was built pretty much on budget, and the work progressed very efficiently, and according to the time frame agreed upon. Peter and I loved the creative experience, and overall, got great joy from building our own home.

The house sits perfectly on the land, and it's surrounded by beautiful gardens and landscaping. We love living in our house. It's comfortable, snug, and easy to live in.'

We did indeed end up with what was truly the house of our dreams. Would we have got the same outcome had I not written that script? I can't answer that. However, there's no way I would build or choose another home without first writing a script.

When it comes to selling a home, scripting is again very helpful.

A woman who attended one of my *'Turn your Dreams into Reality'* workshops complained her house had been stuck on the market for over a year. They hadn't received a single offer.

She wrote a script during the workshop weekend that the house sold in the next month and specified the sale price. You guessed it! I received a very excited phone call six weeks later. There'd been two interested parties. The house had sold at the price in her script.

A woman my husband and I met and chatted to as we ate our gozlemis at the local monthly farmers' market told us that she and her husband had bought a new house before selling the old. Their house hadn't shifted, and they were running out of time. Of course, I taught her ScriptWriting then and there, explaining how to script the sale.

Months later I bumped into her again at a local café. When she saw me, she came over to say, "I had to come and thank you. You remember you taught me how to write a script to sell our house? Well, miraculously, the house sold the next week."

Then there is my Pilates teacher, who received notice to move her practice studio because the building was scheduled for demolition and rebuild. As she fretted about the scarcity of suitable space in the area, I shared how to script an even better studio.

Within a week she had her new, better space, the lease signed and sealed. I still attend Pilates in that new studio.

It gives me so much pleasure when people tell me what success they have had with ScriptWriting.

Travel Scripts

I have often helped clients to imagine their ideal holiday or trip they are planning. *'What would it be like if it went incredibly well? What's important to you on this holiday? What would need to happen for you to feel that you had a wonderful time, and gained all the benefits that you could hope for?'* (See the Travel Values exercise described in Chapter Four).

Once they've imagined that holiday going really well, and installed that 'dream' into their future, I then encourage them to write the script. They do that before taking the holiday, writing it in the past tense, as though the holiday is already over and they're back home again.

Take the scripts written by single people travelling alone, worried about feeling lonely and not having a good time. As per instructions, their scripts have stated instead that they met congenial travelling companions, they were happy and relaxed, had a really good time, and loved their trip. And almost without exception, I've had good reports.

Your dream holiday may be a spiritual pilgrimage, like walking the Camino or a yoga retreat in Bali. It could be trekking in Nepal. Perhaps you have your sights set on a walking tour in New Zealand, or cruising a river or an around-the-world cruise?

You may be attracted to a themed tour, like vineyards in Provence, a solo traveller adventure group tour of Greece, a cooking school in Italy. Or you may be planning a family or school reunion.

Whatever you have in mind, it's worth taking the time to script that it went even better than you could have imagined, and you had a brilliant, never-to-be-forgotten holiday.

You could add how good you've been feeling since you got back, extending the benefits into life at home.

The following script is one that I would write if I were to walk the Camino. The walk is still on my bucket list!

Date (up to a year <u>after</u> the intended walk):

1. We've been home from the Camino for four months, and the feeling of being blessed and grateful is still with us after a holiday that exceeded our dreams.

2. It was an experience like no other. We had hoped it would be spiritual, but it felt like we'd entered a different reality, a realm of magic, healing, bliss.

3. From Day One we were awed by the beauty and variety of the scenery, the challenge and delight of each day's walking, the people we met, the sunrises, the sunsets, the emotional space we dropped into. It was a time out of time.

4. The blisters at the start and the shared accommodation ended up being part of the special thing that is walking the Camino! We slept like babies, and we loved the camaraderie.

5. Each day's walk carried a brilliant sense of fulfilment, as our fitness improved day by day.

6. It was a great privilege to be a pilgrim on the Camino: affordable, delicious dinners, a feeling of being a traveller in a foreign land.

7. The greatest gift of all was the incredible expansiveness, inner peace and joy that were part of the rhythm of the walk. It felt like we had a psyche transplant, like we rose to a new level of humility, connection, oneness and spiritual awareness.

8. Reaching our final destination was hugely rewarding and fulfilling. The last few days were fun and easy, as we revelled in the delight of old towns, new friendships, and our fitness and feeling of achievement.

9. The walk did wonders for our relationship. We feel closer, more loving, more settled and at peace within ourselves, and our commitment to each other has deepened. That shared experience increased our emotional intimacy and feeling of a joint destiny. The lovely thing is the way it has stayed with us in the months since we came home. We agree that it feels like it's brought about a permanent change in who we are as people and as partners.

10. Not everything went according to plan, but the surprises and the unexpected added a touch of adventure. They turned out to be just what we needed, and we met some wonderful people we wouldn't otherwise have met as a result. When we reminded ourselves that the Camino is about opening to the new, it all seemed perfect.

11. We both agree it was the best holiday we've ever had, and we definitely want to walk another leg of the Camino within the next few years.

12. I choose this or something even better for the greatest good of all concerned.

A word of caution: If you're planning some ceremony on a trip, like announcing an engagement to parents who live overseas and don't approve of the match, make sure that you script that the announcement and ceremony went very well, and the parents were supportive and gracious.

In other words, don't omit to script an important event or occasion which you're planning while on that holiday. What you expect is so often delivered on a plate!

Allow that to work for you rather than against you. If you don't script that it went well and you know that your parents don't approve, you'll give your unconscious mind free reign to create from a place of fear or dread.

Scripting your dream scenario gives you the chance of overriding an unconscious doom scenario. And if you keep supporting that by imagining that it went well, you increase the likelihood of a good, or at the very least a better, outcome.

Social Event or Social Life Scripts

Since the aim is to cover every area of your life in your script, social life is worthy of inclusion. I've had clients include friendships with particular people, a special occasion, such as a party, or a wedding coming up in the year ahead, and/or their enjoyment of social life in general.

This part of your script alone can be life changing. As was the case for David, a second-year university student. One of the problems he wanted to deal with in therapy was that he was awkward socially and something of an odd-man-out. He hadn't fitted in with guys at school, nor with his current bunch of acquaintances. He didn't enjoy going out and *'getting wasted.'* He didn't find their jokes funny, nor their testosterone-led conversations engaging. He had a girlfriend but no close male friend.

He drifted between lectures, wanting to make new friends, but worried they would find him stitched up, boring, not their type.

We explored how ill at ease he felt socially, and how much of a field day his inner critic had when he was around his peers. What we also discovered was that, like most people who suffer from social anxiety, David had a running commentary in his head in social situations. *'I'm not their type and they know it!'... 'They're so superficial.'... 'They can tell I'm ill at ease. They're not drawn to me. I'm a misfit, not like other guys. I don't know what to say.'... 'That guy is a joke! Why do I bother?'*

It's hard to relate, to make eye contact, to connect with another person when you're putting up a wall like this. They feel your barrier from the outside, and you feel your barrier from the inside.

The feelings go from awkward and wrong-footing it, to withdrawn and desperately uncomfortable.

I asked David to practise being interested in the person/people to whom he was speaking, rather than...

- Judging them and writing them off as uninteresting,
- Being locked into how bad he was feeling and focusing on his inner critic's judgements of himself.

Create Abundant Possibilities

We role-played active listening, asking open-ended questions to show empathy for, and interest in, what the other person was saying.

For example, '*So what did you do last weekend? Who did you go with?... What did you like about it? Sounds like that was a really interesting thing to do. Tell me more about it.*'

We also teased out his social values, what 'simpatico' friendship would look and feel like to him. For example, the types of guys he'd enjoy being with, their interests, the topics they'd discuss, and so on.

We looked at what sort of people, as an 'intellectual' and a very light drinker, he felt were on his wavelength. We then installed a picture of him enjoying their company into the future.

This is about disrupting your old story of who you are, and your beliefs about other people and what you expect.

Seeing yourself in a new light helps to imagine you're relaxed and enjoying the company of those you're with, as opposed to seeing yourself as unpopular, a failure, dreading meeting up with them.

His therapy also included learning to have compassion and kindness for himself and challenging his inner critic.

David's script had him organising and heading up a debating society (his idea, not mine) and finding that it went incredibly well, and opened doors for him.

He wrote that the friendships he'd made that year were solid, and he was feeling confident and grateful for the way his social life had turned around.

Given that the script covered all areas of his life, he also included things like having fun and getting on really well with his girlfriend and sailing through his exams with high distinctions.

The last time I saw David he was noticeably happier and more relaxed than the David I'd first met. His debating group was going great, and he had a new friendship group of like-minded students.

He'd scored high distinctions in his exams and was starting the new year at university with confidence and optimism, ready to script another great year to come.

Finding Your Voice/Coming Out Scripts

Jade was a sensitive, self-effacing man in his mid-thirties. He had his own home, and a close relationship with his parents and siblings. They lived in the same neck of the woods and spent a fair amount of time together.

Apart from anxiety, one of the things which caused Jade greatest grief was that he had never told his family he was gay. He'd come out to a handful of close friends but kept it well hidden from everyone else, including work colleagues.

> "One of my fears in telling people is that they may react badly. I've been afraid that my friends would say they no longer wanted to be my friends. In myself as well, I'd like to be at a point where it's not important to me whether people like it or not! It's also about me coming to accept myself. I want to overcome that feeling of panic and shame at people knowing and I feel I need some help or some guidance."

He'd managed to get away with non-disclosure because his relationships so far had been short-term. But he'd now met someone with whom he wanted a more committed relationship, and he was petrified at how his family might react.

Not that they were homophobic, but his mum had made the odd remark when he was in his teens, which added to his fear they would reject him if they knew he was gay.

"The approach was to hide it. I got teased for being gay at school. Mum said, 'If someone says you're gay, punch them!' Or, 'Don't sit like that. It looks effeminate.' I think my family would be a lot more accepting if I told them today than they would have been when I was younger."

We worked on Jade's thinking, his anxiety, his shame, his self-esteem, and by our fifth session we were ready to explore his dream of the very best experience possible, when he was ready to come out as gay.

I taught him ScriptWriting, and, of course, encouraged him to write that it was a wonderful, freeing and uplifting experience to finally admit what he'd been hiding. And that it had significantly improved his relationship with his family, as well as his feeling of comfort at work, and given him a huge boost in self-respect and confidence.

He also included paragraphs on issues such as how much his family loved his new partner, and vice versa, as well as describing a great relationship between himself and his partner's family.

You won't be surprised to learn that his parents and siblings admitted they had known he was gay. They reassured him that they had always loved him and always would, and he didn't have a thing to worry about as a valued, welcome and loved member of the family.

> "Things didn't go as planned. I didn't feel comfortable to raise it on the weekend. I put it in an email to mum, dad, my sister, my brother. That went fantastically well. They were very supportive. My brother rang me straight away. 'It's OK, I'll support you. It's fantastic you've told us.' I rang my mum when I got to work. She said, 'I'm really glad that you've told us.' And my dad said, 'I'm so proud you told us. Nothing changes.' And half an hour later, I phoned my sister and she said, 'I'm really glad you've done it.' The only one I haven't told yet is my nan."

Jade's final comments, the last time I saw him: "Since I came out to my family, it's like a huge weight has been lifted and I feel a different person. I'm no longer walking around with tight muscles in my neck and shoulders. It's such a relief! And I like the new me."

A Grand Social Goal

Around 2016, member states of the United Nations elected a close friend of mine as Chair of a UN Committee overseeing the WIPO Treaty on IP and Genetic Resources and Associated Traditional Knowledge.

The goal of the committee was to achieve a binding treaty, rather than a declaration of support - which is a 'soft treaty' and non-binding.

Negotiations to achieve the required unanimous agreement had been ongoing for twenty-five years. Three times a year, 500 attendees and their translators and minders, representing every country in the UN, had converged on Geneva for a week of meetings.

At every meeting, one or two of the richest countries, with most to lose from a fair new agreement, put up road-blocks and objections. Even the countries with most to gain seemed disinclined to bring negotiations to a conclusion.

In the sixth and final year of my friend's chairmanship, I suddenly felt driven to teach him ScriptWriting. I won't say he was a convert, but he respected what I said enough to scribble some notes stating that the treaty he drafted had been adopted.

The wash-up of the story is that despite well over two decades of stalling, the treaty he drafted was signed with unanimous acceptance. It was another victory for the ScriptWriting technique, consistent with the intention *'for the greatest good of all concerned.'*

Short-Term Scripts

I have always supplemented my annual scripts with short-term scripts when extra oomph was needed, or new situations emerged.

I encourage you to be creative and optimistic with short-term scripts. The opportunity may come up to take a holiday – one you hadn't scripted. Well then, write a script dated maybe a month after the end of holiday.

Or a special party or meeting may pop up – again, a great topic for a short-term script. Make sure you apply the usual rules: very positive, specific where possible.

Even if you don't actively do this anywhere else in your life, while you're writing your script, believe that the world's your oyster, the sky's your limit, you deserve to be happy and fulfilled.

In my days as a market research consultant, every week or two a brief would come in to tender for a new project. I would spend a day writing the best proposal I could for the job, present that to the marketing team, then wait to hear if we were the successful bidder.

After I learned ScriptWriting, I invariably wrote a script dated after the likely completion of the particular job I'd just quoted. My script would specify something like this:

The meeting with the client could not have gone better. I was in the flow, the rapport between me and the decision makers was excellent. I walked out of the meeting feeling confident and happy, knowing that they were impressed with my presentation.

Create Abundant Possibilities

(I always supported my scripts by visualising it going well, before getting out of bed on the morning of the meeting.)

The script would then state that:

- *The project was awarded to our company*
- *The job went very smoothly*
- *I enjoyed the entire project*
- *The report and recommendations were very well received*
- *The clients were delighted with what we had done*
- *The money was in the bank!*

We had a good success rate before I learned ScriptWriting, but scripting took that success rate from good to phenomenal. I can truthfully say that if I chose to submit a proposal for a new project, it was rare for me not to get the job.

I wish you every success with your scripting, dear reader, in the delivery of your dreams in whatever areas of your life you choose to script. If you are ready to maximise the effectiveness of your scripts, you'll love the mastery tips in the next two chapters.

6

HOW TO BECOME A MASTER OF SCRIPTING

IS SCRIPTWRITING REALLY THAT SIMPLE?

This chapter shows you how to maximise your likelihood of writing scripts which deliver your dreams — how you can become a master of scripting!

From Day One of my ScriptWriting adventures, most (roughly 90%) of what I scripted showed up in my life. The majority of the clients to whom I've taught ScriptWriting have also enjoyed a high level of success.

As The Seven Steps of ScriptWriting show in Chapter One, the instructions for writing a script are simple. But is that really all there is to it? Well, yes and no.

Does my high success rate in manifesting what I script mean that **everything** I have scripted has eventuated? It does not. Does it mean that everyone is as successful as everyone else in receiving what they've scripted? Again, not so. Some people manifest their dreams more easily and consistently than others.

I will now unpack the secrets, tips and guidelines which have worked for myself and others to increase the success rate of our scripts. These ideas enhance the power of your script and can help you become a master manifester* of dreams. Embrace them as far as you can, but let me reassure you, **however you write your script, it will be powerful anyway. Don't sweat the small stuff, just write a script!**

*A 'manifester' is defined as an individual who creates something by *their actions and makes it visible. By definition, a manifester is someone who is able to materialise ideas into reality. In other words, a manifester is someone who manifests or demonstrates that which they desire to achieve.*

Include the Qualities that Matter to You

Don't take things for granted. I always get a laugh with this one: When I wrote my first script about meeting the love of my life, I omitted mentioning his hair. Had I scripted that the new man in my life had a beautiful head of hair, he wouldn't have been bald.

There are of course limits to this. I'm not recommending an obsessive, totally comprehensive checklist. If you attempt to include everything, it could get cumbersome, controlling, and take the joy out of writing your script.

However, as you describe the partner coming into your life, do include the qualities that really are important to you.

Don't Concern Yourself with the 'How'

When you specify your dream, don't worry about <u>how</u> you will achieve it.

Scripting that I doubled my billings is a case in point. Had I gone into my logical, reasoning, controlling left brain, I would have stepped back and told myself this was a ridiculous ask. I had no idea whether it was even possible to double my billings in a year. I had no idea how I would go about doing so.

However, I stayed in the part of me that is trusting, that is open to possibility. I followed the direction to be super-positive and threw my request into the unknown.

And then, seemingly miraculously, the opportunity presented itself. I was invited to address exactly the audience from which this business could come (pharmaceutical company marketing people and health care advertising agencies) and the rest is history!

The key is to take advantage of the opportunities which do present themselves but in the first instance, merely 'cast your bread upon the waters' with your scripting and be open to, and creative with, what shows up.

Create Abundant Possibilities

So often your script will emerge in a non-linear way. Allow the flow of possibilities and observe when what you've asked for arrives. It may arrive in a slightly different package to what you scripted, and yet, it's perfect! Give it a go.

For example, maybe the man who shows up is not tall and dark. He's medium height and blonde. That'll do. Don't reject him because he doesn't tick every box on your script!

When Opportunities Present, Take Them

With the vision of hindsight, I see that, yes, magic happens. I did meet the love of my life, I did double my billings, I did sell the company for the payout I had scripted.

However, I also see that, **when opportunities came my way, I took them.**

When a PhD program was introduced in podiatry, despite being a busy single mother of two, my stepdaughter Sylvia took the opportunity to enrol. She scripted that she discovered a treatment breakthrough. Her research led her to trial a transdermal nitrate that had previously been used to treat horses, on diabetic leg ulcers.

Miraculously, ulcers cleared up overnight. She is now a sought-after speaker at medical and podiatry conferences. Her work has saved thousands of leg and foot amputations.

Olivia was horrified to discover her husband was an meth addict. His erratic behaviour and the dramatic deterioration in their marriage suddenly made sense.

After an acrimonious divorce, she assured me she felt it would be years before she'd be ready to embark on a new relationship. Nonetheless, when her friend offered to introduce her to a new doctor who'd moved into the area, she over-rode her reluctance and fear, and accepted the dinner invitation. And yes, they fell in love.

Psychology professor Richard Wiseman conducted extensive research with self-professed 'lucky' and 'unlucky' people. They kept detailed dairies of their daily lives. He found that people who considered themselves 'lucky' in fact took opportunities when they arose.

Conversely, people who considered themselves 'unlucky' either failed to take the opportunities or were risk averse. They chose not to follow-up opportunities which came their way.

Wiseman found that he could teach people to become 'luckier.' After one month, 80% of self-professed 'lucky' as well as 'unlucky' participants in his 'Luck School' reported they were happier, their lives were more satisfying, and more importantly, they were luckier.

His 'Four Principles of Luck' are:

1. *Maximise Your Chance of Opportunities*
2. *Listen to Your Lucky Hunches*
3. *Expect Good Fortune*
4. *Turn Your Bad Luck into Good*

In a nutshell, he teaches people to:

- Be more open and look around for new opportunities (if you're wanting to find a partner, don't stay home alone night after night, even though that's what you most feel like doing).
- When opportunities present themselves, expect they'll turn out well, and take them. That's why I recommend that before you hop out of bed every morning, you imagine your day going very well. If there's a special meeting coming up, or some project to tackle, imagine you handled it constructively, and intend that, at the end of the day, you'll think: *'That was a really good day.'*
- Be alive to opportunities. Be on alert to notice the choices available, whereas previously you may not even have spotted things which could represent opportunities for you.
- When opportunities show up, grab 'em! Take more chances, say 'Yes' more, say 'No' less, and become less risk averse – within reason, of course.
- In the words of the aphorism, *'Make more real mistakes and fewer imagined mistakes.'* If it turns out not to be a good

decision, cut your losses and move on. On the other hand, it could be good and if you don't take the chance, you miss out and nothing happens.

Liberate Yourself from Your Old 'Stories' of Who You Are

All I understood when I wrote that first script was that I was learning how to create new possibilities. What I didn't realise was that:

- Spelling out what I longed for, and,
- Allowing my scripts to manifest,
- Was also really about **liberation** from all my **old stories** about **who** I was in the parts of my life where formerly I had experienced problems.

Like two sides of one coin, it's the balance of possibility.

Rather than creating from the unconscious default position of our fears (our old platform for creating), when we harness the potential of scripting, we switch into creating from our dreams (our new platform for creating).

Let me give you a personal example of what I mean by this:

I have been fortunate in that career progress and financial success always seemed to come easily to me. As a result, I didn't need to change my beliefs about career, money, or professional success.

On the other hand, my success and trust in relationships was shakier. I grappled with the burning question; *'Why had my marriage failed? What did I need to learn and change so that I could be truly happy in my next marriage?'*

I recognised that something more than just bad luck had led to my divorce. I was a psychologist. I knew marriage is a two-way street. I knew both partners needed to take responsibility for the things they said and did which contributed to the failure. And I knew the same 'me' would be going into whatever new relationship I entered.

I used my post-separation blues for soul searching. For six months I read self-help books and enrolled in one workshop after another. There I met aspects of myself - inner selves who harboured fears and doubts – aspects which put up roadblocks and sabotaged my relationship. There I learned how I had been relying on losing strategies (like criticism and control) and resorting to misguided attempts to resolve conflicts and differences. I learned better communication skills, more effective ways of getting my needs met. Chapter Eleven *'Keeping the Love Alive'* offers Do's and Don'ts in this all-important area.

The good thing is that, not only did I get to see where I had been going wrong; I also learned what I could do differently to increase my happiness in marriage. I learned how to shift and heal destructive behaviours and communication patterns.

I was able to look at my beliefs, my personality patterns and program about what I expected from men and from marriage.

As an example, I learned to cherish my partner and nurture my relationship for the good of its long-term future, rather than getting my way because I thought I was right.

This gave me tools and skills I needed to stop sabotaging myself and allow my dreams/my script to come true in parts of my life where I had previously struggled.

This is a never-ending journey. I continue to explore, to take responsibility for behaviour which undermines happiness, and to learn new, more effective ways of thinking, communicating and behaving.

What if you too, dear reader, would also benefit from discovering how, and in which areas of your life, you sabotage yourself? **Could you benefit from insights into how your unconscious fears and doubts stop you from getting what you want in career, in financial security, in romance, in friendship, in family life, in fitness, in health?**

Part Two of this book is designed to show you how to do this. It will help you shift and heal old patterns which have held you back from fulfilling your dreams in the past. This will literally be a process of liberation from your old life. It will provide **stepping stones for you to traverse as you turn your dreams into reality.**

The Power of the Words You Use

This may come as a surprise, but the words you use are extraordinarily powerful in influencing what you experience.

I have psychologist and spiritual teacher Amoraea to thank for drawing attention to the power of words in his extraordinary online training, *'Beloved Within.'*

Your words are signals to the universe. You shape your destiny through your language. *'I can't', 'I don't know', 'I don't have'* – we bandy words about like that as though they aren't relevant or important. We don't give them a second thought.

Stop for a moment and reflect on the energy of those words: it's victim energy. Empowerment energy would be *'I can', 'I choose to know',* and, *'I have.'*

Similarly, answers to the question *'How are you?'* like *'Doing OK'* or *'Not bad'*, instruct our obedient subconscious mind to keep us at *'fair to middling'* rather than vibrant, full of energy and enthusiasm, with a strong life force.

Unfortunately, unconscious lack and fear-based thoughts and language are a powerful self-sabotage tool. It's as though your thoughts, your words, your actions cast a spell.

The Law of Attraction and quantum entanglements **work to create exactly what you expect to happen, good or not so good.** You know what it is that you expect to happen. You know this to the very core of your being.

So, when a negative outcome turns up, you may be disappointed, but you aren't really surprised because at some level, that's what you expected. It's like waiting for the other shoe to drop. This is defined as *'an idiom that is often used to describe a situation where someone is* **anxiously anticipating the completion of a sequence of events** *or the resolution of an issue, particularly when the outcome is expected to be negative or uncertain.'*

It doesn't seem fair, does it, but if we combine weak or disempowered words with the body language of insecurity, frowning, shoulders slumped, that tells the universe what we are choosing.

It's also inviting others to take you at your own evaluation of yourself. So, choose to sit straighter, breathe more deeply, use good eye contact. Be vibrant and alive in the moment. Choices like this direct your nervous system, and make you feel more empowered and prepared.

Remember that your cells eavesdrop on your thoughts. When you use the language of put-down, disappointment, discontent and lack, you are instructing your unconscious mind to deliver what your language flags.

Become consciously aware of your thoughts and energy in every moment. If you notice you're being negative and self-critical, immediately challenge that mindset and replace it with optimistic possibilities and self-compassion. Remind yourself of good things about yourself, of times when things have worked out well for you.

That's why it's a great idea to rehearse upcoming events.

For example, if you have a job interview lined up, role play it. It will pay to understand what you will be conveying at an unconscious and felt level about your belief in yourself, and your enthusiasm for the job.

Writing a script before the interview, imagining yourself feeling confident, connecting well with the decision makers interviewing you, will strongly support your likely success.

I often do this with clients before a job interview or an important meeting. With life coaching and mindset tools becoming more prevalent, there's a fair chance that other applicants will have advantaged themselves by doing at least some of this. It will benefit you to load your chances in this way.

By stating; *'I am happy', 'I am loving', 'I find joy in simple moments'* we are expressing empowerment in the present moment. This aligns us with the positive force of the universe.

Avoid using weak language, like; *'I hope this is going to happen'* or *'Maybe it will happen' or 'I'll try.'* Have you ever *tried* to sit down?

You are either sitting, moving from sitting to standing, or standing. There's no trying!

What if you choose to use definitive statements that leave no room for ambiguity? This is an invitation to you to grasp this opportunity to make a new covenant: *'From now on I play at an even higher level of creation.'* This is how we can shape our state (our mood), our very destiny, through our language.

This has direct relevance to the words you use in your script. Bear in mind that the unconscious mind can't process a negative. If I say to you

'Don't *think of a blue tree,'* like most people, you will probably think of a blue tree.

It is crucial that you avoid negative words and ideas in your script. The same applies when you craft your values and visualise yourself living the life that would make you happy. What follows are a couple of examples of 'Don'ts'.

Don't write, *'I'm no longer anxious.'* Instead, write *'I feel confident and calm'.* In other words, write only in the positive, never in the negative. If you have a negative thought, ask yourself 'If things were great, what would I think or feel instead?'

One client, whose marriage ended when her partner cheated on her, wrote: *'I forgive my partner if he cheats on me.'* This is an utter no-no.

To reframe that in the positive, I coached her to write something like: *'My partner and I love each other dearly. We're both honest, trustworthy and faithful to each other. We deal with issues that arise in a constructive way, and our relationship continues to go from strength to strength.'*

I then worked with her in individual therapy to challenge and reframe her fears about unfaithfulness and other limiting beliefs.

Her therapy also included coaching in relationship skills, setting boundaries, being assertive in her communication (respectful and empowered, rather than being a fawning people pleaser, or being aggressive.)

Part Two of this book covers these skills. It shows you how to shift self-judgement and have compassion for/embrace your shadow. It disrupts the old stories of the part of you that has been fearful, that has been hurt and wounded, that expects relationships don't last, that thinks relationships turn sour, that thinks you're not enough (or that you're too much) for someone to keep loving you.

Empowerment IS the Language of ScriptWriting

Setting goals is useful. It gets us to think about what we'd like to achieve; it motivates us to strive towards something. However, in terms of its sheer power to actually manifest, to make your dreams come true, ScriptWriting leaves goal setting in the dust.

This is because there's a darker side to goal setting. In stating our goals, and in our affirmations about what we want, our language can be our undoing. When we 'want' we are coming from **lack**, rather than **abundance**.

When we say:

- *'I want a raise/my goal is a raise'*
- *'I want a better house/my goal is to have a better house'*
- *'I want a loving partner'*
- *'I want to be happy'.*

...the underlying energy or subconscious thought is:

- *'I don't earn enough'*
- *'My house isn't good enough'*
- *'I don't have a partner'*
- *'I'm unhappy.'*

Why is this important? Am I splitting hairs? Compare this 'wanting more' with the language and energy of ScriptWriting, which writes the future as if it's highly desirable and has already happened.

'I was thrilled with the raise I received. My salary increased to $xxx,xxx'.

Some more examples:

- *'We've been living in our beautiful house for the last three months, and it is perfect for our family in every way.'*
- *'I've never been happier or felt more loved and supported. My wonderful new partner and I have been living together since January. We bring out the absolute best in each other. We feel so good and comfortable around each other and love spending time together.'*
- *'Something magical has happened to me. I feel so happy - just happy with me, happy with my life and my world. I now find*

Create Abundant Possibilities

I appreciate the good things in my life. I'm able to be grateful for anything that is good, for the little and the bigger things. The more I do this, the better my life becomes.'

Wanting what you haven't got is the language and energy of **lack**. If you check the dictionary definition of the word 'want', you'll find: '*You have a desire to possess or do something; a want is a lack or deficiency of something.*'

The mistake people make by focusing on what they want is that 'wanting' often comes from a place of lack. '*I want it because I don't have it.*'

So, instead, live in your imagination, as if you already have what you long for. Imagine yourself having that, being happy with it in your life, and that's what you'll attract.

Even if you don't have much in the way of abundance, you can start looking at the abundance of leaves on trees, the infinite number of grains of sand on a beach and breathe in that feeling of abundance.

Instead of going into disappointment that you don't have what you long for, say to yourself; '*I'm so happy it's coming. I'll be celebrating getting it any day now.*' And use your imagination and create that feeling in your body now—in the present moment.

As you shift into using the language and feeling the joy of *'I have this now'* (the words in your script), you come into full alignment with your dreams.

The language of confidence, that you already have what you dream of, is beyond hope and faith. **Because you write your script in the past tense, you're claiming victory <u>now</u>, in the present moment.**

You're stating *'This is what I have. I AM THIS'*, not *'I would like this/I want this'*. You're upgrading your language, you're upgrading what you choose, what you're aligning yourself with.

Beyond Belief - A Mindset of Allowing and Trust

As I revisit my mindset when I wrote my first script, I realise that I was mentally and emotionally open to **possibility.**

When I wrote that I met the man of my dreams, when I wrote that I doubled my billings that year, did I really believe that I would?

I'd have to say that I neither believed it nor didn't believe it.

I didn't get caught up in an argument in my head about whether this was nonsense, how it could work, or even whether or not it was likely to work.

I suspended judgement and analytical thinking. I merely followed the instructions, wrote the script. And had fun writing it.

Almost with the innocence of a child, I loved setting out my dreams of what I wanted, and who I wanted to be.

It was like I was consciously and optimistically writing the next chapter of my life. Think of it as the novel of your life that you are lucky enough to be living.

Insofar as it's possible for you to do that, I recommend you see ScriptWriting as a wonderful opportunity and give it a go.

Your Energy Needs to be a Vibrational Match for Your Dreams

It is essential – and entirely possible if you do the work to release your limiting beliefs and inner saboteurs – to stop listening to your voice of fear.

It is entirely possible for you to unlock your inner wisdom. If you don't, in all likelihood you'll continue to live what you currently experience.

If you do, you will open the doors to wonderful new possibilities which turn into wonderful new experiences. Why is it important to be aware that your energy needs to be a vibrational match for your dreams? Wayne Dyer, best-selling author and spiritual mentor, famously taught *'You'll see it when you believe it.'*

Everything happens twice: First you have the thought, then the experience follows, carrying the energy and spellcasting of your thought. If you are driven by negative emotions - like doubt, fear, anger, sadness, guilt, apathy – this will block your dreams from manifesting.

Conversely, if you major in the higher vibrational emotions, like love and joy, this will be the emotional highway for delivery of your dreams.

Remember the Law of Attraction? The **Law of Vibration** is at its core. This is how manifesting works. It requires constant consciousness, constant choice to be love in action, joy in action, peace in action. Let yourself dream that happiness and abundance are possible for you, write your script, and manifest your dreams.

Having a mindset of allowing trust doesn't mean that I'm 100% trusting all the time, that I have no anxiety or doubt.

When I ask for something in a script, I do sometimes quiver a little, with my mind darting between:

- Trust and peace, and,
- Flickers of doubt and incredulity that this could actually happen.

However, I'm talking about the need to cultivate a high level of **trust**, an almost childlike innocence, and a willingness to embrace the idea of co-creating with a benevolent and loving universe.

If you have a feeling of jaded scepticism, or you insist on being overly logical, clinging to the old, you quash any feelings of wonder and magic of dreams becoming reality.

So, if flickers of doubt come up, I recommend you do as I do. Rather than dwell on them, giving them energy and life, I immediately change the channel on the virtual TV, so to speak. I imagine myself fulfilled in the dream, like focusing on me as a published author before my book was completed, and me as a happily married woman when I was, in fact, still alone and hurting.

This raises a very important question. What is happening if what you script fails to manifest? As a teacher of ScriptWriting I acknowledge that although the majority do manifest their dreams, a small minority do not.

As I look back on the therapeutic journeys of those whose scripts didn't manifest, I see that almost to a person, their dominant emotional landscape was one of fear and blame.

Dr Claire Zammit, trainer of thousands of life coaches, invites clients to say, *'All of life is organising around my success. I let go of control (or waiting) and move into listening, curiosity and receptivity.'*

She also asks the many hundreds of participants in her online workshops to agree to 'zero negativity.' Rather than take on board coaching and skills to change and upgrade their thinking, mood and behaviour, I would say that the people I've worked with who, sadly, didn't manifest their dreams, clung to their old certainties and habits.

I now see this as the critical impediment to their bringing their dreams into reality. This is why I invite you to keep checking your level of consciousness. Aim to focus on positive emotions like love and joy, not negative emotions like grief, guilt, and anger.

If you find you have slipped out of love, joy and peace, into anger, guilt, sadness, do the work to bring yourself back into your heart.

All I can say is that I do the best I can to imagine myself with the things I've scripted. Given that I believe my thoughts create my reality, I allow myself zero negativity, zero scepticism.

This means that if I found myself thinking fearful thoughts, like *'What chance have I got of having my book published?'* I caught the thought and immediately imagined a large display of my books in the bookstore window.

In a similar way, as I sat, newly divorced and alone on my sofa, night after night, I imagined myself feeling nurtured and loved, enjoying being with my lovely partner-in-the-wings.

Since I'm not one of those visual people who create pictures behind my closed eyes, I embodied the feeling and sense that I was happy and safe in the arms of my new partner. And miracle of miracles, when the time was right, he materialised!

Here's a tip if you're doubtful and cynical that what you script could happen. Or if you're someone who is less trusting of life and doesn't understand how you'd be able to feel that way: Identify, then write down your 'doubt' or 'fear' thoughts and ceremoniously burn the paper on which you wrote them.

You might write something like; *'How could I expect this could work. It may work for others. But it wouldn't work for me'*, or *'I've never had a job I've liked'*, or *'I've never had a good partner'*.

Whatever you're thinking, just jot it down. Take a deep breath. Raise your hands, imagining you're lifting the thought(s) above your head. Imagine a brilliant white light is saturating them, and that space above your head, with light. Hold that picture, or sense of it (you don't have to actually see it) for a couple of minutes.

You don't have to do this perfectly. You don't have to feel certain. Even a small glimmer of hope is a good start.

Allow yourself to believe as best you can that those old thoughts are dissolving. Now that you're putting your hand up for help from the universe, step by step, you will begin to change. Notice that you feel lighter after doing this.

You will find many more strategies and practical exercises for changing fear-based beliefs, born of difficult experiences or trauma, as you work through the second part of this book.

Dream Big: A Willingness to Suspend Judgement and Allow Greatness

At the first scripting workshop I attended, we were advised to be **highly optimistic** and **ambitious** in what we asked for. I recommend that you honour this guidance, that this is the spirit in which you write your script. Feel safe to shine your inner brilliance and light!

In her 1992 self-help book, *A Return to Love*, Marianne Williamson - author, self-help guru and spiritual advisor to Oprah - wrote this famous quote, which has often been incorrectly attributed to Nelson Mandela:

> "*Our deepest fear is not that we are inadequate. Our deepest fear is that we are powerful beyond measure. It is our light, not our darkness, that most frightens us. We ask ourselves, 'Who am I to be brilliant, gorgeous, talented, fabulous?' Actually, who are you not to be? You are a child of God. Your playing small doesn't serve the world.*"

Had I been coming from a more modest or doubtful me, a more realistic and 'rational' me, I might have scripted that my billings increased by twenty per cent. That would have been worth having! However, we were encouraged to *'Shoot for the stars.'* So, I didn't hesitate to write: '*I doubled my billings.*'

I didn't give a moment's thought to:

- How this could actually happen,
- Whether such an increase was possible,

- What would need to happen, what steps or actions would be required.

As I look back on how I felt, I recognise that introducing rationality and limits would have been counter to the quintessential freedom, expansiveness and trust which characterised my mood when I wrote that script.

I've used this approach and manifested around 90% of what I've scripted with each subsequent script I've written – which, over the decades since I wrote Script No.1, is a lot of scripts.

How do you feel on a gut level when I mention reaching for the stars? If you are feeling constricted, or this brings up fear for you, as a psychologist I understand.

Many of us experience small 't' trauma - some level of dysfunction in our family of origin, and as we navigate the school system, society, cultural and religious norms in the decades of our childhood, teens and early adulthood.

Or you could be one of the people who experienced big 'T' trauma.

For example, if you grew up in a home with domestic violence, substance abuse, if you were abused or neglected, suffered racial discrimination, if you grew up in poverty, in a war zone, if you suffered serious illnesses - I understand that you may not feel safe to shine. You may feel this is impossible for you.

Research has shown that emotional trauma does make its mark on the brain - on the amygdala, the hippocampus, and the prefrontal cortex.

This explains why people with PTSD (post-traumatic stress disorder), or CPTSD (complex post-traumatic stress disorder), may be fearful and depressed, especially when they are triggered by events and situations which remind them of past trauma. If this sounds like you, I am so sorry you are dealing with such distress.

The work outlined in the chapters on anxiety and depression, as well as the techniques to challenge and reframe limiting beliefs will be helpful to you, opening you up to the belief that you can have the happy future you deserve. If you struggle with severe PTSD, however, I recommend you get professional therapy, to complement the changes you can bring about by following suggestions in this book.

Be Passionate and Fully Engaged as You Imagine Your Dream

Passion and intense feeling as you imagine your joy in having your dream fulfilled will instil life into it. Use your vivid imagination. Your thoughts and your feelings need to work together here, head and heart co-creating.

Your imagination is your ally in this process. Imagine that you are seeing what you'd be seeing, feeling what you'd be feeling, hearing what you'd be hearing, and saying to yourself what you'd be saying if you were right there in the future experience of yourself in your ideal relationship/job, etc. You need to almost taste it, smell it.

As an example, imagine your joy at being back together at the end of a working day, or the delight of your love, companionship and closeness. Allow yourself the gift of imagining yourself feeling joy and feeling bliss.

Hand-Write Your Script, Don't Type It

I believe there's something organic and flowing, a real energetic connection between hand, heart and mind, when you hold a pen in your hand and write. You 'own' what you write. You engage conscious and unconscious mind, allowing an *'Aha!'* moment, a 'eureka' factor, like Archimedes had in his bath when he said *'Eureka, I have found it!'*

Handwriting accesses different parts of the brain, different motor skills, and brings forward more intuitive answers. What if the future you seek is patiently waiting on the tip of your brain for your hand to scribe it out?

Without side-tracking into them here, there are in fact several studies which show that handwriting is better than typing when it comes to retaining information. Interesting, isn't it?

These are all good reasons for recommending you handwrite your script. Test it out on something that doesn't matter... you may be surprised how different the information is that comes from your loving hands and heart.

For the Greatest Good of All Concerned

Ending my script with, '*I choose this or something even better, for the greatest good of all concerned*' has really worked for me.

First, it removed any anxiety that maybe I wasn't sufficiently imaginative and creative to craft a really great script. It allowed for opportunities and possibilities even better than what I, on that day, could imagine.

Second, it meant that nothing I asked for would hurt or diminish anyone or anything else. Win-win. That's how I like it. That's what I recommend you ask for to make your scripting even more powerful. Imagine a world where everyone does this... wouldn't it be infinitely expansive and wonderful!

Don't Keep Checking Your Script

I recommend you avoid checking your script as the weeks and months roll by, keeping tabs on what's shown up, making ticks and crosses. I allowed myself to read my script when I finished, changing the odd word, adding the odd quality, but I didn't dwell too long on 'thinking' while I wrote. Then it went into a drawer till the end of the year, when I pulled it out to see which parts of my script had actually eventuated. I didn't attempt to control, over-analyse, micro-manage or worry about how, when or even if what I'd scripted would happen. I forgot about it, handed it over to the universe, and simply continued living my life.

As Neale Donald Walsch teaches, there are only two energies, **love** and **fear**. Remind yourself that there are a thousand faces of love, and there are a thousand faces of fear.

Keep noticing which you use. As soon as you go into fear, catch yourself and use one of the exercises which help shift you from fear to love, such as reframing your fear-based thoughts. The more you do this, the more you will shift into thinking with love rather than fear. It's an active choice. I do this daily. I recommend you make this a daily practice.

Go with the Flow and Write Your Script Now

Please do the values visualisation described in Chapter Four before you write your script. This will ensure you bring to the forefront the qualities that are really important to you and ones you'd miss if they weren't in your relationship/life.

That way, you can make sure you specify them in your script. For example, you might say, *'My new partner has a great sense of humour, we find the same things funny, and s/he is very affectionate.'*

Familiarise yourself with 'The Seven Steps' (Chapter One) and be highly positive, don't be modest. Be specific where possible.

Then simply sit down and write your script. Go with the flow and have fun with the excitement and creativity of the writing. There's no need to wait until you've sorted out your personality glitches. You can do that in the months after you've set your scripted year in motion by writing it.

While you're writing your script, keep your heart open, write with a lightness of energy and the feeling that **this is your time to be happy**.

If you've learned from your mistakes, done your best to right wrongs, and are now living with full respect, honouring the rights of others, behaving with integrity, you absolutely deserve to be happy.

And if you're not living in this way, you can transform your life today by committing to do so. It will be win-win, I assure you.

Always come from good intentions. Write and desire that whatever you draw into your life is 'for the greatest good of all concerned.'

Use only the energy of **love** and **joy**. Never intend to harm or hurt another (that has a bad habit of coming right back at you). Ask for what you want. Then allow wonderful outcomes to surprise and delight you in their completeness and timing.

7

WHAT IF YOUR SCRIPT DOESN'T MATERIALISE?

THERE'S ALWAYS MORE TO LEARN

Over my thirty years of scripting, I have found it uncanny that what I have scripted has in fact happened. And I've also been pretty impressed with the feedback I've received from most people to whom I've taught ScriptWriting because it has worked for them too!

It is because so much of what I have scripted has happened, that I am so confident and optimistic when I teach ScriptWriting. This experience has etched confidence about ScriptWriting into my very being.

But can I say that I have never been disappointed after writing a script? The answer, regrettably, is 'No'.

My Big Scripting Disappointment

In the early 1990's my husband and I bought an 11-hectare rainforest property with a view of the ocean, two hours south of Sydney. We built our dream home. It was architect designed, had generous-sized high-ceilinged rooms, beautiful building materials, separate guest suites so we could entertain family and friends.

We established cedar plantations, we built bridges over creeks, and we created a beautiful garden. And this project ushered in decades of love of our home, and a lifestyle and social life which we both adored.

The advent of the COVID-19 pandemic and the flood of city

buyers to regional towns was the catalyst for us to put our beloved property on the market. We had begun feeling we wanted a change from the expense and work involved in maintaining our property, and we were tempted by the record prices being achieved in local property sales, so it was time to put the house on the market.

It goes without saying, ScriptWriting devotee that I am, that I duly wrote my script. I specified my hoped-for sales figure, and that we had six months to find and buy our beautiful new home, perfect for us at this stage of our lives.

Although we felt ambivalent about letting our beloved home and property go, we engaged a real estate agent who came highly recommended by friends. As it turned out, the timing was fraught with problems, because this agent was at the start of the process of setting up her own agency and website.

Regrettably, this set-up ran into problems: it took significantly longer than expected. This meant the marketing was delayed and we missed the entire spring-summer sales period. Much as we liked dealing with her, we reached the point where we made the decision to terminate the arrangement and find another agent.

Our new agency made a strong case for auction, and with the dramatic rises in house prices over the mad summer of 2020, we were encouraged to believe we could expect half a million dollars more than we'd been looking for with the previous agent.

My first ScriptWriting error

Dazzled now by greed, I wrote a new script. Of course, it specified the higher figure. At the same time, I also changed the time frame for the sale from the six months I'd specified in my original script, to six weeks, to accommodate the auction.

Both scripts ended with my signature sign-off; '*I choose this or something better for the good of all concerned.*'

However, I left the earlier script hanging; **I didn't specify that the second script superseded my earlier script.** Not that there is a precedent for this, but I later wondered to myself whether it would have been cleaner to have done so?

The energy of innocence and allowing

At the same time, I had gone against one of my strongest recommendations for successful ScriptWriting: Whereas I had written previous scripts with **lightness and almost child-like openness and trust,** in this case, with the pressure of the auction looming, I allowed myself to get swept up in the frenetic energy of the housing market at that time. I became focused on the auction and on 'making a killing', pricewise.

In retrospect I realised that my energy had shifted from that of asking and trusting, which characterised my initial house sale script, to that of being invested and controlling, which characterised my second house sale script.

The advertising campaign and video for the auction sale were stunning. Over the years, we had swelled with joy when friends, family and visitors all raved about the beauty of the house and the property. So, we had high expectations.

Things seemed to be going well. The agent said the level of enquiry was unprecedented. In the week leading up to the auction, there were three parties who had expressed the intention to bid. Encouraged by this, on the Saturday preceding our Wednesday evening auction, Peter and I inspected ten houses for sale.

As luck would have it, we fell in love with one of them. As we walked in and looked over rolling green hills down to a beautiful little beach, I turned to Peter and said, "This is my house."

It was about the right size, I loved the layout and feel, it was within our budget, and it was coming up for auction five days after our auction. *'Perfect'* I thought. I was enchanted by the synchronicity and dazzled that my script was working so well. Just the way it was meant to be.

Unfortunately, that is not what happened. All three would-be bidders dropped out and, on the day, no-one made a bid. I had wanted to cancel the auction, but the agent insisted, *'You have to go ahead and at least register a vendor's bid'*.

The night of the auction was one of the most distressing experiences of my life. I wish I hadn't been physically present. It could have gone ahead without our being there. As it was, I had a raging headache and aching shoulders, and I hated every minute of the experience. I felt devastated:

- Not only because the house had failed to sell at auction and no-one had made a bid,
- But perhaps more-so because my script had been a resounding failure.

What did this mean for me as a teacher of ScriptWriting? What did it mean for me as a would-be author of the book you're now reading? Would this discredit me? How could I accommodate this into my faith in scripting, if my own script had bombed in such an important area of my life?

How was I going to be able to understand and make sense of what had happened? What could account for the fact that I hadn't displayed my usual success in manifesting my dreams? Where did this leave me?

Trust me, I went on a search for answers. It was a time of going within as well as reaching out to my spiritual teachers for help. Uncharacteristically for me, I was highly emotional, confused, upset, deeply disappointed and unhappy in those weeks following the failed auction. Not only because our house hadn't sold, not only because my very faith in myself as script writer and teacher had been shaken, but also because I kept having to field questions like, "Have you sold your house yet?" everywhere I went.

An interesting aside: It's not what happens to you, it's **what you do with what happens to you** that determines how you feel.

For me, the auction was a nightmare, but surprisingly my husband enjoyed it. He still had complete faith that the house would sell, and sell well, and unlike me, he didn't take the failure **personally**.

As a result, he was relaxed and at ease on the night of the auction as well as over the weeks that followed. I did enough worrying for both of us!

Your mindset & energy is crucial

As I looked back on how my mindset and energy had differed when I

Create Abundant Possibilities

wrote Script #1 for our house sale, versus Script #2, I could see that I'd shifted from trust and peace to desire and pride.

In essence, it was my ego, more than my heart, who was author to the second script. One of the most important take-out messages I confirmed for myself, and can now share with you dear reader, about what I learned when my script failed to deliver on time, is that you need to choose and script from soul energy.

What is soul energy? It feels light, expansive, trusting, accepting, and comfortable. You exist in an abundant world where limitless possibilities and opportunities are everywhere.

So, my word of caution is to be careful to NOT script from ego energy.

You'll know if you're scripting solely from your ego because it feels tight, heavy, needy, fear-based, controlling, and comes from a mindset that is imagining a world of scarcity and missed opportunities.

Fortunately, it's never too late to learn how to change that way of thinking!

The trick is to be **grateful** for what's good in your life, not resentful about what isn't good. This is the way happy people live, not because they have more to be happy about, but because this way of thinking **leads** to happiness!

This is the point of the transformational journey I invite you to take in this book. The zone of miracles and dreams coming true is the zone of expansiveness, of abundance, of optimism, of faith, of endless possibility. It is in this zone that miracles show up. They don't show up in the zone of control, doubt, pessimism, fear, scarcity, guilt and apathy.

This is why it is so important to do the work of improving your self-esteem, and self-love, described in Chapter Twelve.

You'll learn how to stop being hard on yourself, focusing on what's wrong with you, and your foregone conclusion that you don't deserve good things to happen, assuming that you'll continue to suffer or have a tough time.

You'll learn to show compassion to yourself instead. You'll begin to love yourself a whole lot more. You'll challenge your critic and your inner pessimist to change their worldview. You'll make your inner child and inner supporter your guides.

Those are voices you'll pay attention to, and not the voices of that snarky inner critic or depressing inner pessimist, replaying dismal experiences from your past (like the date that was a disaster, or when you were fired from your job) as proof that good things don't, and can't, happen to you.

Similarly, rather than focusing on problems, lack, scepticism, pessimism, expectation of failure and trouble, your mindset will shift and lift as you:

- Acknowledge, then reframe your limiting, unhelpful beliefs, following guidelines provided in Chapter Nine, and,
- Implement the strategies to manage anxiety and depression, following guidelines in Chapters Thirteen and Fourteen.

If you're finding it difficult to make these changes by yourself, see a counsellor or life coach to get further help. Your nervous system will thank you for the rest of your life!

In Chapter Four, *'How to Make Your Dreams Crystal-Clear,'* I recommend that you be guided by your dream of what a good relationship, or an ideal job looks like for you when you write your script. That's the point of identifying your values and installing a picture of yourself in your dream into your future.

That you can imagine your dream, and you have been able to articulate it, makes it a real possibility. **Identifying and articulating your dream is an exercise in acknowledging that such a dream is possible.**

Just like in the movie *Sliding Doors*, the 1998 romantic comedy with Gwyneth Paltrow, the movie played with the idea of different possibilities.

When Helen (played by Gwyneth Paltrow), a London executive, is fired from her job, and rushes to catch a train, two scenarios take place.

In one she gets on the train and comes home to find her boyfriend in bed with another woman. In the second, she misses the train and arrives after the woman has left.

In the first, Helen dumps her boyfriend, finds a new man and improves her life. In the second, she becomes suspicious of her boyfriend's fidelity and grows miserable.

Which fork in the road will you take?

As you script your life, writing out your next year - as if it has already happened (in the past tense) - keep your heart open.

As you wait for your dreams to show up, align yourself with optimistic thinking, harness possibility, claim your share of the world's amazing abundance.

That is what **Part Two** of this book is designed to do – to help you shift into the mindset of liberation, optimism, and allowing. Because that is the zone of **flow**, that is the zone of **synchronicity** and **miracles**.

"Be realistic: Plan for a miracle"- Osho

There are many possible scenarios for all of our lives, many sliding doors, of possibilities harnessed, and opportunities taken – or possibilities and opportunities missed or ignored.

ScriptWriting puts you in the driver's seat, where you imagine a wonderful year, a wonderful future. You script it, and trust me, your chances of having it materialise are very favourable, as the scripting success stories in the previous chapters confirm.

Scripting them increases the likelihood that possibilities become probabilities.

This is the thinking and high emotional vibration or feeling patterns that allow your dreams to be ushered in. Claim your share of abundance by cultivating and raising your vibration.

Allowing a Greater Possibility

Another possibility as to why my ego-fuelled script failed was to allow for the playing out of the invitation at the end of my script, *'I choose this or something even better, for the greatest good of all concerned.'*

If this is to be more than merely lip-service, it means that the timing specified in the script may, in fact, not be the right timing for the fulfilment of the dream.

It may mean that what you've asked for may not necessarily be in the best interests of yourself, or of all concerned. It may mean that the request was way over the top unrealistic.

Remember, earlier, I suggested the context of the request needs to be congruent with the request. In other words, you wouldn't script that you were given the prima ballerina role in the next production of 'Swan Lake' if you had never had a ballet lesson! Maybe my additional half a million dollars for our house sale was simply unrealistic?

From another perspective, we saw our land as sacred and saw ourselves as its custodians for the decades we'd been lucky enough to live there. Could the sale have been delayed because the right custodians for the next stage hadn't yet shown up?

On a practical, logical level, with COVID-19 on the loose, we needed to entertain the possibility that it could have been better for my husband and me to ride out the pandemic in our peaceful rural retreat.

In fact, one message I received was that, *'Your angels had to work really hard to derail the auction, because, for now, it is better for you to be living in a rural setting.'* Thanks Angels!

Identifying and Healing Aspects of Yourself which may Sabotage Your Script

All of that considered, I stayed open to exploring other reasons that my house-sale script didn't deliver. I wanted to learn what I might have been doing, at an unconscious level, to sabotage the success of that script.

I found it helpful to identify my fears and limiting beliefs around giving up the home I loved, including my fears that I might not find a home I loved as much, and that we might not be happy with our new lifestyle. I reframed those beliefs, and daily imagined us happy in a beautiful new home, using the guidance in Chapter Four.

If there are areas in which your script fails to manifest, you could use these guidelines to reframe any limiting beliefs and flush out your fears, your 'inner saboteur'. By doing so, you actively shape a new narrative and a new life experience.

My House Script Did Manifest – Just Later than Expected

The good news is that reframing my limiting beliefs, and a dose of patience (not that I had the choice) did the trick!

Within six months, our house sold at the higher price I scripted, and we were fortunate enough to buy the next house of our dreams, with all the features I'd scripted.

Peter, my husband, now says, "We moved from Paradise A to Paradise B."

That's what it feels like, and we are deeply grateful. The other feature of my script which manifested is that the buyers of our property seem ideal as custodians of the rainforest.

They fell in love with the land and the house, enabling us to breathe a sigh of relief as we handed the property over to their safekeeping.

8

TOGETHER, WE CAN CREATE A BETTER WORLD

YOU AFFECT YOUR LIFE, YOU AFFECT OUR WORLD

Not only do you have the power to script and create a happy future for yourself. You also have the power to script and create a better future for your world, our beloved planet.

In this book I have provided plenty of evidence that what we focus on exerts a powerful influence on what we experience. There is no such thing as a thought, an expectation, a belief which doesn't matter, which doesn't have some influence on your life and on your world.

The thoughts and actions of each and every one of us have consequences. If I'm angry with you, if I judge you as being rude or mean or uncaring, you will feel and pick up on my judgments, and that will influence the way you react to me.

You may choose to be compassionate, understanding, forgiving, and/or sorry that I judged you, and behave with great maturity and generosity. Or you may be highly reactive, become defensive, and hit back, aggressively or passive-aggressively. Whatever you choose, I will have influenced you. And whatever you choose, you will influence my next response.

Insignificant as each of us may seem as one individual in a world population now numbering billions, each of us is our own sphere of influence. Our beliefs, our thoughts, our expectations about, and our behaviour towards, other human beings, other life, animal, vegetable or mineral, influences their fate. We wage war — or not; we slaughter, we mow down — or not; we dig up, mine and crush — or not.

We are inherently connected with all that and with whom we share this exquisite gift of a planet. Each of us has free will. We choose, moment by moment, how we will **be** in the world.

What Are You Choosing?

Ask yourself about the choices that you make:

- Will I be responsible or irresponsible?
- Respectful and caring?
- Disrespectful and careless in my relationship with food sources?
- How will I treat the environment, the forest, the flora?
- How about other life forms such as animals, insects, birds of the skies, fish of the seas?
- How do my choices on the products I buy affect others?
- How do I dispose of the waste I generate?
- How will the way I travel affect the planet?
- How about the way I treat (and think about) members of my immediate family, my extended family, my community, and my fellow human beings around the globe?

Acceptance of reality is the path to inner peace. Will I live in judgement, greed, blame, railing against the circumstances of my life? Or will I practise acceptance of **what is**, with gratitude, open-heartedness, forgiveness, compassion, non-judgement and non-violence, knowing that everything rises and passes over the course of time?

> **The choice is mine. The choice is yours. And make no mistake. This is a choice. Every moment, you and I are making a choice.**

The reason this is so important is that the choice I make, the choice you make, today, tomorrow, and the day after that will affect the world we live in, the world our children and grandchildren live in. We are part of a global collective.

As beings who are over 70% water, we are all connected at a cellular level whether or not we want to be. Explore the work of Veda Austin, where she demonstrates the responsiveness of water to its surroundings. Seeing her evidence could change the way you live your life!

If I harbour envy, greed, unkindness, prejudice, hatred, shame, superiority, my energy will spill over, touching all with whom I come into contact, dragging us all down.

Offending from the victim position, according to Terrence Real, is at the heart of all prejudice, abuse, violence, war. Viewing others with resentment and dislike will curdle relationships. It will push them into the losing strategies that are so common in our relationships, like criticism, defensiveness, retaliation, verbal and physical abuse, control, withdrawal.

On a bigger picture, *'no man is an island.'* Not caring about the suffering of others – people of different gender, different racial or religious groups, the poor, the disabled, the disadvantaged – will be my tacit agreement to allow prejudice and the suffering to continue. My careless choices will fuel further problems. My thoughtful, caring, loving choices will help uplift myself and humanity.

I am fascinated by the possibility of the 100th monkey effect. You probably know the 100th monkey experiment is a hypothetical phenomenon in which a new behaviour or idea is spread rapidly by one group to all related groups. This happens once a critical number of group members of one group exhibit a new behaviour or acknowledge a new idea. Even in a population now numbering in the billions, once the tipping point is reached, any one of us could be that 100th monkey, and set in motion dramatic global change. Which way we tip is up to each of us, individually, given the gift of our own free will.

Our Earth is in a State of Transition

We seem to be getting closer and closer to tipping points. We have all recently witnessed an increase in natural disasters (flood, drought, fire), and experienced lockdowns in response to a global pandemic that lasted for years. The pandemic response by governments has brought changes to the very fabric and structure of society as we know it and continues to have an impact in many unexpected ways. Having our financial security, our livelihoods, our very lives threatened, has taken us into our individual and collective vulnerability. Our realisation and remembrance is that change and renewal are inevitable parts of life.

Many people are now reflecting on the way they live their lives, and on the sustainability and integrity of many of our political and commercial practices. Greed, inequality, corruption, discrimination, squandering of our beautiful planet's finite resources, have increasingly come under the spotlight.

Consider this quote from David Suzuki:

'The way we see the world shapes the way we treat it: If a mountain is a deity, not a pile of ore; if a forest is a sacred grove, not timber; if other species are biological kin, not resources; if the planet is our mother, not an opportunity - then we will treat each other with greater respect. This is the challenge, to look at the world from a different perspective.'

One if the greatest thinkers of our times, Albert Einstein, exhorts us to wake up:

'A human being is part of the whole called by us the universe, a part limited in time and space. He experiences himself, his thoughts and feelings as something separated from the rest, a kind of optical delusion in consciousness. This delusion is a kind of prison for us, restricting us to our personal desires and to affection for a few persons nearest to us. Our task must be to free ourselves from this prison by widening our circle of compassion to embrace all living creatures and the whole of nature in its beauty.'

We, you and I, vote with our feet. Not only the choices we make (what and how much we buy, how we live our lives, what's important to us, for whom and what we vote) but also how we hold society in our minds, affects the future of our planet, our children's and grandchildren's futures.

Collectively, this amounts to a powerful force for change.

Let's Shape the Earth's Next Chapter Together

This is a book about scripting, about transformation. It's about choosing different (and abundant!) **possibilities**. Poised at this moment in the history of our planet, we - you and I - have the power to **choose** what kind of world we want to live in.

I have been privileged to learn how to script a positive future for myself, and I see much of what I've scripted come to fruition. I have been encouraged and inspired that many people with whom I've shared scripting bring their dreams into reality. They have literally changed the course of their lives and the lives of people around them through their courageous choices.

This is an awesome, effective process with proven success. If each of us scripts our dream for mental and physical health, peace, fairness, respect, wise government, integrity, wisdom in use of resources and distribution of wealth, love, enlightened non-violent relationships, and enlightened child rearing, it's possible that, together we can create a new way of being in the world.

From my wide-ranging experience eliciting many clients' values for their relationships, their careers, their family life, their health and lifestyle preferences, I have been encouraged that these **values are invariably positive, invariably beautiful, invariably loving and hopeful.** In other words, there is a part of all of us that has a picture or a sense of ourselves living with **love, integrity, respect, ease** and **joy.**

Each of us has our own individual, unique solutions or preferences for Mother Earth right now. Your brilliance is needed!

No-one wants an angry, abusive, bossy partner who doesn't care what they think; no-one wants to be badly treated and underpaid at work. And no-one wants a violent, chaotic society and a corrupt government.

> **I feel pretty sure that your values for our wonderful planet are positive, beautiful, bountiful, hopeful, peaceful and loving too. Rather than fear the future, let us shape it according to our dreams of the best possible solutions.**

I therefore invite you, dear reader, when you write your script for the year ahead, to include a section on your dream for our beloved gift of a planet – Gaia or Mother Earth.

You might also want to script your dream for this planet five years from now. You're harnessing and creating possibilities for your future self, for the type of world in which you'd like yourself, your children, your grandchildren to live.

If you were its creator:

- How would you see the economy/financial recovery/job prospects in your country and the global community?
- How would you see the distribution of wealth, what would you script in terms of fairness and corporate taxation and profits?
- What laws would you want to be enacted, and practices adopted to protect forests, to protect animal and plant life, biodiversity and threatened species; to restore the natural system of checks and balances, including our precious ocean currents and weather patterns?

You might also want to include your dreams for:

- World peace
- Religious freedom, religious tolerance
- Gender equality in the home, in the workplace, in the world
- Work/life balance, physical, mental and spiritual health
- Teaching of self-esteem and relationship skills, meditation, the skills for conscious, loving child rearing and learned optimism in schools and other places of learning
- Improved health and wellbeing
- And any, and everything else, that truly matters to you.

Although our scripts may not cover the identical areas, nor will our requests be identical, this principle that all of us will have a positive vision for our planet will mean that, collectively, we will ask for a wonderful world.

The more each of us imagines those dreams coming true (rather than imagining mayhem and disaster - as the news often teaches us to) the more likely we are to experience the prosperous, fair, peaceful world we long for.

What to Expect in Part Two

Hopefully, this book, so far, has taken you on a journey of possibility and hope. Hopefully it has inspired or will inspire you to write your own script. Hopefully it has encouraged you to want to understand and break free from old unhelpful limiting beliefs, discarding the 'stories' you tell yourself, which have held you back from fulfilling dreams – from reaching for the stars.

Part Two is the toolkit that provides you with life coaching, via practical, grounded steps of transformation on your journey of possibility. Not only will this help you disrupt and ditch old habits. It will also help you stay conscious, regularly updating your thinking and choices in ways that enhance the dreams your scripts bring into your life.

From beginning to end, this book is therefore designed to be a complete cycle of transformation. What I mean by this is that it will have the effect of changing your understanding of your life story, giving you a new perspective on your past. It will also introduce you to many life changing concepts and practices to assist your growth, changing your experience of 'reality'. Both will have a ripple effect on the way you see and live your life.

The book ends with an extensive list of resources including inspiring books, workshops, and trainings which have informed my writing and my practice. I recommend you follow up those which resonate with you. They will orchestrate the next stages of your own personal growth and self-actualisation.

∼

PART II

THE TOOLKIT TO HELP YOU
FULFIL YOUR DREAMS

PREFACE TO PART TWO
TAKE YOUR OWN PERSONAL DEVELOPMENT JOURNEY

Self-Sabotaging Beliefs and Patterns

Why the need for a second part to this book?

Like mine, some of the zones of your life will be more satisfying and flow more easily than others. Maybe you struggle with money, with career, or love?

Your zones of struggle could become the parts of your script which don't arrive, until you work with and release your limiting beliefs, fears, blockages and addictive or self-sabotaging patterns.

Your 'shadow' contains the parts of you that you don't want others to see, as well as the parts of you that are hidden, even from you!

Shadows shroud and obscure. The **Shadow** was the term first coined by Carl Jung, famous Swiss psychiatrist, psychotherapist and pioneering evolutionary theorist who founded the school of analytical psychology in the late 1880s.

He used this term to refer to the blind spot, the hidden, dark side of the psyche. These are 'disowned' parts of us which live in our unconscious, where the unwanted, unprocessed parts of Self are stored. These are parts of us we want to avoid at all costs.

Therapeutic work, such as inner child work, and certain spiritual practices, like meditation, encourage us to make peace with those parts

Preface to Part Two

of ourselves we find unacceptable and uncomfortable: parts of ourselves we find shameful, embarrassing, frightening, disgusting. We repress them, but try as we may, we cannot get rid of them - until we do the inner work. And the reward is freedom, peace, joy.

Whether or not you are consciously aware of them, these beliefs, these patterns, these habits, lurk in your shadow. In the past, they have stood in the way of you getting what you want. Having learnt Script-Writing, you don't want to give your old personality saboteurs free run to make their familiar mischief and undermine the dreams your script has made possible.

For example, you may have manifested a loving new relationship. But have you learned different and better ways of communicating, setting boundaries, resolving the conflicts which inevitably arise in intimate relationships?

If not, you may well find problems you hated in your previous relationship re-emerge in your new relationship, for example, explosive arguments, or feeling unheard or unloved. Hence the chapter 'Keeping the Love Alive'.

There are also chapters on 'Confidence,' 'Unhook from Anxiety', and 'Shift Depression' for the same reason.

If you've grappled with debilitating low self-esteem, anxiety and depression, they could take the shine off the dream relationship or the dream job you've just successfully scripted into your life. It's far better to be **proactive**. Far better to use these teachings to learn and apply new skills and strengths which increase confidence, which shift and heal anxiety and depression before they can undermine the new you.

In a nutshell, Part Two shows you how to transmute and deprogram your old paradigm stories of what is wrong and your limited beliefs of lack.

This will support and guide you in nurturing your new story about yourself. What better time could there be to do that than NOW?

An Opportunity to Heal, A Step to Liberation

Life coaching and therapeutic help can liberate people who are trapped like a deer in the spotlight, or being held to ransom by crippling, fear-based limiting beliefs and mental illness.

Preface to Part Two

To gain full value from ScriptWriting, I take my workshop participants and individual clients on the journey, or those parts of the journey, which their particular issues require.

Part Two of this book offers you practical, actionable processes, exercises, skills and tips to help you get your needs met in better ways, so that you experience more pleasure and inner peace. This can help you beat saboteurs, inner critics, the inner selves, or aspects of personality which could put up roadblocks to manifesting your scripts.

You may remember it was December when I wrote my first script, asking for my dream partner to show up in October. I embarked on an intensive program of personal development between that December and that October.

I wanted to deprogram my old beliefs of lack, my fear of relationship going wrong again. It wasn't enough for me simply to ask for my dream partner to be delivered. I knew I needed to learn new relationship skills so I could do better with him than I had done in my failed marriage.

Indeed, when my new love showed up, I was better equipped to create a growth-oriented relationship. And it didn't end there. I have continued to upskill, get help, and evolve as my partner and I have juggled the ups and downs of marriage.

The material in this second part of the book draws on my own experiences and my emotional, mental, and behavioural shifts for the better, as well as those of many clients who have walked this path before you.

There may be chapters that really speak to you, and others which may be of passing interest, rather than having direct relevance to your life. For example, you may have a great marriage, but struggle with career satisfaction and finances. Or vice versa.

Dear reader, take from Part Two what is relevant to you and your dreams and leave the rest.

And please get professional help if you feel drawn to it, so that you boost the likelihood that you fulfil your potential and keep making your dreams come true. **The world awaits your magnificent creations**. Whether personal or professional, they will make a difference to your local community and our shared world!

9

FREE YOURSELF FROM OLD STORIES
RELEASING LIMITING BELIEFS

Time and again when I work with my clients, I find their beliefs are fearful and confused in the areas in which they struggle. Psychology calls these limiting or unhelpful beliefs. If you have done any Cognitive Behavior Therapy (CBT) you will have learned how to challenge and change limiting beliefs and mindset blocks.

Conversely, in those areas in which your life is working well, beliefs are almost invariably more positive and optimistic.

As early as the 17th century, in *Paradise Lost,* English poet John Milton wrote, *'The mind is its own place, and in itself can make a heaven of hell and a hell of heaven.'*

Bestselling author and public speaker Wayne Dyer said, *'You'll see it when you believe it.'*

Recapping on the Law of Attraction, what you focus on is what you draw to yourself. Hard and unpalatable as this may be to believe or accept, your thoughts have the power to manifest in your life. Your thoughts attract experiences which match your expectations, a kind of, *'I told you so!',* or, *'I knew that would happen!'*

Some examples of how this works:

- If you believe relationships can be supportive and loving and

- visualise yourself in a happy relationship, you attract the opportunities that make these desires a reality
- If you believe money is dirty, that wealthy people are dishonest and greedy, it's likely you'll be someone who finds it hard to earn what you need to support yourself in the way you'd like
- If you believe men are insatiable and not to be trusted, or your father cheated on your mother, you may generalise from that that men stray, and end up with a partner who cheats on you
- If your inner critic gives you a hard time about your looks, and tells you no-one would really want you, you may find it difficult to meet anyone, or you may attract partners who don't stay for the long haul.

Remember to question that voice!

Deepak Chopra warns us that our 'cells eavesdrop on our thoughts.' This means that our very health, the way we age, the sweetness or otherwise of our relationships are strongly influenced by what we tell ourselves. This includes what we tell ourselves both on conscious and unconscious levels.

I therefore invite you to become conscious of your habitual thoughts and beliefs. If they would create what you'd love, keep thinking and believing them. If they'd create something you don't want, challenge them, reframe them, then wait for the improvements to show up in your life.

I saw this on Facebook, author unknown:

'Your brain constantly rewires itself to suit the information you feed into it. If you constantly complain, blame, gossip, find excuses, it will make it much easier to find things about which to be upset, regardless of what is happening around you.

Conversely, if you constantly search for opportunities, abundance, love, and things to be grateful for, it will make it much easier to attract those things to you.

> *It takes practice and commitment, but over time, this is a powerful way to reshape your reality.* **Our thoughts make what we see beautiful or ugly, not our eyes.** *The whole world is in our minds.'*

Weird, huh? But it's a notion that gains more and more traction year by year. There are many books, and best-selling authors like Dr Jean Houston and Eckhardt Tolle offering brilliant online workshops on the subject if you want to explore it more deeply.

For example, in her state-of-the-art online training, *'Quantum Powers'*, Jean Houston inspires her readers and course participants to use their imaginations to reach for the stars and see themselves as powerful co-creators and shapers of their world. She explains that *'A clearer mind creates a clearer field of possibility and accomplishment.'*

She recommends this daily meditation:

Exercise: Daily Hygiene Meditation

> *'Every day, you clear away the old, useless weeds of your mind. Give heed to what you think and banish sorrow and dismay. Do not allow yourself to dwell on failure. Give up your notion of obstacles, and the obstacles will give up their notion of you. Think of open doors, opportunities, paths unfolding under your feet leading to marvellous events (and) fulfilling happenings. This is the pattern you have to use to supplant the one that does not work for you.*
>
> *This simple technique is based on the oldest of all techniques, breath or breathing. You breathe in, you breathe in new life, new possibility. You breathe out, you banish all the old stuff that no longer works. You breathe very, very deeply new life, new possibility. Feel this new life, this breath, just moving through your whole body/mind. You breathe out, you expel the toxic, old thoughts. You breathe in new life, new possibilities, new energy, what you truly wish to bring into manifestation. You breathe out the dregs and toxic worries that no longer are part of you. It's breath; it's based on breath.'*

It has been mind-blowing how several of my clients' experiences changed within weeks of doing the above as a daily meditation.

Someone who was single for years met the man of her dreams a week after doing this; someone who had been unhappy in his job for some time received two job offers in the ten days after he started practising this meditation!

This chapter is about limiting or unhelpful beliefs, and more importantly, how to reframe them. And by doing so, how to reshape your reality, how to change the story you have been living into a story you would prefer.

Examples follow from my clients who did just this, then found that their lives improved. They are shared to inspire and encourage you. I invite you to be hopeful. You too can learn how to challenge and reframe your limiting beliefs and change your life for the better.

How Reframing My Beliefs Changed My Life

Had I not learned how to reframe my limiting beliefs when I wrote my first script, I doubt that the part of my script which brought my new husband into my life would have worked. At the time, I had some very limiting beliefs about love and marriage.

I had attended a workshop because I was unhappy about what had happened in my first marriage. Clearly, enough had gone wrong to make me become one of those divorce statistics. In the pain of the breakup, I managed to garner enough insight and honesty to recognise I needed to heal the baggage I must have brought into the marriage for it to have ended. I was certainly up for learning how to do better in the relationship stakes next time around.

My Limiting Beliefs and Fears Around Love and Marriage

According to the Australian Bureau of Statistics, one-in-three Australian marriages end in divorce. And according to the American Psychological Association, around one-in-two first marriages in America end in divorce.

Second marriages in both countries record a two-in-three failure rate! If this were to include the de facto relationships that fall apart, the statistics would look even more dismal.

Much of the role modelling we learn from our parents is less than optimal. Many of us grew up witnessing arguments, incompatibility, blaming, criticising, dysfunctional patterns, infidelity, power imbalance, control, narcissism, emotional (and sometimes physical) abuse, addictions, divorce – the list of less-than-optimal situations is long and discouraging.

I was no exception. While I certainly didn't experience most of the above in my family of origin, my parents, probably like yours, were far from perfect. When the famous public speaker John Bradshaw was asked whether he agreed with the assessment by Virginia Satir, (known as the 'Mother of Family Therapy' in the US), that 95% of American families are dysfunctional, he said he disagreed. In his view, 99% are dysfunctional!

So, most of us are in the same boat here, in terms of family patterning of unhelpful ways of trying to solve problems and behave in marriage. We either do the opposite of what our parents modelled, or we blindly repeat their behaviour, even when we dislike it and know it's destructive.

Exercise: Identifying Limiting Beliefs

The day before we were taught ScriptWriting in the *Future Pace* workshop I referred to earlier, we focused on identifying our limiting beliefs and learning to reframe them – a fairly straightforward process.

How to Identify your Beliefs

- **Step One:** Choose an area you want to work on, like relationships, career, health, or money. I chose relationships.
- **Step Two:** Head the page **Old Beliefs**. The quest is to uncover the beliefs which drive you. These often lurk in our subconscious minds, with most of us being unaware we hold them.
- **Step Three:** Think about the important adults in your life when you were growing up – mainly mum and dad, but perhaps uncles, aunts, grandparents, teachers, religious leaders etc.
- **Step Four:** Write what you believe as a result of what you've observed and been taught under **Old Beliefs**. Say you're

> working on relationships: these beliefs could be about love, marriage, how women/men behave in marriage, how you yourself behave/what sort of partner you think you are. They can be wordy, or in point form. They might cover one page or several pages.

I identified around twenty beliefs in this exercise. There are two beliefs I discovered about myself that day which were most significant and meaningful to me. As I looked back on my childhood, I zeroed in on the fact that:

• My mother had suffered from severe migraine headaches. Predictably, she'd have one pretty reliably about every two weeks,

• My father had fussed over her, trying to stop her from worrying so she wouldn't develop the next migraine.

Much as my father adored my mother, even as a child I strongly disliked this symbiotic dynamic playing out between them. During that *Future Pace* workshop I realised that when I married, I sure as hell didn't want to be fussed over, adored, managed and controlled by my husband like my mother had been loved and fussed over by my father.

My first husband - lovely, highly intelligent, funny man that he was – turned out to be pretty self-sufficient, unaffectionate and stitched up in the emotions department. Walled off, not available for deep emotional intimacy. As the years rolled by, I longed, so I thought, for more affection and emotional intimacy. But as I wrote my stream-of-consciousness beliefs about men, what popped up were old beliefs that I'd held onto for years:

- If I have a man in my life who is affectionate and loving, like my father, I'll end up being weak and sick, like my mother.
- Men don't really love women who are strong, powerful and successful. They may admire them, but they don't love them. To be truly loved, you have to be weak and sick like my mother. (The fact that my mother had warned me to hide my cleverness because men don't like clever women, didn't help.)

Create Abundant Possibilities

These beliefs were a revelation to me. I'd had no idea that they were part of my mental landscape, influencing my love life!

I came to see that my first husband was the perfect choice for a woman who believed what I believed. I'd chosen a man who wouldn't show me a lot of affection or fuss over me. And much as he admired and respected me, he didn't show me the deep caring and love my father had shown my mother.

The point was, according to my unconscious belief system, it wouldn't have been safe for me to have a really affectionate, loving husband. Much as I longed for that, I wasn't prepared to pay the 'price' of being weak and sick.

This thinking isn't conscious, it isn't rational. We're aware of the 10% of the iceberg above the surface. We're not aware of the 90% of the iceberg which is below the surface, and it's that 90% that drives our emotional decisions and behaviour.

Even I, who made the choice, hadn't been aware that this was what led me to choose the man I married – a man with his personality, his traits, his upbringing, his childhood experiences.

I often see unconscious drives play out while I work with clients struggling with relationships, careers, money, and many other problems. If you hated your father's drinking, or his violence, your radar for abuse is on high alert.

And by a strange quirk of fate, even though this is what you think you're desperate to avoid, the statistics are that you have a higher-than-average likelihood of ending up with an alcoholic or physically abusive partner!

The way this works is that what we saw and experienced as love as a child - in this case, a violent or alcoholic father- is indelibly entangled with love in our mind. You are vulnerable when it comes to discerning this potential in a future partner.

When the violence strikes, it's almost as though you always knew it was going to happen. You'd been waiting for the other shoe to drop. Your childhood fears and beliefs that men are violent hit pay dirt. And you stick around and put up with it, where a woman with different childhood experiences, different beliefs and high self-esteem would end the relationship immediately.

If this is what you've been unfortunate enough to experience, the psychotherapy path will likely include counselling to identify and reframe your limiting beliefs, build your self-esteem, set boundaries, learn good communication and relationship skills, as well as management of depression, anxiety, and so on.

All of this is covered broadly in this toolkit so that you can get started on changing your beliefs and patterns today.

Exercise: How to Reframe Your Limiting Beliefs

Having identified my limiting beliefs about love and marriage, the time had come for me to reframe them to create my **New Beliefs**. This is how I did it:

Step Five: Under the heading **New Beliefs**, write the total opposite of each **Old Belief**, one belief at a time.

You are, in effect, converting the pessimistic into highly optimistic ideas and language. This is not just a matter of challenging your beliefs in the way recommended by Cognitive Behavioral Therapy (CBT). That's helpful and good too, for example. saying *'What would a friend say about this belief?'* or *'What else might be true here? This is not the only way to handle it. What is the bigger picture?'* However, **reframing** is like CBT on steroids. You're not just reframing your unhelpful beliefs. You're turning them on their heads. You're in fact converting them...

- From being problems which, if you continue to believe them, will continue to attract problems
- Into optimistic solutions, which will attract good things into your life. The dark becomes the light, the shadow becomes the strength.

Step Six: Under the last of your beliefs, write:

'I acknowledge that I have believed these old beliefs and manifested them fully in my life. I have served myself well with them and learned what I needed to learn. I now choose to let them go completely. I now believe these new beliefs and manifest them fully in my life.

Date:_____ Signature:_____

. . .

This is how I reframed my limiting beliefs:

Old Beliefs:

- If I have a man in my life who is affectionate and loving, like my father, I'll end up being weak and sick, like my mother.
- Men don't really love women who are strong, powerful and successful. They may admire them but they don't love them. To be truly loved, you have to be weak and sick like my mother.

New Beliefs:

- When I have a man in my life who is loving and affectionate, it's like the wind beneath my wings. It makes me become even more than I already am.
- The man in my life loves and adores women who are strong, powerful and successful. My intelligence is one of the things about me that he finds very attractive.
- He loves and adores me, and our relationship goes from strength to strength.

Exercise: Integrating Your New Beliefs into Your Framework of Consciousness

Reframing doesn't end here. The next step is to <u>integrate</u> these new beliefs – the opposite of what you've believed until now – into your current framework of consciousness. This helps you to manifest these new beliefs in your life.

After reframing my beliefs, I followed the instructions in **Step Seven** below - the same instructions I give to clients when they reframe their beliefs.

Doing this process will also help you step beyond your limiting beliefs.

. . .

Step Seven: Instructions for integrating your new beliefs

1. Read the old beliefs once (one after the other).
2. Say the litany (*'I acknowledge that I have believed...'*) at the end, and the first time you do this, date and sign them, owning them.
3. Read each new belief four times.
4. Do the above every day for four-to-six weeks.
5. For at least a month to six weeks, before you go to sleep, see a computer screen in your mind, bring up one or two of your most important old beliefs, then clear the screen.
6. Silently say the litany.
7. Bring up an abbreviated version of the reframed belief and repeat it four times.

Remember, our thoughts can make a heaven out of hell, and a hell out of heaven. Imagine what you would create if you were running your old beliefs tape constantly in your head, often unconsciously, but exerting a powerful influence anyway.

As you scan your new beliefs, think how different life will be for the new you, the person running this new recording. This practice is life changing. The new beliefs are what you are putting in place. This is what your body language will convey. This is what you will draw to you.

NOTE: At first, the new beliefs seem like lip-service, because you believe the opposite. But keep up the focus on the new beliefs, and habitual, pessimistic patterns of thinking will shift into wise, optimistic and empowered thinking. Change your mind-set. It <u>will</u> change your life.

Stay with the Process

The process of integrating your new beliefs into your life, as detailed above, may look like a lot of work, a bit of a drag. You may be wondering whether it's worth bothering, given all the other demands of your life.

When I learned reframing, I left the workshop with this promise to myself. *'If this works, it's going to work for me, because I'll give it every-*

thing I've got!' I admit that repeating this exercise nightly for a month or so was boring. But I was 100% conscientious in doing it.

Did it pay off?

Suffice to say that the man I scripted into my life, whom I married, is romantic and affectionate. In fact, he's a published author of a string of romance novels.

Moreover, he's a master at fulfilling my primary love language – words of affirmation and admiration.

Remember that the universe responds to the frequency at which you are vibrating, rather than to your 'wants'. Although at a conscious level I longed for a man who was affectionate and loving, my deeper belief was, *'If I have a man in my life who is affectionate and loving, like my father, I'll end up being weak and sick like my mother.'*

When I was vibrating at that frequency the universe answered my underlying request or energetic imprint to keep an affectionate, loving man as far away from me as possible.

For the universe to send me a loving, affectionate, admiring partner, I had to change my frequency to that of the new belief, *'When I have a man in my life who is loving and affectionate, it's like the wind beneath my wings. It makes me become even more than I already am.'* And to do that, I was willing to put in the hard yards described above.

For the new to be born, the old needs to die

I now believe that without this personal development work, the literal reframing and shifting of my fear based limiting beliefs about men and love, I would have chosen (or the universe would have delivered) another man who was as unaffectionate and emotionally detached as my first husband.

Instead I chose a very different man as my second husband. I *'chose'* a man whose daily greeting to me is "Hello Beautiful!" Admiration and affection are his middle names!

He often tells me that he loves me, rather than being walled off and taking me for granted, as my first husband had. I shifted my beliefs of what was 'safe' for me in a husband. Changing my relationship operandi stopped me from repeating my mistakes. It also really did deliver my dream.

To increase the power of this process and maximise the positive changes you now attract into your life, combine this cognitive reframing work with the daily inner hygiene meditation (earlier in this chapter), which operates at the level of unconscious mind and imagination.

Other Reframing Success Stories

What follows are a few of my favourite tales from people I've taught reframing.

Consider Samantha, a disillusioned university student.

Old Beliefs

- I feel there's no hope for my generation with boys. The males of my generation are selfish. Boys seem to have only one goal: sex with girls. And that's not the sort of friend I want, even though I've always felt more comfortable with boys than with girls! For that reason, I've got only one male friend.
- A lot of girls encourage or go along with the one-night stand thing. It seems like a never-ending cycle, like I find this boy and he seems really nice, and then.....it's hard to be positive about relationships when that keeps happening.

New Beliefs

- There are many lovely boys out there, just as there are many selfish boys. I now meet and have easy friendships with lovely boys.
- The sort of relationship I choose is with a respectful boy. In a long-term relationship they're like friends, with the extra bonus thrown in. The reality is that all I need is a relationship with one boy who respects girls, and who realises the value and joy of meaningful connection and friendship. I now attract and have a wonderful relationship with a boy like that, a boy who loves me, and is happy that

Create Abundant Possibilities

> I'm not like those other girls. He's trustworthy, respectful, considerate, caring, and a good friend. For us, sex is a beautiful extra. That makes both of us very happy.

Within months of that belief reframing, Samantha met her respectful and caring young man. When her therapy came to an end, she was still happy in her relationship with him.

Then there's Gina. She's my daughter, a psychotherapist herself, and she is happy for me to use her real name.

Years ago, as she graduated with English Honors from Sydney University, she phoned me in tears. "I thought I'd get the University medal for English. I didn't get it!"

Having recently learned reframing, I said, "What fears or beliefs do you think blocked you? Did you think you'd put Andrew's nose out of joint?" (Andrew, her husband, was also finishing his last year at university). She snapped back through her tears. "Mum, I hate it when you talk such rubbish!"

The next day she phoned, jubilant. She told me the committee had called another meeting and decided to give two English medals. So, she received her medal, after all.

Simply acknowledging your fear can be enough to remove the blockage and change what you experience.

Then there was the lovely young man – let's call him Steven – who came to see me very distressed because his de facto relationship wasn't going well:

Old Belief

- I'm no good at relationships. They never last for me.

New Beliefs

- I'm getting better and better at relationships.
- My partner and I communicate really well when issues arise.

- We learn and grow together, and our relationship goes from strength to strength.

Last I heard, they were married and looking forward to a happy future together.

Another favourite story concerns Matthew, a young father who confided his bitter disappointment in his parents' lack of involvement with his children.

Old Beliefs

- I'm bitterly disappointed with my parents' relationship with my children. They are cold and uninvolved.

New Beliefs

- It's been a delight to me that my children now have a wonderful relationship with my parents.
- They've become caring and loving grandparents, and it's a pleasure for me to see them together.

It may seem too good to be true. How could something like that change so quickly? Yet within weeks he told me there had been a marked improvement in the relationship.

When we put someone in a box and hold that as a truth (e.g. my parents are cold and uninvolved), our body language and tone of voice contribute to the problem, fixing it in place. I've witnessed ample evidence that holding the best possible outcome in mind helps change the situation, as it did in this case.

We make choices and behave in ways that provide evidence that what we believe is true! Like Matthew being edgy and resentful when he and his children visited his parents – which influenced the way they reacted. When he opened his heart and was warmer to them, they showed up differently around the children. It's estimated that:

- Only 20% of what we experience is purely **situational**.
- 80% of what we experience is consistent with our **beliefs** about what we are like, what other people are like, and what we can expect from life.

In other words, the way we approach life, our thinking and behaviour, are major contributors to what shows up for us! Remember the Law of Attraction?

This is why I invite you to:

- Identify your limiting beliefs about whatever topic/s you want to focus on (just brainstorm and write down what you believe, even if you believe some of these things only some of the time),
- Reflect on insights/beliefs you may not have realised you held,
- Change or 'reframe' your old stories and addictive thinking and behaviour (turn those beliefs on their heads) to achieve far more favourable outcomes.

In doing this exercise, you're effectively coming up with your own solutions for your future. You're liberating yourself from old stories about who you are, what other people are like, how life is, and what's possible.

This new understanding and new perspective give you the opportunity to see your full role in what appeared to 'just happen' to you. This allows you to view your past through a different lens, effectively deconstructing your past.

You can now create the possibility for new and different experiences, rather than having the same experiences repeatedly.

As an example, rather than believe *'people take me for granted,'* reframe this as *'people show me support, friends are caring and genuine, I'm praised and acknowledged for what I do'*.

This will help you create a new story for yourself and attract experiences into your life consistent with your new beliefs. That said, you then need to be willing to change and behave in ways that support and reinforce your new story.

If you catch yourself slipping back to your old mindset, say, *'people take me for granted',* challenge that fear.

For example, imagine yourself relaxed and happy in the company of new friends. You can also call on other techniques and strategies described in this book, such as practices to relieve anxiety or depressed, self-critical, victim thinking.

Beliefs About Career Success and Money

I've already alluded to this but let me use the example of my career and finances – a part of my life which had always seemed pretty flowing and easy for me.

My beliefs around prosperity and career are clean and positive. I seem to have been born under a lucky star when it comes to abundance, prosperity and success in my career. I'm not being egotistical when I say that. I say it not with arrogance but with gratitude and the recognition that I have been blessed.

Not that I didn't study and work hard, not that I didn't have goals, and an eye on long term security. Not that I didn't take opportunities when they came my way and put in the effort required to bring them to fruition. But I have been fortunate in that success seemed to come relatively easily to me, with many more ups than downs.

Back when I did that life changing workshop and learned how to identify and reframe limiting beliefs, as I looked at my beliefs about money and self-worth, I realised I didn't seem to have sticky or limiting ideas. No reframing was needed in that area of my life.

We all have our strengths as well as our weaknesses. I'm grateful that that has been one of my strengths. Fulfilling my awesome dream of doubling my billings via my first script, then my dream to sell the company for a great price via my second script, seemed to come on a platter. Love and relationships were a different matter for me. That's why I worked on identifying and reframing my beliefs about myself in a relationship. If you run into problems in your career or finances, do the process described in this chapter around your beliefs about work and money. You will uncover your underlying beliefs. You can then reframe those that are fear- based and negative.

By the way, there's an excellent book that I recommend to help clients who have difficulty with prosperity and career: *'The Billionaire Buddha'* by Jane Monica-Jones. The sub-title *'Guiding you From Financial Struggle to Serenity,'* says it all. Jane takes you through your family-of-origin experiences, your track record, your beliefs, then leads you through the healing that you need to bring yourself into a healthy relationship with work and money.

Ollie's Story

Reframing certainly made a big difference to Ollie's life at work, as demonstrated by his story.

Ollie is an engineer in his late 30s. Tall and good looking, blonde, olive skin, nicely built, pleasant manner. He'd come to see me because he wanted help as he navigated his way through a particularly nasty divorce.

Ollie was a people pleaser, but he hadn't managed to please his wife. A very angry woman, she was hard to please and full of complaints. It seemed that the more he caved in to her demands, the more demanding and discontented she became. The last few years had been dominated by a lot of fighting, with relatively few ups and many downs. He recognised it wasn't all about her.

He was keen to understand what he had brought to his 50% of the relationship; how his beliefs about himself and his behaviour had contributed to the breakdown of the marriage. He welcomed coaching about what differentiates good marriages from those that are troubled, as well as ways to manage his anxiety and low self-esteem.

The therapeutic process guided Ollie through significant personal growth. Being a loving father was a high value for him. He structured his life to enable him to co-parent his three young children well. When he announced that he was ready to look for a new partner, I reminded him to write a script majoring on his dream partner. Months into therapy this is how Ollie felt he'd changed.

"I'm an extremely loyal person. But looking back, jeez, there was a lot of stuff I was putting up with. I was pushing things down, not being true to myself. You lose your sense of identity. I didn't actually know who I was. I had all that growing up to do from when I first met my wife. I was in my man box: men are tough. I hadn't been taught it's OK to be angry, embarrassed or to show emotion. That's where I was in terms of my own self-respect: showing emotion is weakness, I thought. Worrying all the time. What do I have to say or not say? I've come a long way. I have a sense of pride, happiness. I love to be able to show my kids what love is, give them what they need, teach them my perception of good. It's a warm feeling."

His life was going well. We lost touch. When he returned a couple of years down the track, he reported his relationship with his children and his new love life were excellent. "I met the woman of my dreams. It is ridiculous, Wendy. She is exactly who I scripted".

He'd come back to get help with anxiety, which was undermining his confidence and enjoyment at work. Ollie's problem was that he felt undervalued. He sensed his hard work went unnoticed. He'd been passed over when it came to promotion, with jobs he wanted being given to less competent people.

His story about himself at work flagged that career and prosperity were an area where he struggled. Remember that limiting and fear-based beliefs inevitably underpin struggle. And limiting beliefs about lack, not being good enough and being hard-done-by, cry out for reframing! I therefore set about asking him what he believed about work and prosperity, and this is what he came up with:

Old Beliefs

- I'm unappreciated. I'm not valued. I haven't been recognised.
- They're qualified and I'm not. I'm under-qualified. I'm incompetent. And I don't know what I'm talking about. I'm wrong.
- Wealth depends on decisions you make. It's easy for some and not so easy for others. I see people I don't value making

good money and not doing much to earn it. I seem to be putting my hand up and doing the tough work and not being rewarded for it. But I want to keep pushing. Maybe I want to prove them wrong!
- They don't have to work as hard as I do. Things come more naturally to others. They're smarter than I am.
- I feel hopeless about the future. I feel like I'll be made redundant. I feel like I'm high up on the list of being made redundant at the first pick.

As Ollie's story of personal disempowerment emerged – a story of low self-esteem, feeling under-valued and unimportant – I would have been willing to bet that this stemmed from his childhood.

The next step was to revisit his childhood to uncover his early memories of anxiety in his family and at school. Ollie admitted his relationship with his father had always been strained. Remember his angry wife, difficult to please, full of complaints?

His description of his father was much the same as his description of his wife. He had, in effect, married his father! This seeming coincidence, that your partner resembles one of your parents, is common in couples presenting for therapy.

> "As I reflect on it now, I remember the red flag went up soon after I met my wife. There were times when she'd be really mean to me. I was used to my father speaking to me like that. My father did a lot of yelling. I would be worried when he came home. Was he going to be a nice guy today, or a shit! He'd play my brother and me off against each other. My feelings were second. I was a lot more worried about his feelings than my own."

Discovering vulnerability like this in a client's childhood, which is still playing out in adult life, is like gold to a therapist. There are many ways to work with it to bring about healing and to disrupt the old pattern, the old story. One of the things I did was to help Ollie reframe his Old Beliefs.

Please note how radically different his New Beliefs are from the Old. The Old Beliefs have been turned on their heads.

New Beliefs

- Things have changed in miraculous ways. I now get regular feedback that I am appreciated. I keep noticing how I am being recognised. I allow myself to really feel the pleasure of being seen and acknowledged, knowing that this is what I have earned and richly deserve.
- I'm well qualified, as well qualified as my peers. I am highly competent, and I've become my best supporter. I often remind myself that I definitely know what I'm talking about. My confidence has grown by leaps and bounds, and I'm enjoying and taking pride in my work. Like everyone else, I'm imperfect and wonderful at the same time, and if, like everyone else, I make an error, I quickly find a solution. I can count on my inner Wise Adult to show compassion and kindness to myself. This reassures me that errors are human and that, overall, I'm highly competent and a valued employee and they're lucky to have me.
- I've become one of those people who makes good decisions and for whom wealth is now easy. I'm abundant and prosperous, and building my assets in ways that fulfil my dreams. I sometimes put my hand up for tough jobs, and I sometimes don't. I take my own feelings and needs into account and choose when to put my hand up and when not to. I make those decisions with confidence and clarity. My judgement is good, I give, and I receive in a fair and balanced way. I'm relieved and delighted that I'm rewarded, acknowledged and appreciated for both the tough and the other work.
- I now work at the level that makes me feel good about myself. I work as hard as I need to and in order to contribute what I want to contribute to my workplace. I'm me, they're them, and I'm not interested in comparing myself. I make smart and responsible choices from a place of self-respect, self-care, integrity, efficiency and wisdom. I'm super-smart, and I now allow myself to recognise and reward that in me. I am fully connected to myself. I stay tuned to how I am

feeling, and how I can best look after my needs in accordance with my integrity, my standards and my values, for the greatest good of all concerned
- I feel optimistic about the future. I look forward to the future. I feel safe and comfortable in my workplace, and I believe management sees me as a trusted, hard-working and highly competent member of the workforce, integral to its continuing success.

As per the instructions spelt out earlier, I asked Ollie to work with these beliefs daily, or close to daily, for the following month.

Your Core Identity

Before moving on from Ollie, I'd like to drill down to a deeper level than the beliefs he was able to articulate when I asked him what he thinks about himself in his workplace, and his beliefs about prosperity.

Driving our beliefs, and even further out of sight of our conscious awareness, lies our **core identity**.

I did my training to work with core identity blocks through Women Centred Coaching, the brainchild of Claire Zammit. She explains how we all have barriers which block us from deep connection, vulnerability and love.

In her words, "*Identifying your core identity block or false identity makes visible the unconscious strategies of 'stuckness' or separation. Discovering the barrier that has been holding you back, and receiving a 'map' helps you break free to make a huge leap.*"

In her PhD, Claire researched and developed the Transformation Matrix of core identity blocks or false identities which represent the glass ceilings that hold most of us back from fulfilling our highest potential - in relationship, career, health, self-actualization.

In ten years, she has built a still growing US $100 million online transformational learning and life coach training business. One of the reasons for this phenomenal success is that what she teaches is brilliant in empowering women to rise above their limiting self-concepts and break through their inner glass ceilings. When I discovered Claire's work, I felt I'd found the holy grail!

If you want to do further work to turn around patterns of disappointment and failure that dog any area of your life, I recommend you enrol in one of the online 'Feminine Power' courses. Claire lists twenty-one identity blocks, which form as we experience hurts, disappointments and traumas when we were growing up. Go to her website at https://femininepower.com/ and check out the courses.

Of these, the 21 identity blocks, three she sees as foundational are:

1. *I'm Invisible (a.k.a. I'm Not Seen, I Don't Exist)*
2. *I'm Not Enough*
3. *I'm Alone (a.k.a. I'm On My Own).*

Each matrix maps out the common beliefs about self, other people, and expectations about life and the world which characterise that core identity block.

The exceptional transformational power of working with these core identity blocks lies in the fact that Claire has designed highly positive, super reframes for each block, or false identity, which she calls the Deeper Truth.

The Deeper Truth is about who you really are, your true identity. In the case of the *'I'm Invisible'* false identity, the Deeper Truth statement is, '*I came here to be seen and to have a profound impact on the world, and it is my responsibility to be visible wherever I go.*'

Ollie's story sounded to me like a core identity problem of *'I'm Invisible.'*

When I put this idea to him, he admitted that is exactly how he feels. As I led him though the common beliefs about self, others and the world of people who believe '*I'm invisible*', he admitted that most of them fitted him like a glove.

We worked through Claire Zammit's *'I'm Invisible'* matrix map, which detailed:

Create Abundant Possibilities

- Skills and capacities to cultivate to evolve beyond this false identity, such as, *'The ability to recognise and name your own feelings, needs and desires; the ability to say who you are and what you have to offer in ways that truly represent your greatness and therefore get you invited to participate in ways that would generate more visibility in the world,'*
- The gifts such people typically have, such as *'You possess a deep capacity to see what is invisible; the ability to hear what is not being spoken and the capacity to discern that which has never been made known,'* and,
- Additional encouraging Deeper Truth statements, such as *'The more I am present in my needs and desires, the more I empower myself and others.'*

Belief reframing, combined with working on disrupting his *'I'm Invisible'* core identity paid off handsomely - and quickly. Ollie literally freed himself by creating a new story about himself and his life experiences.

At the follow-up session a month after we'd done the belief reframing, and he'd been given the notes instructing him how to work with the Deeper Truth statements about his identity, Ollie walked in a totally different man.

Imagine my delight as he told me how his life at work had gone from receiving zero acknowledgment to an experience of frequent compliments and thanks. All in the space of a month. That's what to expect if you're willing to do the work!

> Ollie noted, "The reframing feels validating and gives me relief about who I am. Being acknowledged and appreciated is a big one for me – not just at work but in my life as a whole. This has helped me be more confident. I've been able to reflect on who I am and what I've done. Now I'm feeling surer of myself. It really changed the ball game at work.
>
> People are telling me, 'I appreciate what you're doing', 'You really know what you're doing.' My boss said, 'You're a gun.' I'm not surprised any more. It keeps happening. I put it down to the reframes. I'll keep projecting those thoughts to the universe and hopefully it'll

keep happening. And it's happening in my personal life too. My partner tells me she appreciates having me in her life. It's going so well we've decided to move in together."

What About Reframing Positive Beliefs?

When it comes to your positive beliefs, you may not need to reframe them. However, you might choose to instead **upgrade** them to an even higher level of possibility.

When we peel off the outer layers of the onion of who we are, we may discover deeper layers of limiting beliefs and/or blocks.

For example, earlier in this chapter, I shared how I reframed my limited belief that it wasn't safe to receive affection. That opened the door for a loving, admiring partner to enter my life.

It was only many years later, as I did the training with Claire Zammit, that I discovered that below my fear of affection was a core belief that *'I am alone.'*

This led to profound work to move further into my heart and my ability to give and receive love - dropping the judgements which had acted as a way of keeping distance between me and others.

The point is that the more we become aware of, and release, old patterns of behaviour, and old beliefs and stories of who we are, the more of our conditioning and programming we transform and transmute, the brighter our light shines.

After years of working on myself, I am still on the journey of rising higher in consciousness and self-actualisation.

This is the gift of possibility: What more is possible? How big do you dare to dream?

How much more love, compassion, forgiveness, grace, joy and freedom can I embrace? Who do I choose to be now?

That's what I mean when I say you may choose to **upgrade** to an even higher level of possibility. I acknowledge that we're all different. We're not all on the same path. However, in my view, and certainly for me personally, the journey is ever ongoing and the sky's the limit.

10

GET TO KNOW YOUR INNER CHILD
YOUR INNER CHILD HOLDS THE POWER

We all know the saying '*All roads lead to Rome.*' It means that all paths or activities lead to the same place. Its literal derivation is that in the days of the glory of the Roman Empire, all the empire's roads radiated out from the capital city, Rome.

Rome in the world of personal transformation is your **inner child**. Any deep healing work inevitably leads there.

You may be familiar with the phrase '*The child is father to the man.*' This idiom was first coined by William Wordsworth in his poem '*My Heart Leaps Up*'. The most accepted interpretation of this apparent paradox is that **the adult is the product of habits and behaviour developed in youth.**

There's simply no getting away from the fact that our childhood casts a long shadow. Much of what we do has its roots in the things we observed and experienced when we were children.

Getting to understand the existence and influence of your inner child – the memories of the child within you – is essential if you are to fully understand the patterns that play out in your life again and again.

Your inner child formed in response to the good as well as the vulnerable and traumatic experiences of your childhood, starting when you were very young, perhaps as young as only two, three, four. What we want to do is to retain the pure, innocent, loving, happy parts of our inner child and recognise and release the frightened, angry, traumatised, disempowered parts of our inner child. They're the parts that wreak havoc on adult life.

Take a child whose parents did a lot of arguing and fighting, including physical violence. To create meaning in their life, their inner child may have decided, *'Life's not safe;' 'I'm not safe;'* or *'I don't matter.'*

You met Ollie in the previous chapter. His father had mood swings. Ollie never knew which dad was coming home. He learned to be on permanent high alert, in case it was one of those bad days where his father would take it out on Ollie and his mother and brother.

Digging into his childhood experiences, we found out that his core identity was actually, *'I'm Invisible'*.

His father's behaviour led him to believe that his needs didn't count. These beliefs were then buried and forgotten, but you saw how they dictated the way he showed up in his marriage and his career. Both were a direct mirror of those beliefs hidden at the level of his core identity.

Especially if you are not even aware that you have an inner child, you may be astounded to learn that it is your inner child who is driving you.

Your inner child is the 90% of the iceberg below the surface of the water; the author of many of the beliefs you have about yourself, about other people, and about what you can expect from life. They are the hidden architect of what is present in your adult relationships and experiences.

Scratch anyone battling problems like choosing a good partner, making a marriage work, enjoying and succeeding at work, raising their children, managing their health and wellbeing, finding meaning in their life; you'll invariably find unhelpful, fear-based patterns and mindsets laid down in their childhood to be at the core of the problem.

These beliefs, the world view of the inner child, have been locked away in the subconscious mind, out of sight for far too long already.

Despite being out of sight, it is these beliefs, attitudes and resultant behaviours which have created the patterns which show up as our life experiences. Like good fortune - or not - in financial affairs; like being lucky - or not - in love.

For example, if we think we're not lovable, we will run into problems with relationships because the way we show up in the world influences how others respond to us. The problem is that we see the world through the lens of our own conditioning, projections, desires, fears and habits. We focus on *'them'* and *'what they did to us'*, rather than on *'us'* and *'what we did'* as the cause of our woes.

Take a woman unlucky in love, who has been betrayed by her partner(s). At a subconscious level, she chooses men who are exciting but unfaithful. This then provides evidence for her belief and experience that, *'Men are fickle. You can't trust them.'*

Worse still, not knowing she's doing this, she keeps these patterns in place.

We tend to bring the same energy, mindset and behaviours which influenced our responses to our last partner, into the relationship with our new partner.

There is hope, however. Many avenues of healing are available to help the inner child heal and evolve. The right kind of therapy and life coaching can teach you to:

- Recognise the existence of your inner child, and where his/her beliefs came from
- Reframe beliefs of lack and fear, disrupting the old story of 'who I am', the false identity that created barriers in the past
- Increase self-love, confidence and optimism
- Script and visualise dreams coming true
- Be coached in practical skills and capacities to fill your skills gaps and change old behaviours, bringing about better future outcomes.

Becoming more aware of, and empathic to, the feeling of our inner child allows our adult selves to become more whole and better functioning. Reconnecting with our original innocence and creative awareness of possibilities takes us to a place of liberation and authenticity. This acts as an aid, an ally, in maximising our likelihood that our scripts will manifest. That achieved, it then helps us nurture and look after the wellbeing of our new story, of ourselves in our new life.

Carmen's Redemption

Take Carmen. At 35, attractive, successful, with a lot to offer, she's worried she'll never meet the man of her dreams, never have a loving partner and the support and family she craves. She's had a string of failed relationships. Men are interested. There've been a few de facto relationships. They start with promise, but don't last. She feels them drawing away. Then comes the moment when they explain they aren't ready for commitment. And each time, Carmen is plunged into heartbreak and despair.

When I first saw her, she'd almost come to terms with being single all her life.

"What did you observe in your family of origin, Carmen?" I probe. "What was your relationship like with your mum and dad?"

Even thinking of her father distresses her. He walked out on her and her mother when she was three and that spelt the end of her relationship with him. She has vague memories of yelling. The picture her mother painted of her father was not flattering. She never re-partnered.

The childhood Carmen describes is lonely and deprived, her mother battling to keep a roof over their heads, exhausted, with relatively little family support or social life.

As she shares her beliefs about men, it becomes apparent that Carmen has a dim view of their likely reliability. She expects they'll walk out on her, that they don't really care. Just like her father walked out on them, because he didn't care. Coupled with this, she is insecure about how desirable and able she is as a partner. She judges herself as socially awkward, not sure of how or who to be around men, trying to second guess what to say and do to please them. With her *'I'm Not Enough'* core identity, and her belief that she doesn't really matter, it's not surprising that Carmen has had a dismal relationship history.

Beliefs like these become a self-fulfilling prophecy. It seems to be a run of bad luck, as if these unfortunate experiences are coming from the outside. To Carmen, it seems a coincidence she's attracted one man after the other who is commitment shy.

The truth is, however, that these expectations about herself and men hold these recurring problems in place. Her insecurity about how to behave and be authentically herself made her a people-pleaser, behaving in ways that undermined the comfort and ease of emotional intimacy. Her romantic experiences were, in fact, an out-picturing or mirror of her expectations, her experience being an external mirror of her internal beliefs.

The door to redemption was through Carmen's disadvantaged inner child. The first step of getting to understand her inner child, and of how she had come to be like this, enabled the design and direction of the remedial work.

Her therapy included building her self-esteem, helping her understand she was no longer the frightened, abandoned three-year-old. She'd become a competent, wise adult, with a successful career under her belt. Coaching helped her to:

- Recognise herself in empowered mode at the times when she's in her element
- Bring the wisdom, empathy, kindness and support of this wise adult part of her to re-parent her wounded, insecure inner child
- Learn new relationship, social and life skills
- Reframe her limiting beliefs about herself and about men
- Have the courage to ask for what she wants
- Identify her relationship values – developing a crystal-clear picture of the type of man she'd like to attract and what the relationship would need to be like for her to be happy
- Script this as an exciting, desirable future and a loving relationship.

The good news is that she was able to drop her old story of who she was and create a new one which opened doors into a new way of being for her. After she had worked through her therapy, the next man who showed up stayed. And he was the best of them all!

Meet Jimmy's Inner Child

Jimmy is a young man crippled by anxiety. Fear hounds him and limits his life. It's a particular problem in the workplace. When his workmates are loud, or when he gets ordered around or criticised, he feels a rising tide of panic and it's all he can do to stay functional.

We trace his severe anxiety to screaming matches between his parents when he was a boy. He also remembers violence, usually his dad beating his mum, but occasionally copping it himself if he was in the firing line. He recalls cowering under the blankets at night, hoping the fighting would stop, hearing the rapid beating of his heart.

Once again, as commonly happens in therapy, the road led back to his inner child.

Wendy: *'You know that feeling of fear and dread at work, Jimmy? Show me where that is in your body. Great. And on a scale from 1 to 10, where 1 is very low and 10 is very high, how intense is that fear?'*

Jimmy: *'It's a 10.'*

Wendy: *'And how old is the part of you feeling that fear?'*

Jimmy: *'I'm about four'*

Wendy: *'Right, it's a very young part of you?'*

Jimmy: *'Yes'*

Wendy: *'Jimmy, I'm so sorry it was so scary and tough for you when you were little. Just stand up now and take a couple of deep breaths into your diaphragm. Now shake your hands and jump up and down a few times on the spot to let that feeling lift off.'*

Minutes pass. I smile at him.

Wendy: *'Sit down again Jimmy. Are you ready to try something different?'*

'Yes', he says, somewhat tentatively.

Wendy: *'OK, what is there in your life that you really enjoy? A time that you feel happy and relaxed?'*

Jimmy: *'When I'm surfing. Nothing I love more than being out on my surfboard, cracking the waves.'*

Wendy: *'Describe the feeling. And say what's going on in your head when you're doing that.'*

Jimmy: *'I am free, powerful. Nothing's going on in my head. All I'm aware of is me, in that moment, flying along, water around me, the smell of the ocean, the sound of the waves, the feeling of freedom.'*

Wendy: *'Wonderful. That's the part of you that knows the experience of being in the moment, feeling happy, confident, powerful? How old are you now?'*

Jimmy: *'I'm 29.'*

Wendy: *'Great. We'll come back in a moment and call on this adult, powerful part of you. For now, though, I want you to go back briefly to that anxiety that so often walks with you in your life. Put one hand on the place where that sits in your body'.* He clutches his stomach.

Wendy: *'Now I'd like you to invite that powerful, confident surfer in you to flow in from above your head all the way down into your hips, your legs, through the soles of your feet and into the ground beneath you. And anchor that part of you into your body, placing your other hand below your first hand. That's good.'*

He smiles – a wide happy smile.

Wendy: *'How does this older part of you differ from the frightened little 4-year-old boy, Jimmy? What are the things he knows about and can do that the little 4-year-old doesn't know and can't do?'*

Jimmy: *'He's had a lot more experience, he's good at surfing, he's physically big and strong, he can look after himself, he has fun with his surfing mates.'*

Wendy: *'That's right. And he doesn't live with the little 4-year-old's parents anymore either! Now repeat after me: 'I'm grown-up 29-year-old Jimmy. I'm a really good surfer, I really take care of myself on the waves, and I have mates who are surfers, and we have a great time together'* Jimmy repeats this.

Wendy: *'Now say; 'I'm big Jimmy, and I'm here to take care of you from now on. Please notice that you no longer live with your parents. And notice that you're no longer dependent on parents who don't know how to look after themselves, let alone look after a beautiful, sensitive little boy!'* Jimmy repeats this.

'Now say; 'You no longer need to be afraid because I'm here now and I'll always be with you. I love you and I'm strong and I will protect you from now on. I'm going to check in with you every morning to ask you how you're feeling, and whatever you feel, I'll listen and keep loving you. And you can ask me for help any time of day or night. Just call me. I'm here for you. You'll never be alone anymore.'

By this stage, Jimmy is crying, so I ask him *'How is little Jimmy feeling?'* Through his tears, Jimmy says, *'He's so relieved. He's climbed up onto big Jimmy's lap. His arms are around his shoulders and his head is nuzzled into 'big' Jimmy's neck.'*

Wendy: *'And how's his anxiety?'*

Jimmy: *'He's feeling safe now. He's much calmer. Thank you so much. That was wonderful.'*

This was the start of Jimmy's healing journey. It began with connecting him with little Jimmy and went on to have him show empathy, compassion, kindness and support to little Jimmy. His ongoing therapy included anxiety management, building of confidence and self-esteem, and many other interventions.

So many of our problems in life, health, finances, mental health, and relationships stem from experiences locked inside our inner child. These examples of work to heal Carmen's and Jimmy's inner child reveal how much done on therapists' and life coaches' couches goes to the very core of the problem—what is carried from childhood, hidden inside, into adulthood.

Childhood problems don't refer only to Big 'T' traumas, like abuse and neglect. Small 't' traumas include myriad circumstances and experiences such as sibling rivalry, parental mental illness and other dysfunctions, parental divorce, emotionally immature parents, problems at school, prejudice, gender issues, socio-economic or other inequality, shyness, low self-esteem – all of these and many more qualify as childhood trauma.

Even so-called 'normal' families go through difficult times, perhaps financial stress, job loss, illness in the family, or emigration.

It is in times of stress that our inner child lays down limiting, fearful beliefs about how worthwhile and deserving they feel, how trustworthy other people are, how safe, abundant, and fair life is, and what they can expect from the world.

Few of us get to adulthood without some 'marking' of our inner children, without building some fearful thinking into our navigational system for interacting with the world.

Meeting My Inner Child

As a participant in the *Master Track Women's Coaching Program* with Claire Zammit, when we did the work to uncover our identity blocks, I was surprised to discover that my core identity block is *'I'm Alone'*.

I've had a pretty relationship-rich life and enjoy a good social life, yet lurking beneath my style of relating was this feeling that when the chips are down, I'm on my own! Even though I've been fortunate to have received a lot of support and cooperation in my personal and business life, my false beliefs were:

- *'I'm the one who has to make things happen.'*
- *'I can't really rely on anyone else. '*

As I trawled my earliest life experiences, I remembered my father telling me how my mother had cried for three days after my birth and called me Michael. She refused to accept that I was a beautiful girl, not the boy she'd set her heart on. She rejected who I was. I know I decided in those first few days of my life on earth, that I'd chosen the wrong mother!

If she was who I had to rely on, I'd have a tough time.

When I looked at the matrix of beliefs about self and others held by someone whose core identity block is *'I'm Alone'* I found I ticked many of the boxes. I started working with the Deeper Truth Statement beyond my *'I'm on My Own'* block:

> *'I was not born to be alone. I came here to love and be loved, and I have the power to create deep and meaningful connections with others.'*

When things are going well, my inner child is pretty sunny, optimistic and confident. But as I gained a deeper understanding of how identity blocks work, I identified my pattern as one of extreme self-reliance. I'd far rather give than receive help.

A bit of an *'I'll go it alone'* person. I'm an *'I'll grit my teeth and do what needs to be done'* type. The price I've paid for this belief is feeling alone, not willing to be emotionally vulnerable and not reaching out for help when I most need it.

Remember when my script hit a temporary glitch, when our house failed to sell at auction? It was this barrier I slid behind. I retreated into feeling we'd just stay where we were, because I couldn't even rely on the benevolence and help of the universe anymore!

The truth is that auctions are a mixed blessing, with variable rates of success. In retrospect, I was unnecessarily pessimistic about the saleability of our property. I could see that this was the distress of a disappointed child, not a rational adult.

As I grappled with doubt and worry, I recognised it was time to do some healing work, to bring a wiser, adult part of me in to show my inner child compassion and reassurance. Using a process outlined at the end of this chapter led to a wonderful dialogue between my inner child and the capable, optimistic adult I usually am.

Little Wendy revealed how disappointed and frightened she was that no-one wanted her beautiful house. She felt as though she had somehow failed. She had been rejected, just like she had initially been rejected by her mother.

The wise, mature part of me was able to show her great love and understanding and reassure her that it wasn't her job to be looking after the sale of the house. Her job was to play and have fun and leave the arrangements for sale in the hands of competent, adult Wendy. There was a virtual handing over of the baton as little Wendy relaxed, expressing her relief that she no longer needed to be in charge.

Through this dialogue, the over-functioning, fear-based inner child in me was liberated to be a child. My anxiety about the house being on the market reduced considerably after this wise adult-inner child dialogue. You may find dialoguing with your inner child similarly liberating. The guidelines for dialoguing are spelt out at the end of this chapter.

Your Inner Child Is Behind Problems in Your Relationship

Who would believe that when the 'grown-up' version of you is in the middle of a stand-up fight with your grown-up partner, it's not actually the grown-ups who are arguing. It's really two children. They're using the strategies for survival which they developed when they were upset in childhood.

Create Abundant Possibilities

To understand this, we need to briefly revisit the 'fight-or-flight' arousal of alarm, resistance, exhaustion. When you're emotionally flooded, you exit your **executive** 'upstairs' brain, your **prefrontal cortex** and your **amygdala**, part of your more primitive 'downstairs' brain, takes over.

Your amygdala prepares you to 'fight' for survival, to take 'flight' for safety, or to 'fix it' for control. This is exactly what you did back in childhood when you felt unsafe or confused. You felt rebellious (fight), or you shut down (flight) or you tried to fix things (control). That's what's playing out in relationships everywhere when couples trigger each other.

In his *New York Times* relationship best-seller, *'Us: How Moving Relationships Beyond You and Me Creates More Love, Passion, and Understanding,'* Terry Real describes the Adaptive Child as a kid in grown-up clothing, the child's version of the adult we cobbled together in the absence of healthy parenting. When your partner cuts you off, or doesn't take your side, or criticises and belittles you, you step straight into your Adaptive Child.

Think about it. When you're arguing with a partner, are you a Wise Adult, conciliatory, flexible, realistic, a good listener, relaxed in your body, nurturing the relationship? Or are you an immature, angry or frightened child, who is black and white, rigid, certain, relentless, harsh, tight in your body, and risking the relationship?

The Adaptive Child is a young part of you – aged perhaps three, four, five - that learned to cope the best way it could at the time. That may have been angry, screaming and attacking, or terrified, going quiet and hiding.

We need to be respectful of the exquisite wisdom of this younger part of ourselves who made the choices it did back then. However, the essential learning is that while it was adaptive as a child's survival strategy, it's maladaptive now. As an adult's survival strategy, it could cost you your relationship and your happiness.

Your Adaptive Child's dysfunctional way of behaving will never get you what you want.

Take Lenny. He loves his partner, but his habit of flying off the handle, turning on his partner and losing it, is what's brought them to counselling.

When I ask him "How old were you when you first did this?" he admits that his parents tell stories of his legendary temper tantrums. Their attempts to soothe him were singularly unsuccessful. They ended up gritting their teeth until the tantrum subsided. He'd been allowed to get away with this as a child, and he's still doing it!

However, Lenny behaving like an angry three-year-old as an adult, is pushing his partner to question whether or not it's worth staying in the relationship.

Angry pursuit of your partner is an Adaptive Child's dysfunctional stance, just as withdrawing and cold-shouldering your partner is an Adaptive Child's dysfunctional stance. You will rarely get closer to your partner by getting mad at how distant they are, or how they withdraw when you complain about things you don't like. In a similar way, becoming defensive or withdrawing will never repair the problem, or help your partner feel understood and heard.

The model of couples therapy I favour, Relational Life Therapy (RLT), includes coaching to:

- Shift the Adaptive Child into the thinking and behaviour of the Wise Adult,
- Effectively re-parent a dysfunctional inner child, and,
- Get the Adaptive Child to take his/her hands off the steering wheel.

Among other things, it models and teaches what Wise Adults do when they encounter relationship problems. We learn to replace the relationship-sabotaging behaviour and thinking which we bring to the party when we 'whoosh'--or unconsciously react– into being our Adaptive Child.

So what is our true inner child like, before it loses its innocence and adapts to survive what Shakespeare's Hamlet calls *'the slings and arrows of outrageous fortune'*?

By this Hamlet is referring to his fate and the outrageous situation he finds himself in.

His 'old story' is the stuff that plays are written about! The ghost of his father, the King of Denmark, tells Hamlet to avenge his murder by killing the new king, Hamlet's uncle. Hamlet feigns madness and seeks revenge. Fearing for his life, his uncle devises a plot to kill Hamlet.

Fortunately for us, most of our family-of-origin dramas are a lot less dramatic than Hamlet's. Nonetheless very few of us have been lucky enough to have had a childhood totally free of pain and family dysfunction.

Let's come back to the really good question of what our inner child was like before its loss of innocence. Let's explore that and remember!

Who is Your Inner Child, Really?

In his excellent book *'Journey into the Light'* Tim Carter introduces us to our true self, the self we would be if we experienced an idyllic, problem-free childhood in a peaceful, loving local and global community.

The true self within each and every one of us is creative, spontaneous, vulnerable, feels emotions, and is intuitive. This self loves play, fun, not taking life too seriously. It is able to just **be**.

This is our true self, and it is this self that we lose sight of as we grow and adapt to the requirements of our families, our communities, our schools, our religions, our institutions, our cultures.

As we comply with such requirements, as we experience the disappointments of big "T" and small "t" traumas, as we lose our innocence and trust, our true selves go into hiding within the subconscious part of ourselves. Before very long, we have put in place a false identity.

We have reached a point where we have forgotten our playful, inner children, our true selves.

The cost of this loss is emptiness, like something is missing in our lives. Maybe this feeling is familiar to you too?

When our false self takes the place of our true self, instead of being able to just be, instead of being intuitive and playful, we become busy. We seek behaviours, experiences, people, places, things outside of ourselves to fill our emptiness.

This often goes hand in hand with a host of dysfunctional, negative coping mechanisms and defensive behaviours, including a workaholic or driven lifestyle, perfectionism, obsessions, life dramas, mental illnesses and addictions.

. . .

These are the characteristics of the inner child versus the adaptive or false identity most of us present to the world:

Inner Child (True Self)	Adaptive or False Identity
Feels feelings	Denies or hides feelings
Naturally intuitive, picking up information that supports us emotionally and spiritually	Merely logical/rational
Vulnerable	Pretends to be strong
Open to the unconscious	Blocks subconscious material
Trusting	Distrustful

The Need to Reconnect with Your Inner Child

Inside every adult is an inner child asking to be let out. Our inner children are constantly trying to get our attention, asking for our intervention and help.

When we ignore our true feelings and our intuition, we are ignoring our inner child. Feelings are our inner child's way of communicating with us. So many of us find it difficult to recognise and manage our emotions. This is largely because we have lost contact with our inner child and our inner child's trapped emotions. We push these feelings away because they are too painful.

This lack of contact with our feelings, this lack of recognition of the emotional distress of our inner child, can lead to profoundly serious physical and mental health problems.

If you are so out-of-touch with your inner child that it is imprisoned in your grown-up persona and you refuse to listen to it, it may eventually try to get your attention via chronic illness, low energy, compulsions, addictions, challenging relationships and other physical and emotional problems. Such problems often lead to a dark night of the soul and may, ironically, act as a wake-up call and be the catalyst for healing and growth.

Our inner child is longing for us to reconnect with it, to acknowledge its presence and to listen to it.

Because a wounded or unhappy inner child, a false identity underlies so many of today's emotional and relationship problems, many styles of therapy have been developed to help people reconnect with, re-parent and heal their inner child. The stories of Carmen and Jimmy at the start of this chapter reveal how such types of therapy can be of immense help.

Exercise: A Way to Reconnect with your Inner Child

I referred earlier to the author of *'Journey into the Light'*, my colleague Tim Carter. We run workshops together, with an emphasis on manifesting dreams and understanding and working with the inner child. One of the ways we invite participants to connect with their inner child is to write a letter to him or her, as follows:

Part One:

Starting with your **dominant hand,** address your letter to your inner child. You could start with something like, *'Dear little*...(your name)

- Let her/him know you will always love and support her/him unconditionally
- Promise you will check in with her/him regularly to see if she/he needs help
- You may, gently and respectfully, mention certain beliefs, emotions or behaviours that you might jointly want to look at, and if appropriate, change. (Negative coping mechanisms, like addictions, workaholism, or obsessions could be worth addressing here.)

Part Two:

With your **non-dominant hand**, write a reply from your inner child to your adult self. Don't censor anything, just let ideas flow. You might be surprised at what comes to light!

. . .

Simple as this may seem, this is a very powerful exercise, able to unlock lost memories and buried emotions.

The left hemisphere of the brain is the logical side, which controls verbal and analytical processing. The right hemisphere is mainly non-verbal and looks after visual and spatial perception, emotional expression, imagination, and intuition.

Your letter to your inner child and their reply is a dialogue between the two of you, where the use of your dominant versus your non-dominant hand allows access to the different hemispheres of your brain. It allows your left and right brains to converse.

If the deep emotional parts of your brain have been sealed off for a long time, you may need some patience to break through the feeling of emptiness and create connection.

Remember it's the **feelings** that count as you attempt to understand your inner child's responses. If you're unsure whether your inner child feels safe or has her/his needs met, simply ask. Do a 'right - hand-left -hand dialogue' and consult her/him.

This is an exercise and a practice you can do alone, starting now, if you want to. Before you start, I invite you to set the scene by honouring how profound an experience you are inviting in.

Find a place and time where you'll be able to have space and be on your own. Perhaps light a candle, perhaps start with a meditation, or by centering yourself with a few deep breaths. Set the intention in your mind and heart that you will find this a richly rewarding and invaluable experience, deepening the connection with this precious part of you.

Bear in mind that once you make the promise that you will consult with your inner child on a regular basis, you need to honour this as your inner child trusts you to make good on your promises.

In Tim Carter's words;

> *'As you begin to nurture your inner child on a regular basis, in a gentle, empathic way, you may find that you become more open-minded, more flexible, more vulnerable. You will then begin to experience freedom, courage, self-validation, love of self – things that you perhaps never believed you could experience. Long-buried emotions will surface, some happy, some sad, some loving, some fearful. Feeling these emotions and*

letting some go, will heal and help you become whole again. Your feelings of emptiness will disappear.

Part of the beauty of this process is that it frees us up to say no without feeling guilty, to state our beliefs without fear of ridicule, and to know that it's OK if we make mistakes. It's important to set aside a regular time to connect with your inner child, to have fun and play. When you do this, congratulate yourself because this is of great value not just for your inner child but also for your Wise Adult wellbeing.'

- Journey into the Light by Tim Carter.

As you drop your old stories and personality, your old identity, and truly open your heart to gratitude, forgiveness of self and others, acceptance of what is, there will be a resurrection of **innocence**. You will become a child again. But not a naïve, inexperienced child. Rather an evolved, healed, compassionate adult, a child reborn. The nature of this child-like innocence is the ultimate goal.

11

KEEPING LOVE ALIVE

HOW TO STOP MAKING THE SAME RELATIONSHIP MISTAKES

The magic of ScriptWriting puts you in the place of identifying the relationship you dream of, then visualising yourself in it.

That's the first step. If you've run into problems in the past, the second step to maintaining a happy future is to learn new skills so that you don't repeat previous patterns. The truth is that many of us do a pretty dismal job of keeping the love alive when we meet the partner of our dreams, or worse still, when we settle for the next best available.

As a 'second-time-arounder' myself, I assure you I've had my fair share of learning in the marriage stakes. Sure, I had scripted Mr Right into my life. Though he was Mr Right, he wasn't Mr Perfect. Guess what? Mr Perfect doesn't exist. Not for you, not for me. He wasn't perfect and neither was I.

Each of us brought into our new relationship our family-of-origin baggage and the bad habits we'd developed as our first marriages had run into trouble.

Our honeymoon lasted for years. But then as problems arose around blended family issues and work pressures, we weren't getting on as well as we had been. I wasn't going to do what I did in my first marriage — think that it was his behaviour and his attitudes that were the problem. This time, I realised the only part of the problem over which I had any control and could change, was my behaviour and my beliefs.

Running into glitches in my second marriage motivated me to understand the underlying dynamics of couple interaction. In particular, my intention was to learn ways of dealing with the ups and downs of coupledom, especially the downs, so that I could create harmony and happiness in my relationship and in my life.

And I hit gold! Trust me, there are ways of raising problems with your partner, and ways of responding when your partner raises problems, which can either increase trust and cooperation, or spell doom for the relationship.

This chapter introduces you to some communication skills and behaviours which can help you contribute your best, rather than your worst, to your relationship. It can help you make your relationship one in which you (and your partner) will want to stay.

How Do You Nurture Your Relationship?

You deserve to be happy. So does your partner.

Do you want to nurture and grow the new relationship you script into your life? Or do you want to rebuild emotional intimacy and fondness in a relationship which has grown stagnant?

Flying blind, repeating mistakes learned from your parents, or making the same old mistakes which caused problems in previous relationships will not deliver you the relationship harmony or longevity you hope for.

Couples often sit up and take note when they hear that research psychologist Dr John Gottman found that by watching just fifteen minutes of how a couple handles conflicts or differences of opinion, his researchers could predict with better than 90% accuracy, who would be divorced in five years. Gottman quotes this research in his best-seller, *The Seven Principles for Making Marriage Work*.

In other words, it's the way that you **handle the problems** which you inevitably encounter, and the ways you react when triggered by something your partner says or does, which are critical to the ongoing health of your relationship.

In a nutshell - and this is not rocket science – behaviour has consequences.

You behave in a certain manner, you say certain things, and this calls forth certain responses from your partner. You won't be surprised to hear that when you are angry or critical, he/she will respond differently than when you are loving and admiring.

You have a choice. You can **choose** how you react. Couples who are happy together are not simply lucky because they have better partners. Rather, they know or have learnt how to manage the ups and downs of their relationship. They do so with mutual respect, understanding, compassion, generosity, forgiveness, responsiveness, love and flexibility. They have learned not to be critical, blaming, aggressive, defensive, retaliatory, vengeful, withdrawn, sulky, demanding, rigid, hard-line, self-righteous or controlling.

There's no point in buying a beautiful new car, then failing to have it serviced and repaired when it runs into problems. In the same way, I would be failing you if I taught you to script the partner of your dreams into your life, without teaching you how to nurture your longed-for relationship.

Mills and Boon romance novels and boy-meets-girl movies often end at the beginning of the relationship. The skills needed to woo and win your partner are not the same skills you need after you've moved in together. I'm sure we all know people who easily attract new partners into their lives, but for whom relationships don't last. You'd probably agree that it's easier to be charming, fun and understanding when you're courting than when you're fielding and managing the problems which crop up as the years roll by.

But what if you kept up the romance, the wooing, the affection and kindness to each other that tends to characterise the courtship? As time passed, your relationship would look very different from the angry, name calling, blaming, controlling, bitter or distant relationships that often end up on the psychologist's couch.

There's no getting away from it - relationships are work. If you want a growth-oriented relationship, you need to separately nurture romance, shared interests and activities, friendship, forgiveness, compassion, and understanding, as well as contributing, with good grace, your share of the workload and responsibility required to keep a relationship or family functioning well.

You also need to take care of your mental health and learn from your mistakes, choosing not to repeat them again and again, even though they're not giving you what you want.

You're responsible for **your fifty percent** in the 50/50 two-way street called marriage or de facto relationship.

What you do—or don't do—profoundly influences the way your partner responds to you, profoundly influences the quality of your relationship.

You need flexibility, you need generosity, you need kindness, and you need to strike a balance. At times, you need to put up with micro-disappointments for the good of the relationship, giving in as gracefully as you can. At other times you need to stand up for yourself respectfully and call it when your partner is out of line.

If you're doing more anger and withdrawing than loving and reaching out to your partner, get help. See a relationship counsellor to get a relationship in the doldrums back into the sunshine. Or, you can also explore a few of my favourite relationship self-help books that you'll find listed in the appendix at the back of this book.

An Example of Couples Therapy in Action

In the middle of an argument, both partners believe they are right and their partner is wrong. The dynamic driving the conflict and the solutions are often out of sight. The following session shows how therapy:

- Helped Matt understand why Larissa was so upset, enabling him to be more empathic and,
- Helped Larissa learn to ask, respectfully, for what she wanted, rather than blaming him and turning on him in anger.

In a de facto relationship, Matt and Larissa were a glamour couple, in their early thirties. They were intelligent, fit, sleek, and good looking. This was the fifth time I'd seen them, as they worked through the arguments and problems which sometimes made them question whether theirs would be a long-term commitment.

Matt, the Innocent Victim

Session five opened with Matt confidently asking, "Can we talk about an incident that happened a couple of weeks ago?"

Setting the context, this was in the middle of the global pandemic. There had been a 'run' (no pun intended) on toilet paper in Australia, and the supermarket toilet paper shelves were often empty.

> **Matt:** "We were running out of toilet paper. We were down to two rolls. I asked Larissa if she could buy some. I ended up having to go myself on the way home from work, and buy some for an exorbitant price. The issue arose over miscommunication on the phone. She said the toilet paper had been sold out. And I said 'You would have had to shop early in the morning to get some.' That was like the last straw that broke the camel's back! The conversation turned very quickly into a blame game. I felt I was under attack till the call ended. It was very charged because she thought it was unfair, given that she'd been saying for weeks that we should be stocking up on toilet paper. All this emotion!
>
> There are two points I want to raise. One, she admitted later that sometimes the only thing that stops her verbally abusing me is to give me the silent treatment. I think there could be a better way than that. It's not a good solution. Two, the emotional reaction I got was way out of proportion to the toilet paper issue."

Matt feels like the innocent victim here, and thinks that it's Larissa's behaviour that is the problem.

Larissa, the Innocent Victim

There are, of course, two sides to every story, so I asked Larissa for hers.

> **Larissa:** "What happened was that I brought this up a few weeks ago, that we needed to buy toilet paper given that it had become so hard to get. He kept saying that I was being ridiculous, that we didn't need toilet paper. I brought it up three times, and three times he laughed at me and said 'You're being ridiculous!' What upset me (she said, looking

at him) was that you then expected me to have bought some when you kept telling me not to do it."

Matt: "I wasn't combative at all when I said you should have gone (to buy it) early in the morning. It would have been a lot nicer if you hadn't adopted that tone of voice and turned on me."

The session went on to explore:

- How Larissa had felt each time Matt had dismissed her request to buy toilet paper, calling it ridiculous ('Really disrespected, not understood', Larissa said)
- How explaining that to Matt early in the piece might have been a better way for her to look after her feelings and needs
- The value of small, controlled burns (raising the problem by admitting she felt invisible and disrespected when he made fun of her request to stock up), rather than her biting her tongue again and again, letting her resentment build, then ending up with a screaming match and a major conflagration
- How Matt could have registered that, if Larissa kept raising this, it was really important to her
- How Matt could have been more empathic and said, after the second or third time she said that she thought they needed toilet paper, 'OK, I hear you're feeling concerned. Why not? Let's just get some.'

The Plot Thickens

At this point in the conversation, Larissa proudly admitted that she had done a controlled burn.

Larissa: "We were out with friends and Matt kept making jokes about me wanting to stock up on toilet paper – like all the people who'd stocked up when there was no need, and created the shortage in the first place. When we got home, I told him I didn't appreciate his making fun of me. I nipped it in the bud."

Create Abundant Possibilities

This was like gold in the therapeutic situation. As a therapist, I took the opportunity to explain that it is an absolute no-no to make jokes in the company of family or friends at your partner's expense. When you complain that you feel hurt, your partner saying, 'Where's your sense of humour? You're over-sensitive. It was only a joke!' is passive aggression.

I asked Larissa to consider how different she might have felt had he responded in a more empathic and respectful way, like, "I get that you're really concerned about the toilet paper shortage" ('Much better', she said) — rather than expressing contempt and shaming her in public with put downs like "You're being ridiculous!"

How to Be More Responsible and Emotionally Available

As Larissa explained the steps in the lead-up to her 'losing it' when Matt had complained she should have shopped early in the morning so as not to have missed out on toilet paper, the full extent of his failure to be more responsible and emotionally available to her became crystal clear.

I felt he needed coaching to help him become more empathic and aware of Larissa's feelings, as well as being willing to be more vulnerable and accountable for what he said and did in response to Larissa's requests.

I recommended to Matt that, instead of regularly criticising Larissa, before he speaks, he pause, take a deep breath, and ask himself, *'How is she going to feel if I say that?' 'How might this affect our relationship?' '**Am I crushing her confidence?**' 'Might this make her angry and defensive towards me?'* (The same applies in a parent's relationship with his/her children.)

By this stage in the session, Matt was sounding a little less sure of himself.

"This is helpful. I didn't think about my contribution to the situation, what I'd done. At the time, I thought, 'Where did this come from?' I did feel like an innocent victim. It is helpful to get reminded that in every situation, you're contributing."

The Shifting Roles of Persecutor, Victim & Rescuer

I also introduced Matt and Larissa to the Karpman Drama Triangle, the brainchild of psychiatrist Stephen Karpman, which highlights the destructive and shifting roles we play when we get caught up in emotional dramas.

The following diagram maps out this typical relationship conflict interaction:

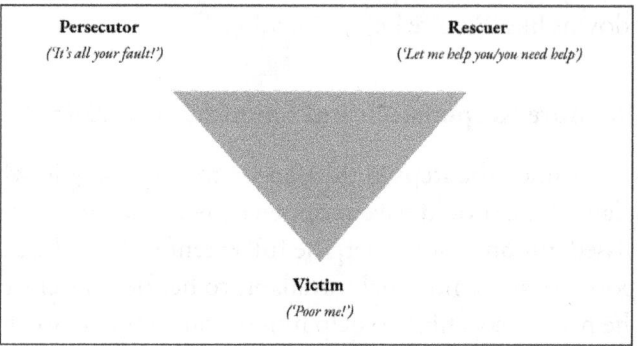

When you're in the negative interaction cycle, playing persecutor-rescuer-victim roles (we all do this), the pattern of talk-fight-exhaustion can go on for hours.

It looks like this... you both:

- Argue loudly,
- Interrupt frequently,
- Value only your own opinions and interpretations of what's happened, rather than ask for information and listen to hear, and,
- Take it all emotionally and personally.

Breaking the negative cycle requires you to move into the centre of the triangle, refusing to play an exaggerated or complementary role to a Victim, Rescuer or Persecutor. This requires you to be **vulnerable**, to reach out and to be persistent in constructively working through issues together.

It requires you to become **outcome-oriented** (focusing on goals,

Create Abundant Possibilities

solutions and desired outcomes), instead of problem-oriented (focusing on what's wrong).

By failing to look after her own needs to stick up for herself and tell Matt how hurt she felt when he belittled, dismissed, and then continued to belittle and dismiss her repeated requests, Larissa became the victim, stuck in the problem, letting the resentment build.

Then she 'lost it' when he complained she hadn't shopped early enough, without admitting that he'd contributed to the incident by repeatedly ignoring her warnings about serious shortages.

Unfortunately, unleashing her bottled-up fury turned her from **Victim** (one-down and laughed at) into **Persecutor** (one-up and angry — *'It's all your fault.'*)

The healthy position is the centre of the triangle, where she could have said how she felt about his complaint, without becoming angry and punitive.

Worse still, in Matt's point of view, her anger let Matt off the hook. It enabled him to avoid taking responsibility for the disrespect he'd shown her earlier. He became the innocent victim as she switched from victim to persecutor. Remember how he'd started the session secure that he was totally in the right and citing her overly emotional reaction as out of proportion to the gentle tone of his request as the problem?

A Healthy Approach to Decreasing Drama

At the heart of the Karpman triangle is the healthy position. In it lives:

- Authenticity and the wisdom of mature, adult emotion,
- Being able to really listen and be empathic about what your partner feels, even though you disagree,
- Being willing to be flexible and accommodate minor disappointments or disagreements for the good of the relationship,
- The choice to let go of taking things personally, having to be right, fighting and arguing.

In intimate relationships, there is no one truth, no one objective reality. Rather, there are just two people's perspectives. To keep the relationship sweet and loving, both need to be willing to hear each other's point of view, then find a solution which honours both.

In the remainder of that session I coached Matt and Larissa on objectivity battles. I questioned Matt: "In this battle are you sticking with your reality? Or are you open to being objective?"

In particular:

- "Did Larissa, or did she not, over-react to your benign request for her to buy toilet paper?"
- "Is Larissa justified in getting angry that you expressed disappointment that she hadn't shopped earlier in the day, given the shortage of toilet paper which she had been pointing out for weeks?"

Being able to be **objective** about a situation outside of perceived good/bad and right/wrong style judgements is key to restoring harmony and balance in relationships.

Following the Relational Life Therapy coaching model, I then suggested to Matt that his way of thinking and responding was not the only possibility open to him. "What if you respond in this way… When Larissa is upset or feels you've let her down or misunderstood her, the response which will nurture the relationship is not your being right, **not** your saying 'You're wrong to have overreacted. I did nothing wrong.'"

I asked them to imagine how different the outcome may have been when Larissa was so upset if Matt had:

- Looked into her eyes,
- Taken care to use a soft, gentle tone of voice,
- Said, 'Darling, I'm sorry, I could have listened better. I'm sorry you feel bad. I didn't mean to make you feel that way. Is there anything I could say or do right now that could help you feel better?'

When I role-played Matt doing that, tears of joy welled up in Larissa's eyes. She had at last been heard and understood.

Create Abundant Possibilities

. . .

Today's individualistic society is grounded in a winner takes all mentality. It's not restricted to the corporate world. It also shows up in our relationships and is alive and well in our living rooms.

The trouble is that as a model for managing intimate relationships, the individualistic *'I'm right, you're wrong'*, 'you' versus 'me' style of relating takes a severe toll. It leads to repetitive fights that go nowhere and feeling alone in your own marriage.

Relational Life Therapy offers a diametrically different way of doing relationship: it places **cooperation** and intention to **nurture** the relationship front and centre.

In a nutshell, it teaches that if you strive to cherish your partner, working to maintain the sweetness in your relationship, the question is not *'Who's right and who's wrong'*, it's *'Who cares?'* It was this that I recommended to Matt and Larissa, suggesting Matt put the following words on his shaving mirror:

'Darling, I could have listened better. I'm sorry you feel bad. Is there anything I could say or do right now to help you feel better?'

Couples therapy coached:

- **Larissa** to make a point of giving Matt feedback in a soft, vulnerable way when she finds his behaviour hurtful or demeaning: 'I felt hurt when you said'... 'I'd have liked you to have acknowledged that there was an out-of-stock problem brewing, and to have been respectful of my opinion even if you didn't agree.' This is the use of soft power; the skill of standing up for yourself with respect at the same time as cherishing your partner and your relationship, rather than winning and having 'power over.'
- **Matt** to understand that if something is a problem for Larissa, it's a problem for him. His being dismissive will make her resentful. It made the point that it is important that he listen to her views in a respectful way, **whether or**

not he agrees with her. Making fun of her, especially in front of family or friends, is a total no-no!

We can, of course, all benefit from adopting such communication skills in our own relationships. The good news is that Larissa and Matt are now married. They report that they put into practice this and other new relational skills and the relationship is travelling well.

If you encounter problems and disillusionment in a new relationship you've scripted into your life, or in an existing relationship that you'd like to revitalise, I hope this case study encourages you to believe that relationships which run into problems can be healed.

Of course, this means making changes. If nothing changes, nothing changes! I hope Larissa and Matt's story also opens your mind to the fact that both of you will need to make changes to your side of the story if things are to change.

If, and when you hit a rough patch in your relationship, I invite you to ask yourself what part of the problem you can take responsibility for? What did you do, or not do, think or say which contributed to the problem?

Whether or not you feel more 'sinned' against than 'sinning,' I invite you to ask yourself what you can do to make your relationship sweeter and happier. The next step is to do it! This is the win-win, rather than the win-lose model of relationship. It guarantees both of you will be beneficiaries.

There are plenty of great books and courses on how to make relationships work, and times when seeing a skilled couples therapist can make a big difference. Instead of letting problems simmer until they boil over, take the steps that will keep your problems easily fixable with a little effort.

12

CONFIDENCE
SILENCING THE INNER CRITIC

If you hang on to old critical beliefs about yourself or if you put yourself down when things go wrong, this chapter provides an opportunity to practise ways of increasing your self-esteem and self-love so that you can express yourself confidently.

Do you flinch at the idea of acknowledging what's good about yourself or even worse, loving yourself? Do you judge people for loving themselves? If so, this is your invitation to discover the beauty and magic of you! Everyone is invited to play!

There is not a person on this planet that doesn't deserve to love themselves into a life of joyful, loving abundance and freedom.

The Slings and Arrows of Outrageous Fortune

So many of us are held back in our lives by self-doubt and self-criticism. In general, even in the West, women have a lower level of confidence than men. This is not surprising, given that our self-concept is rooted in the power dynamics of patriarchal culture.

Research shows that when things go wrong, women are more likely than men to attribute it to their very identity; who they are or what's "wrong" with them. Men are more likely to dismiss their feelings, or blame others, circumstance or something they did, rather than attribute something going wrong to their very identity.

Women's self-concepts often fail to match their actual possibilities. For example, it is estimated that on average, women under-estimate their earning potential by as much as 50%.

When future generations look back on the past couple of centuries, I hope they will be shocked to discover that many of our social structures and cultural norms loaded the dice against certain types of people or certain groups of people.

Prejudice and bias has been directly responsible for creating false notions of individual and self-worth. It has been a major contributor to many of the injustices and problems on Planet Earth.

Cultural, societal and religious norms restrict women's freedom, denying them privileges accorded to men. Yours might be a culture with marked socio-economic, class, caste and ethnic differences. Yours may have been a family that valued self-sacrifice, believing that looking after your own needs and desires is selfish. You may have grown up suspicious of 'tall poppies', being critical of people who are 'too successful' or proud of their own success.

Add to that religious and political judgments about who is right and who is wrong! Then there's the whole gamut of minority group differences, including cultural, ethnic, economic, gender, disability, etc. and their associated disadvantages.

And that's before we even look at the widespread common denominator of traumatic childhood experiences, including family-of-origin dysfunction, the less than perfect parenting which has so many of us carrying baggage into our adult lives.

Little wonder that most of us grapple with issues of self-worth and self-esteem. The trouble with this is that we tend to take ourselves at our own evaluation of ourselves. This results in under-performing or aiming low. It also saps joy and inner peace.

Confidence and self-esteem are your ally if you are to manifest and continue to live your dream. Part of what holds us back and limits our potential in work, love, health and life in general, is that many of us don't believe in ourselves or don't even like ourselves.

If we believe we're not clever enough, or able enough, if we believe we're unlovable, or incapable of a great love, instead of fulfilling our true potential, we settle for less. We live a less happy life than is our divine right to enjoy.

As we look at healing your limiting notions of 'not being good enough', I invite you to open your mind and heart so you can:

- Be willing to move into a stance of believing that we are all both flawed and magnificent, at the same time. (This includes you and me!) This allows you to accept your mistakes and limitations with compassion, while concurrently embracing your gifts and championing your good points;
- Be willing to be uncomfortable and to grow outside of your comfort zone. You need to expand your current beliefs about yourself if you are to live the life you dream of and enjoy the happiness you are here to experience. You need to be willing to champion yourself, rather than play the more familiar role of putting yourself down;
- Know that you will be learning new skills and cultivating new capacities which will better equip you to live the new story of happiness and success you've scripted into your life. You are the author of your life. You are also its hero or heroine!

Your potential is longing to be expressed. Being kind to yourself, having compassion for your mistakes and acknowledging and celebrating your strengths opens the door to becoming your best self.

Changing in the ways you need to change is your transformation journey. It's a journey we all take sooner or later. May as well start now!

Watching someone who has been unhappy and disempowered shake off the yoke of the low self-esteem of their past to become more confident is one of the great joys of being a therapist and coach.

Janine's Story

As people become more confident, invariably their lives improve and they become happier. I reassure you that I've seen this happen for many clients, and it can happen for you, too. Janine offers another great example.

As I asked what she hoped to get out of therapy, Janine's face crumpled and the tears flowed. Fortyish, overweight, dark hair pulled back in a ponytail, she was an accountant and sole breadwinner for her family of de facto partner, Mark, and her three year-old son Paul. She also did all the cooking and housework.

Mark was the stay at home dad. He was the sort of partner you walk past on eggshells, because of a lack of emotional safety and trust. Bipolar and unmedicated, he'd often turn on her, criticising and blaming her, yelling and name calling. "It is always all about him. I just can't keep him happy. You can say things to a normal person and expect an appropriate response. We aren't close, like being able to talk to each other."

Profile of a People Pleaser

What made Janine accept such an unsatisfying relationship? At the heart of her problems lay Janine's low self-esteem, fed by a harsh inner critic. "I don't really like myself very much. At work, I'm confident. I know what I'm doing. But who am I outside of work? I just try to be whatever someone wants me to be. I'm surprised when somebody likes me."

Typical of fawners and pleasers, she put herself last. She fawned and said 'yes' when she meant 'no.' She said she agreed when she actually didn't because she didn't want to cause an argument. She put up with things that upset her. She did things she didn't want to do because she didn't want to reveal how she really felt.

She did not know how, and didn't have the courage, to set boundaries like, "No thank you. I don't want to do that.", "I don't like it when you say that. What I would have preferred is this."

She wanted to ask for help but was too scared to do so. The cost to herself and her relationship was the build-up of a dungeon of resentment and discontent below her outward appearance of being easy-going and accommodating.

Faulty beliefs like these made Janine put up with Mark's bad-boy behaviour, her thinking being:

Create Abundant Possibilities

- *It's better to say nothing. It will only make things worse.*
- *I have no right to expect to be happy.*
- *Other people won't like me. I'm not attractive or likable. I'm overweight.*
- *I'm not popular, so there's no point in saying what I feel or asking for what I want.*
- *It's probably my fault. I shouldn't have done what I did.*
- *I shouldn't have said what I said.*

During the conversation we discovered that her mother's post-partum depression had stopped them from bonding. The mother-child relationship held the key to her perception of her low worth as a woman.

"I tell Paul I love him a million times a day. I do that because mum never ever told me she loved me. I remember thinking she must be a wicked step-mum. She was always unhappy with me, always sending me to my room. She wanted me to have done all the housework by the time she got home from work. It was so unfair. My brother did nothing, yet he was the one she favoured. I believed that unless you don't argue, you won't be loved. It got to a point with Mark where as long as he wasn't being abusive, I was happy to have him around. I thought that was good enough."

We've touched on this before in this book: It's almost uncanny how as children of five, four, or even younger, we make decisions outside of our conscious awareness. This encompasses decisions such as what we need to do to get love and care in our family, how safe life is and what's actually possible.

For example, someone with an abusive or traumatic upbringing may well live with the belief, *'It's a cold, scary world. No-one's there for me.'* Conversely, someone brought up in a stable, loving home may live life believing *'I'm surrounded by love. Life is good.'*

Such life narratives cast a very long shadow, becoming a virtual blueprint for how we experience life. Our beliefs become self-fulfilling prophecies.

Fortunately, personal development, therapy, life coaching, and a willingness to learn and change, can open doors to healing and a brighter future. They can encourage you to dare to dream. They can help you nurture and maintain the dreams your scripts deliver.

Turning Janine's Life Around

For Janine, the first step in building her confidence was to help her notice her inner critic, and understand the havoc it was causing in her life.

Next, she needed to change her relationship with herself to become her own best friend, rather than her own worst enemy, as she had been.

Perhaps something in this is familiar to you. The steps for challenging your own inner critic and instead fostering your own **inner supporter** are outlined next.

Your Inner Critic – The Enemy

If you want to shift depression, anxiety and pervasive unhappiness with your life, a powerful place to start is by raising your self-esteem. Low self-esteem often goes hand-in-hand with an over-active and nasty inner critic.

Dr Jennice Vilhauer, director of Emory University's Outpatient Psychotherapy Department of Psychiatry and Behavioural Science in the School of Medicine implores us to come face-to face with our inner critic, *"The inner voice in your head that judges you, doubts you, belittles you, and constantly tells you that you are not good enough. It says negative, hurtful things to you – things that you would never dream of saying to anyone else. I am such an idiot; I am a phony; I never do anything right; I will never succeed."*

She adds: *"The inner critic isn't harmless. It inhibits you, limits you, and stops you from pursuing the life you truly want to live. It robs you of peace of mind and emotional well-being, and, if left unchecked long enough, it can even lead to serious mental health problems like depression and anxiety."*

Working with clients who believe their inner critic has shown me how this sabotages and slows them down. Listening to your inner critic makes you doubt yourself and what you're capable of. Conversely, when you are kind to yourself or forgive yourself, your morale and motivation skyrocket.

Do you realise **your inner critic has been your hidden script writer, scripting disappointment and failure, condemning you to ongoing anxiety, shame, fear, loneliness, procrastination?**

Banishing your inner critic is about letting the old stories and scripts go. These are invisible scripts you didn't know were creating your future. What would be possible if you wrote your own scripts more consciously?

Following a process designed by Dr Vilhauer, the expert on healing the inner critic, if you have a strong inner critic, I recommend the exercise below.

Exercise: Keep an inner critic log for a week

Every time you notice you're being self-critical, make a short note about:
- **The situation**, e.g. 'argument with husband,' 'son rude to me', 'manager short with me.'
- **The criticism**, e.g. 'I'm not lovable,' 'I'm a bad mother,' and, 'I'll be the first one fired.' Just log what your inner critic says.

In tandem with keeping an inner critic log, again following Dr Vilhauer's process, I recommend you:

> **Keep a journal where, each day for a month, you note two or three things you liked about yourself that day.**

The key is to read everything you've liked about yourself so far, each day, so that by Day 30, you're reading a long list of things you like about yourself.

By becoming aware of your critical voice, noticing how often it steps in, and how nasty and disempowering it is, you're opening the doors to placing yourself in a position where you can challenge it.

This simple process of banishing your inner critic and installing a virtual inner supporter leads to personal empowerment. You aren't being grandiose or egotistical when you remind yourself that there are good things about you, that you have strengths as well as weaknesses. You're not comparing yourself with other people and giving yourself a tick or a cross. You're simply setting the balance straight in your own psyche by reminding yourself of what's good about you, rather than focusing on what isn't.

Putting this into practice helped lift Janine's spirits. I was delighted to see the change in her. I have witnessed this in many clients who previously spent too much time thinking about what's wrong with them and not enough time acknowledging what's right with them. Simply doing these exercises changes that tendency, lowers depression scores, and helps people hear and accept compliments.

Set Clear Boundaries

Janine's over-functioning, over-delivering, people-pleasing attitude held the imbalance of her relationship firmly in place. She was so out of touch with her own needs that she put up with things which she disliked, let herself be taken advantage of, and was an almost non-existent advocate for what she wanted.

I asked her to buy and read *'Boundary Boss,'* by psychotherapist Terri Cole. This took her into new territory, as it does for many people. She discovered how to express her preferences, desires and deal-breakers and set firm boundaries.

We role-played her standing up for herself, and pushing back when Mark was unreasonable and unyielding. She was literally terrified, and needed considerable coaching and encouragement to create healthy boundaries for herself.

Learn to Enjoy Compliments

Do you have a hard time accepting compliments paid to you? Do you find yourself thinking compliments aren't deserved or aren't sincere?

As we allow ourselves to drink in that we do actually do things which are helpful, effective or attractive, we become better able to allow compliments in. That is because they align with the improved view we now have of ourselves.

If you find it hard to accept compliments, or feel it's big-headed to tell yourself what's good about yourself, it's important to recognise this is one of the ways you sabotage yourself and keep your insecurities in place. I invite you to turn this around. I invite you to allow more good things to flow to you.

How do you accept compliments? Do you feel embarrassed and try to negate the compliment? *'You don't mean that, ha ha.'* or *'No, I don't look good!'* Or, do you wonder what the ulterior motive is of the compliment-giver? Or do you ignore it completely?

Here are a few ideas that may help you accept the next compliment you receive:

- A simple, "thank you"
- Let the compliment land inside you…start learning to allow yourself to feel the pleasure that comes with being acknowledged, or admired. Take a deep breath, slow down and start feeling a little smile inside.
- Let yourself reflect on the compliment. Open your heart and have compassion for yourself if you are one of those people who were neither trained to receive compliments, nor to feel good about yourself. Resolve to react differently next time someone pays you a compliment. Practise, practise, practise.

In summary, when you're no longer cringing and being limited by the put-downs of your inner critic, you give yourself the gift of personal empowerment. You walk tall. You stop doubting yourself. You stop being distracted and hijacked by a fearful, anxious mind. You stop procrastinating and get on with simply doing the tasks you need to do. As you experience quiet satisfaction, you find yourself attaining more of your goals and your confidence grows.

Assertive Communication is Respectful & Empowering

When a new couple presents for counselling and you ask them how their relationship would look if it was the way they'd like it to be, one of the things they invariably say is their communication would be better. Most admit the way they try to resolve problems makes their problems worse, not better.

One of the models I use – just one of the many models available to improve communication skills – is **Assertive Communication Skills**.

This may sound a touch strident, but this model of communicating really does provide practical, easily actionable guidelines for good communication. It identifies three styles of communicator:

1. At one extreme, you have the **pleaser**, whose mindset is, *'You're OK, I'm not OK.'*
2. In the middle, in the position of healthy balance, you have the **assertive person**, who believes *'I'm OK, you're OK.'*
3. At the other extreme, you have the **aggressive person**, who believes *'I'm OK, you're not OK.'*

The following table highlights differences among these styles of communication:

Pleaser/passive aggressive, non-assertive	Assertive, empowered, respectful	Aggressive, bullying, controlling
I'm not OK, You are OK	I'm OK, You're OK	I'm OK, You're not OK
• 'I just want to keep the peace' • 'I'll pretend it's OK, but I don't like it'	• 'We may need to disagree on this.' • 'It doesn't really matter to me'	• 'Do it my way, or else!' • 'It's all your fault'
• 'That's fine with me, but don't be surprised if someone else gets mad'	• 'I think I understand what you're saying but I don't agree' • 'Thanks for your suggestion but I'm not going to do it that way'	• 'You need to change. I'm right and you're wrong' • 'I'm not giving up on this'
CURDLES RELATIONSHIPS	**HEALS RELATIONSHIPS**	**CURDLES RELATIONSHIPS**

'Pleaser' and 'Passive Aggressive' Communication Styles

Pleasers may find it difficult to acknowledge their anger and fail to express their feelings and needs. Failing to confront another person and say *'No!'* allows, even invites, domination by others. It often ends up in misunderstandings and a build-up of anger and resentment. This bottling up of resentment is called gunny-sacking – tantamount to carrying around loaded ammunition.

People who do this lack confidence, self-esteem and self-respect. They tend to say, *'you feel'* or *'people feel'* when talking about themselves, rather than *'I feel.'*

Their communication is not open and honest. They may give the silent treatment, or they may appear cooperative while silently doing the opposite. Moreover, after months of putting up with what they don't like, they may suddenly erupt like a volcano. Relatively frequent slow burns are better than occasional explosions.

Where does a non-assertive, or passive-aggressive communication style come from? What underlies and drives this style are:

- Limiting beliefs about self that came from childhood
- Payoffs or rewards that provide some comfort because they offer peace and a lack of conflict (e.g. *'It's not worth the risk. If I say what I feel, I could end up getting hurt.' 'I won't get rejected.' 'Better to say nothing. It could make things worse.'*)
- A harsh inner critic and/or critical self-talk
- Non-assertive role models *'I'm like my dad. He was really quiet and took the back seat.'*

If you're a people-pleaser, super-empathic, failing to stand up for yourself or your beliefs and putting others' needs ahead of your own, you may well end up attracting a narcissist.

To understand the narcissist dynamic, there is no better book than *'The Wizard of Oz and Other Narcissists',* by Eleanor Payson. It will give you a lot of insight into and guidance on how to cope with the one-way narcissistic relationship in work, love and family.

Aggressive Communicators

Aggressive behaviour give-aways include:

- Statements such as: *'you should...' 'you never...' 'you make me...' 'you always...'*
- Criticism, blaming, threatening, discounting, putting down, ridiculing, withholding, or hurtful sarcasm
- Non-verbal: ranges from a harsh stare, a raised eyebrow, to physical abuse
- Passive-aggressive: deliberate acts that aim to punish or hurt others, which may be camouflaged or even disguised as 'a joke'
- Displaced anger: projecting aggressive feelings/blaming others for being aggressive, rather than owning your anger.

Lurking inside the aggressive, angry person is:
 • Low self-esteem (being aggressive to others often boosts feelings of self-worth),
 • And a background of aggressive role models.

It almost seems like a contradiction in terms, but aggressive people tend to dominate others because they lack confidence, lack respect for self and others, and have low self-esteem.

Assertive Communicators

Assertive communicators are respectful and empowered.

- They are self-aware, especially of their thoughts, feelings and emotions, and of their wants and don't-wants. They set and maintain **firm and well-defined boundaries**.
- They resolve issues, speaking up in a respectful way when there are problems.

Create Abundant Possibilities

- They feel comfortable to be assertive or not, and to have the right in any situation to be assertive or not.
- They don't gunnysack (keeping hurts, resentments, etc. inside).

Assertive people don't try to control or dominate others and don't allow others to control or dominate them. They are generally confident, with high self-esteem. They respect themselves and others. People who are assertive speak for themselves. They use *'I feel'; 'me'; 'my',* and *'mine.'*

Since this is a communication style which heals relationships and maintains harmony, I recommend you cultivate it. Again practise, practise, practise.

Tips for becoming assertive:

- Take ownership – use 'I' statements, e.g. *'I feel unhappy about what happened yesterday. I'd like us to talk about it. I'd have preferred you to have done...'*
- Maintain eye contact
- Learn to say *'No.'*
- Voice your desires and needs confidently.

The Quiet Revolution of Self Love

Acknowledging our strengths and having healthy self-respect goes hand-in-hand with looking after our own needs and setting healthy boundaries.

You may know people who think that they are being selfish if they look after their own needs, without constantly falling over backwards to please others.

Some women in particular — certainly many in our mothers' or grandmothers' generations, and still today in certain cultures — have played out the woman's role as that of service, compliance and even martyrdom.

This is a far cry from today's teachings that, before we can attract and maintain love and approval in our relationships —whether with our partner, our children, our parents, our co-workers and managers — **we need to love ourselves.**

Quite simply, we aren't doing ourselves and the people in our lives any favours if we fail to love ourselves. That said, there's no need to be perfect before you can attract love!

If we feel not good enough, unworthy or ashamed, what we project onto and accept from those around us causes dysfunction and inequality.

We either:

- Allow or give tacit encouragement to grandiosity or superiority in our children, partners and work colleagues
- Or we teach our nearest and dearest to have similarly low self-esteem to our own and to have low expectations for their lives and their relationships.

If you're a parent or teacher, is this what you would like for your children or students?

The great teacher of transformation, Louise Hay, defined self-love as a cornerstone of good mental health and loving relationships. It enables you to recognise and value your own worth, complete with your strengths and your weaknesses. You don't have to be perfect before you can love yourself!

As your love of yourself builds, your need for external validation to prove that you're OK fades. This makes you less vulnerable to approval of others, less dependent on how they feel, before you can feel good about yourself.

Your growing self-love also makes you less likely to be hurt if others disapprove. Self-love empowers you to build relationships based on mutual respect, understanding and trust.

To deepen self-love further, you can practise looking into your eyes in a mirror and telling yourself something positive, like 'I love you'. If you're interested in following this up, I recommend the book *'The Art of Extreme Self-Care'*, where Cheryl Richardson describes this and other ways to love yourself more.

Create Abundant Possibilities

Janine's Climb Up the Self-Esteem Ladder

The climb up the self-esteem ladder outlined in this chapter formed one of the most effective parts of Janine's year-long therapeutic journey.

Step One: While learning to challenge and separate from her nasty inner critic was a must, that shift alone didn't go far enough to build her self-esteem.

Step Two: Concentrating on installing her inner supporter took her one-eyed focus off her weaknesses and mistakes. In its place, she became more compassionate and kinder to herself when she made a mistake or felt bad. She also observed and acknowledged her strengths and the things she did well.

Step Three: Discovering new skills such as how to challenge the pleaser's legacy of self-sacrifice and over-giving helped her become a more assertive communicator. She practised asking for what she wanted and not going along with what she didn't want.

> "I've been proud of myself. I was exhausted. I've been practising saying no. People can take advantage. With Mark, if I give an inch, he says "Can you just do this, can you just do that?" When I first said no, I felt sick, pacing the house, waiting for repercussions. When there weren't the repercussions I expected, I felt better. I'm feeling much more empowered."

Step Four: Looking into her own eyes in a mirror and saying positive things about herself activated self-love. To feel truly, authentically confident, our self-approval needs to rise all the way to self-love.

. . .

Week by week, Janine reported pleasing improvements in her dealings with colleagues at work and with her mother and brother.

Her mother, whom she had never been able to please, stepped up in the role of helpful grandmother to Paul. Although Janine saw her often, she still maintained that her mother neither liked nor approved of her. What she wasn't acknowledging was that she neither liked nor approved of her mother.

I challenged her to, "Take your mother out of the box you've put her into, and make room to see, acknowledge and be grateful for anything good between you."

One day she came to therapy with a touching story. They'd been playing a game with three-year-old Paul, where they asked, 'Who loves Paully?'

"I said 'Mummy loves Paully.' Then mum said, 'And grandma loves Paully.'

Then I asked, 'And who loves mummy?' Paul said 'Paully loves mummy.'"

Then followed the words that Janine had never heard, nor ever thought she'd hear: "And grandma loves mummy."

The next moment, Janine was sobbing. And so began the journey of dropping her guard with her mother, talking about her own feelings, asking her mother about hers.

"Mum admitted she had postnatal depression after she had me. She does get upset really easily and I didn't want to spoil that moment, so I didn't say how awful it was for me. I just said, 'That must have been awful for you.'"

Since that day, Janine has worked on becoming more approving and loving. She continues to 'out' her inner critic and practice being compassionate towards herself. And she reminds herself every day about small things she approves of about herself. She notices and celebrates 'small slices of joy.'

"Mum is a very good grandmother. She does have a good heart and doesn't mean to be hurtful. I've started asking her for a hug."

Create Abundant Possibilities

The Crunch for Janine and Mark

Ideally, couples putting in place healthier communication, boundaries, and other improvements in their relationship, achieve personal growth as well as relationship changes.

When one partner goes it alone, and the other stays stuck in his/her dysfunctional patterns, it may not augur well for a failing marriage.

The crunch for Janine and Mark came one day when Mark was being especially demanding and insulting. Suddenly, Janine had had enough. She'd been pushed too far. She lost her temper and demanded he move out.

Unfortunately for Mark, living without him made Janine happier than she had been living with him. She went from strength to strength.

The last time I saw her, she was planning a holiday with her mother and son. She claimed that she was feeling more relaxed and happier than she had been in her living memory.

> 'I'm generally feeling a lot better and more relaxed. There's still work pressure, but it doesn't feel overwhelming like it used to. I feel really sad that I stayed with Mark as long as I did. I'm being more assertive at work, too. A couple of years ago, I felt insecure, and people took advantage of me. I feel more confident now than I ever have in my life.'

Then, six months after her therapy, Janine sent me a thank you email.

> 'Things are going well. I'm going on a cruise with Mum and Paul for two weeks, leaving tomorrow, so I'm really looking forward to relaxing in the South Pacific. Thank you for all your help last year. I never realised how much easier my life could be, just by changing my perspective! What I learned at a time when I couldn't see the wood for the trees has made me much happier than I was in those dark days.'

Building a Positive Narrative about Yourself

As I completed this chapter, I put myself in the shoes of someone feeling as disempowered as Janine had at the start of therapy. I wondered how I could encourage someone with low self-esteem similar to Janine's to believe that he/she could climb the self-esteem ladder and even come to love him/herself.

Although I did neither of these with Janine, what follows may help you to build a positive narrative about yourself, using a hypothetical script and a hypothetical values exercise.

My hope is that they provide stepping stones to inspire you to craft a script and imagine yourself being confident and happy, even if you are at the low end of the self-love ladder right now. This would be like me, scripting myself into a loving relationship when I was single, and the dating horizon looked pretty bleak. But I wrote the script, and before the year had ended, I was in my dream relationship!

Example of a Confidence Script: (Date a year down the track from now)

1) I've had the most amazing turn-around in the way I feel about myself and my life in the past year. I now feel really, really good about who I am and what I stand for. I have become a lot more assertive, asking for what I want, setting boundaries and looking after myself. I have been taking a positive, self-approving me into all my experiences this year, and I intend to keep doing that for the rest of my life.

2) Having started off feeling phoney doing the mirror work, like 'This isn't true for me', as I stuck with it, my self-perception shifted. I started feeling fondness and respect, and even love for myself, for who I am and what I've achieved. That feeling built and it's continuing its upward trajectory. I caught myself when the old pattern showed up and consciously reminded myself of my good points.

3) I recognised that it was high time I gave myself a pat on the back for how well I did at school and uni. I worked hard, I got great results, and I've deserved the career satisfaction and financial success in my life.

4) I've been kind and helpful to many people over the years, putting them before myself. While I've stopped putting my desires and needs on the backburner, I can acknowledge I am a kind, considerate person and I've made the lives of some people easier. I do care about how other people feel, and that's something I like about myself.

5) In my role as mum, I love and am proud of who I am. I love

Paully so much and I am thrilled I was courageous enough to decide to become pregnant and give myself the gift of the joy of motherhood. I'm a great mother. I'm rewarded every time I see Paully's smile and delight when we're together. Mothering comes easy to me. I seem to have good instincts for how to handle him. I love this beautiful little soul.

6) My work-life has gone from strength to strength over this last year. I've picked up a couple of great new clients and my earnings have increased by 50%. I know I deserve this, as I work hard, I'm conscientious and I give great service.

7) I've been enjoying my relationships with my partners and the staff much more than I used to. I think the fact that I now stand tall, value myself and stand up for myself, has increased their respect for me. I find the office a nice place to be.

8) My relationship with mum has transformed. As I let my guard down and my confidence in myself grew, mum seemed to become more admiring and approving of me, which is a good feeling. She sings my praises for the way I mother Paully. When she admitted she had been in a bad way when I was a child, and said she wished she'd been a better mother to me, I was able to let my resentment go and forgive her. I also felt more compassionate to myself for the difficulty of my childhood. Mum's a supportive, reliable grandmother, and we're a great team around Paully.

9) I've been doing a good job on the home-front too, as the one who cooks our meals and looks after the house. It's no small thing to be the sole breadwinner and manage the cooking and cleaning as well. I'm really proud of my effectiveness and competence, and that I do it with good will.

10) The only area where I've made less progress than I would have hoped is in my relationship with Mark. I find there's a big gap between what I'd like and what I've got. I need a partner I can trust and feel safe with, emotionally. I need someone I enjoy being with. Though I've tried, we are still unable to talk about problems in an adult way and I'm disappointed and angry with the way he takes advantage and isn't willing to be more cooperative. At this stage, the signs aren't good. I believe I deserve better. For now, I'm biding my time. I'll see what happens.

11) I choose this or something even better for the greatest good of all concerned.

Date:_____ Signature:_____

While some of what the above script claims wouldn't have been true of Janine early in therapy even after I'd introduced her to assertive communication and mirror work, most of what it describes as her strengths were actually present right at the start of therapy.

The only problem was that she had been so hard on herself, drowning in shame and a feeling of worthlessness, that she hadn't realised this about herself.

Perhaps you can identify with that? If you are someone who is hard on yourself, and more likely to worry about what is wrong with you than to acknowledge things you can be proud of, if only you'd let yourself see them, then I hope this imagined script makes you realise how you could script a happier, more self-loving you.

Another way you could paint a more optimistic picture of your worth could be to imagine how you would look if you were **already confident**. To do this, follow the guidelines in Chapter Four for clarifying how your dream would look.

Imagined Confident You

Imagine while you are asleep tonight, a miracle happens, and your self-esteem and confidence skyrocket. After this miracle occurred, what would you be feeling, thinking and hearing in every area of your life? What would be there in your life as a mother, in your career, when you wake up in the morning, in your relationships, etc.?

Again, what follows are my words, not Janine's.

- **Feeling good in the morning**: I'd wake up feeling at peace and good about myself. I'd be calm and anticipate the coming day with a feeling of confidence and pleasure. I'd have a smile on my face as I thought about saying 'Hello' to Paully, dropping him at kindy, and then having a rewarding day at the office.

Create Abundant Possibilities

- **Knowing I'm a loving mother**: I'd think of Paully with love and joy, knowing how much we love each other. I'd be thinking how lucky I am to have such a beautiful, sweet son, whom I adore. I'd glow with pride at what a good mother I am. I'd picture the way his face lights up when he sees me.
- **Being grateful I have a great career**: I give myself a pat on the back that I am such a competent accountant with a great practice and clients I like. I feel confident that I really am good at what I do, and grateful it's a job I enjoy. I feel privileged that I'm a woman with a career I value, knowing that for me to study accountancy was the right decision. I'm happy that I had the ability, opportunity and education to be able to have such a satisfying career.
- **The company I'm with**: I enjoy the positive feedback I get for how well I pull my weight and the contribution I make to the practice. I'm glad I like my business partners, and that we have a good team of staff members. I appreciate that we mainly get on well, and that it's a supportive and cooperative environment. It feels encouraging that we keep picking up new clients, and that word of mouth works in our favour.
- **Financial independence**: I'd be super grateful that I am doing so well financially. I'm proud of how much I earn and how well I'm able to cater for my own and my family's needs. I love that I'm able to be independent and live a life of prosperity and abundance. I know that's a privilege not everyone enjoys, and I relish my success and accomplishment.
- **Feeling respected and valued by my clients**: I enjoy my relationships with most of the clients. I feel valued and respected by them. I often get thanks for the advice I give and the work I do, and that contributes to my confidence and self-esteem.
- **Feeling good about my home and my role as a homemaker**: I let myself enjoy the fact that I do a pretty good job managing my home, given that I'm a working mother. I feel happy about the food I serve and my cooking,

and I'm satisfied with my standards for keeping the house clean and looking good.
- **I have a good relationship with Mum**: Things have improved between mum and me. I appreciate the support she gives me with Paully, and I like the way she is as a grandmother. Maybe seeing me show so much affection and love to Paully has made her realise that she could be more loving to me. We are now pleased to see each other, and we're hugging and being more affectionate.
- **Learning to love myself**: The mirror work is getting easier, and more believable. I know my most important relationship is with myself, so I'm working on loving and approving of myself, because that is who I take into everything I do. I believe I deserve to be loved. I know I'm as flawed and as magnificent as everybody else. I soothe and am compassionate to myself when glitches happen, and most of the time, I'm in a good mood.
- **Intimate relationship**: I am reflecting on what I want and need from my intimate relationship. I know that for me to be happy, it needs to be respectful, equal, where we both pull our weight, kind, understanding and loving.

I hope that this imagined narrative of a Janine with high self-esteem is helpful to you in garnering ideas for how to imagine yourself as a confident, grateful person, even if that's not how you feel yet.

I should note that this huge gap between her current relationship and her recognition of what is important to her, would probably have orchestrated an end to her life with Mark. The same would be true for you. If there are large, unbridgeable gaps in your life, this probably signals a need to re-evaluate those areas, and perhaps make changes, so you can become the version of you you'd like to be.

∼

13

UNHOOK FROM ANXIETY
CREATE A LIFE OF PEACEFUL PRESENCE

Increasing the likelihood that you will fulfil the dreams you script into your life requires you to unhook from addictive and unhelpful old thought patterns, behaviours and emotional responses that hold you hostage. This means this book cannot avoid opening a window onto the psychologist's bread and butter, namely, **anxiety** and **depression**.

Are some people more prone to anxiety and to the way it disrupts their happiness and inner peace? Absolutely! Can they do anything to minimise this disruptive and corrosive influence on their lives? Again, absolutely!

This chapter explores simple yet effective tools for exchanging worry for relaxation, what creates anxiety and how we can create a life of peaceful presence by using tools which gently decrease persistent anxiety.

How to Feel More Relaxed, More of the Time

I'm pleased to tell you that if you battle with anxiety, there are ways you can manage it so that it doesn't hijack your life. Before moving onto a brief handle on understanding what anxiety disorder is and the mental and physiological mechanisms behind it, I'd like to introduce you to three helpful, easily actioned ways to relieve anxiety, so you can start getting some benefits right away.

1. Your **thinking** triggers your emotions. It's important to notice what you're thinking, because when you change what you think, you change what you feel.
2. **Worry-based thoughts** sap your energy and stop you from being fully present in whatever it is you are doing.
3. Worrying about things over which you have **no control** is counterproductive. Think instead about what you CAN change or create.

Let's explore each of these actionable ideas in more detail.

Exercise: Your thinking influences how you feel

Based on my extensive clinical experience treating anxiety, I have found that if you think about frightening or worrying things, guess what? It makes you feel bad. And if you're feeling bad you are more likely to think sad, frightened, worry oriented thoughts. The loop goes around and around until you stop it. If you change one, you change the other.

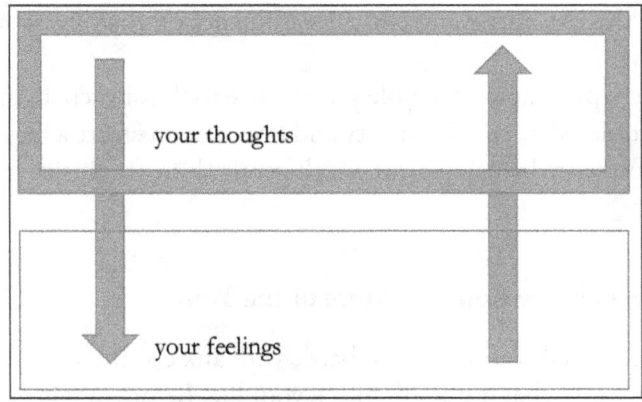

Doing the two-minute exercise which follows will clearly show you how closely your thoughts and feelings are interrelated.

Create Abundant Possibilities

- Close your eyes and imagine war-torn Afghanistan: It's hot and dusty. You can see the rubble of destroyed buildings, hear the sounds of bombs detonating, the screams of terrified, wounded people.
- Now, notice what you feel... Is it dark and heavy, or light and relaxed? OK, open your eyes and take a deep breath. Stand up, jump up and down a couple of times and shake your hands.
- Now sit down and close your eyes again. Imagine you're walking in a beautiful rainforest.
- The temperature is perfect. You see dappled sunlight filtering through the leaves. You hear birdsong and water gurgling in a creek. Tune in to how that makes you feel. Dark and heavy, or light and relaxed?

If you're like almost every person I've ever asked to do this, imagining war-torn Afghanistan makes you feel dark and heavy, whereas imagining walking in a rainforest makes you feel light and relaxed.

In other words, **what you focus on, where you allow your thoughts to go, exerts a very significant influence on how you feel. And the effect is lightning fast.**

Instead of letting automatic, addictive thoughts manage you, you can choose to be conscious of where those thoughts are leading you. Then move the dial on your thought radio and choose to think about something uplifting or beautiful, like a glorious sunset.

Exercise: Worry oriented thoughts sap your energy

Imagine yourself as a ball of energy. That's 100% of who you are. Now imagine that:

• 20% of your day, you find yourself worrying about your relationship – it's not going too well,

• 15% of the day, you worry about your job security – perhaps you don't feel confident about your performance, perhaps you don't get on with your manager,

• 20% of the day, your thoughts turn to your kids - you worry something may happen to them, or you worry about their behaviour,

- 10% of the day, you worry about your parents – they're ageing, they have problems with their health.

This adds up to 65% of your waking hours where you are distracted by uncomfortable and anxious thoughts. Those thoughts are sapping your energy and stopping you from being in the moment.

- You - the potential: 100% of you is present in the moment
- You - the reality: only about a third of you is present in the moment

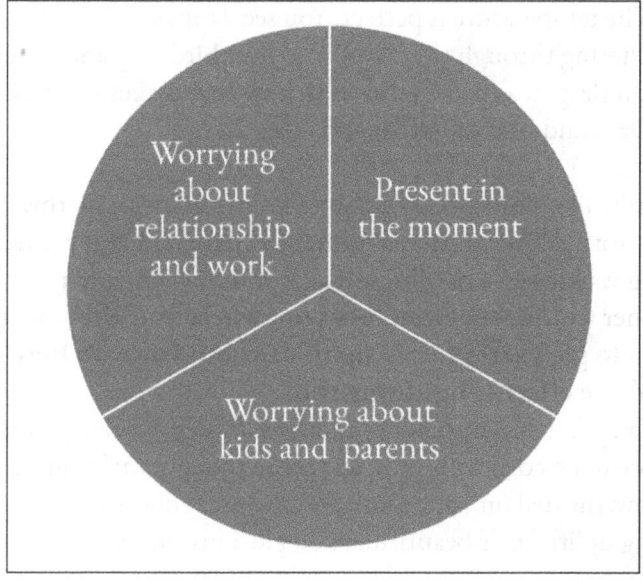

When your mind busies itself with those worries, as in the above diagram, that leaves only about a third of you available to be fully present **in the moment**, concentrating on what you're doing and creating.

Imagine yourself with your kids, but instead of fully engaging with them, your mind is elsewhere. Or, imagine that you're at work but you're on automatic. You're not fully engaged. You're not concentrating fully on your work. You're marking time, and not really enjoying what you're doing. Quite simply, you're not really present.

Create Abundant Possibilities

This means that through much of your day, you're merely going through the motions.

The irony of that is, when you're home with your kids you're worrying about work. And when you're at work, you're worrying about your kids. Short-changing both experiences. Not being fully present or giving your best to either.

Now you know that getting stuck in your mind and worrying interferes with your concentration and stops you from being fully present, I invite you to **practise being mindful instead.**

Whatever you are doing, whether it's eating your dinner, brushing your teeth or having a conversation with your partner, make that activity the focus of your mindfulness.

What I mean by that is that you give that activity **100% of your attention**. If your mind wanders, as soon as you become aware you've been time sharing, consciously bring your attention back to focus on what you're doing.

When you're eating, instead of barely noticing the food, focus your attention fully on the colour and the appearance of your food; the taste, aroma, the texture. Notice yourself chewing, notice yourself swallowing, be present in the moment. If your mind wanders, bring it back. This is called **mindful eating**.

When you're brushing your teeth, notice the taste, the smell, the texture of the toothpaste. Practice being present and stilling your mind. That's where calm and inner peace lie.

These questions should help you put your priorities into the correct perspective:

- What's the most important **time** in your life?
- What's the most important **place** in your life?
- Who is the most important **person** in your life?

Here are the answers:

- The most important time in your life is this **present moment.**
- The most important place in your life is **where you are right now.**

- And the most important person in your life is **whoever you are with** right now.

Those are trick questions, but if you make the person you're speaking to at any given moment the most important person in your life, your connection with people and your relationships will flourish.

The opportunity is that when you're with your children, your partner, you do them the honour of paying them full attention, of truly listening. You listen as though what they think and say matters, as though you're actually interested in them, rather than longing to get back to your phone, or turn on the TV, or speak to your friend!

If you become aware you've been half listening, thinking about something else, or wishing they weren't bothering you, bring your full attention back to your child or partner.

The amount and nature of the attention you give them (or don't give them) shows them how much you value them. It shows them how much you care. Even if we are unaware we're doing this, we all read each other's tone of voice, body language and words.

Where we focus our attention is a choice we make. It influences how we respond to each other, in an endless chain of 'this causes that', or simple cause and effect. There are no coincidences in what is created; it is a predictable chain of events.

We can observe the chain clearly. If we make the effort to reflect back on our behaviour and what we said, we get to see how this choice caused that outcome! I invite you to take responsibility for what you are creating, moment by moment. You will either reap the rewards or pick up the pieces.

Start making a point of noticing where your mind goes when you're doing tasks or interacting with others.

This is a practice in being awake and conscious in the moment, of being grateful for the food you eat, for the people in your life and the simple things that make up your day. Notice the many small moments of joy.

Rather than take the food you're eating for granted, barely noticing it as you lose yourself in your thoughts or your phone, eat mindfully.

Rather than being only partly present with your child, or your partner, half listening to them while wanting to get on with something

Create Abundant Possibilities

else, do them the honour and pay them the compliment of giving them all your attention. This is the immense power of unwavering presence.

Focus your energy and thinking on the present moment.

Most of us are distracted in our daily lives with everything except what is right in front of us. I call this **time-sharing**.

Do you find yourself doing one thing yet thinking about another? Do you spend hours scrolling on your phone becoming totally absorbed by social media?

How much of your day would you say that your attention is actually **fully focused** on what you're doing, whether at home, out exercising, shopping, at work, or socialising?

How much time do you spend in your waking hours thinking of something other than what you are doing, like going over things that upset you or worrying about problems in your life?

Over the next seven days, notice what you are thinking. You could even make a quick note of your thoughts every 30 minutes or so. Patterns will emerge!

Whenever you find yourself time-sharing, STOP.

Then concentrate fully on the task at hand. Especially if what you're thinking is negative, thinking about it will make you feel bad. Not focusing on it will lighten your mood.

Each evening, review or make notes on what you found yourself thinking when you were time-sharing. Journal how you felt when you honoured what you were doing by giving that activity/task/person your full attention. Observe what was happening when your mind was quiet/quieter.

At the end of the week, notice:

- How much easier did it become for you to stay in the moment?
- Has this improved your concentration, your effectiveness and your enjoyment at work?
- How, if at all, has it affected your feeling of closeness to people in your life?

- Do you think other people have noticed any difference in your attitude or the way you behaved?
- What helps quieten your mind?

Exercise: Worrying about things over which you have no control

This diagram models your circle of influence, your **locus of control:**

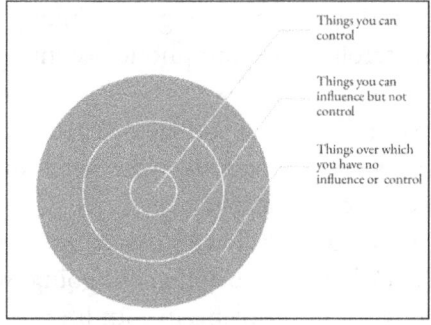

Imagine yourself at the centre of these three circles. The inner circle contains **the things in your life you can control,** for example:

- Being reliable and putting in your best effort at work; or being unreliable and getting away with doing as little as you can.
- The way you treat your partner — with love and respect, or disdain, resentment and criticism.
- The way you are with your children — present, patient and kind, or impatient, not present and irritable.
- Your relationship with your food choices, lifestyle and work-life balance.

The middle circle comprises **things over which you can have some influence, but can't control,** such as how you treat your children, or how you react when your partner does something you like or don't like.

The outer circle contains **things over which you have absolutely no control** — like whether your children or your partner are involved in an accident; whether you or someone you love develops a severe illness; whether the economy thrives or slumps; which politician wins or loses an election.

I once attended a professional development workshop on anxiety. The presenter asked the twenty or so psychologists to name the thing they feared most. I noticed as one person after another divulged their worst nightmare, each and every one related to something that might never happen!

What they most feared was not a problem already present in their lives, but something that hadn't happened, and probably never would, like *'my partner dying'; or 'my child being in an accident'*.

The important point here is that **worrying about something we cannot control won't and can't stop that thing from happening.**

As individuals, we cannot directly control or prevent things like a recession, a war, or a severe weather event. We cannot ensure that we or our family members will never be struck down by a dreadful illness or will never be run over by a bus.

Not only is it pointless worrying whether such a tragedy might befall us or them, it is actually detrimental to our mental and physical wellbeing to worry about such things, or to worry at all. Worrying undermines our health and wellbeing. With worry, there's **no gain, only pain.**

Creating a Life of Peaceful Presence

Peaceful presence is possible when we move our energy and attention away from catastrophising and towards **creative (and abundant!) possibilities**.

You are inherently a **creative being**. When you acknowledge what you've been creating, it opens the doors for change. New choices will emerge when you shift your energy and mindset.

If you've lived a lifetime of intimately knowing that gnawing anxiety inside, it seems impossible for it to dissolve. When you realise that this knot in your solar plexus, or the ball in the pit of your stomach, is simply your nervous system signalling that some change is required for it to relax, living in **peaceful presence** becomes much more believable as a possibility or a choice you choose to make.

Living without anxiety is life changing. And so much more enjoyable! As you start living without anxiety, your choices will expand. Your presence will be more powerful. Your curiosity and enthusiasm for life will have expanded capacity for taking you on the most wonderful of adventures. Remember your script? It's waiting for your nervous system to catch up!

What is Anxiety, Really?

Anxiety is an emotional, physical and behavioural response to a perceived threat, to something going wrong, e.g. financial problems, a child's illness, an argument. Anxiety heightens our ability to detect threats and provides the rapid surge of energy required if we are to avoid danger — the fight-or-flight response. Its direct relevance to anxiety means we need to revisit the fight-or-flight response.

This intense arousal is usually accompanied by familiar symptoms such as increased heart rate, sweating, rapid breathing and dryness of the mouth. This arousal helps us to either stay, defend and fight, or run away. The fight-or-flight response was essential to our caveman ancestors who may have needed to flee from or attack a mammoth.

But in today's world, threats are much less likely to be of physical danger, and more likely to be emotional, like financial stress or unhappy relationships. In this context, becoming highly aroused and ready to attack (fight) or flee (flight) are both more of a liability than a support.

We're living in the modern world, saddled with an archaic brain. In this current world fighting/arguing or fleeing/withdrawing in response to emotional upsets exacerbates communication and relationship problems.

Worse still, it adds additional problems, like a stress headache, an upset stomach, exhaustion, insomnia, involuntary twitching, or panic attacks. This is behaviour driven by our **primitive limbic brain**.

The healthy response to such problems is to stop, take a deep breath, become resourceful, flexible, conciliatory and a wise decision-maker. Healthy responses like these are guided by our **executive brain, the prefrontal cortex**, which is more suited to the times we're living in. Seeing a psychologist or couples counsellor can teach you how to regulate your nervous system. This is a better option than escaping or dissociating from emotional upset through addictions like alcohol, substance abuse, being a workaholic.

Anxiety Disorders & the Sympathetic vs. the Parasympathetic Nervous System

Your nervous system is intimately involved in how well you deal with threats and problems, and how well you let go in the aftermath. That's the story of anxiety!

Your **sympathetic** nervous system has an opposite role to your **parasympathetic** nervous system.

The job of your **sympathetic nervous system** is to put your body's systems on alert. It's this system that activates the flight or fight response when you're faced with a perceived threat or danger. Being relaxed and calm in such circumstances could be very costly to your health and wellbeing!

The job of your **parasympathetic nervous system**, on the other hand, is to restore your body to a state of calm after the threat has abated (the attacker has left the scene), or the need for high performance and action is over (you've finished your exam, you've delivered your speech, your bid at auction has been successful.) It is now safe, and good for your body, to relax.

Each is perfectly designed to play its own specific role. Both are not only extremely valuable; both are essential! They ensure that when you need to be wide awake and on alert, dealing with current demands and problems, you can be, and when you need to relax and let go, you can do that too.

An anxiety disorder raises its ugly head when you have an overactive, out-of-control sympathetic nervous system, and an underactive, under-utilised parasympathetic which fails to counteract your sympathetic nervous system response.

Instead of doing its job, and then switching off, your sympathetic nervous system stays on high alert even when the specific problem has been dealt with, or when there's nothing you can do about the problem but accept it, learn to live with it, and be happy anyway.

That's called accepting what's so! With that comes calm and inner peace.

Everyone experiences anxiety from time to time. While anxiety is a normal response to threatening situations, if it often interferes with our ability to function, it becomes an anxiety disorder.

There are several types, such as generalised anxiety disorder, panic, social phobias, obsessive compulsive disorder (OCD), post-traumatic stress disorder (PTSD), complex post-traumatic stress disorder (CPTSD), and specific phobias like fear of flying.

Some people are more prone to anxiety than others. They may react to situations which don't really threaten their survival as if their very lives were at stake. Moreover, once the threat has passed, they find it harder to let go of the anxiety, or to stop it invading other areas of their lives.

What Can You Do to Relieve Anxiety?

Exercise: Keep a Worry Diary

I discovered the Worry Diary at a talk given by Dr Sarah Edelman at a *Happiness & its Causes* conference several years ago. I have since asked many clients to keep a Worry Diary.

Most have found it highly effective in changing their relationship with anxiety.

(For the reader who would like to delve into a more comprehensive understanding of anxiety disorders, depression and CBT (Cognitive Behavior Therapy), I can recommend no better book than *Change Your Thinking* by Dr Edelman.)

For two weeks, keep a Worry Diary. Your worry diary can be a small note pad, which you carry around with you, or the notes in your phone. Whenever a worry – big or small – sneaks into your mind, jot it down, e.g. *'worried I'd be late'* or *'did I say the wrong thing?'*

Commit to yourself that every night you'll go through your worry diary. As soon as you've noted it in the diary, stop thinking about it. Think about anything but that!

If the same worry comes up again, tally it in your diary. Again, immediately you're aware you've thought it, think about anything but that worry. Preferably, think of something that gives you pleasure!

Keeping A Worry Diary

- **Step One**: Whenever you have a worry, jot it down in your diary, then IMMEDIATELY stop thinking of it. Add a tally stroke if it comes up again that day.
- **Step Two:** That evening, go through Day One's worry list. Write '*Yes*' or '*No*' alongside each one, in answer to the question, *'Is there something I can do about this?'*
- **Step Three**: Anything with a 'Yes', that you think you can do something about, brainstorm possible solutions, then take action.

An example of **a 'can-do-something-about it' problem:** *'I'm worried that I'm suffering from depression.'* There definitely is something you can do about that. You could see a GP and get a Mental Health Care Plan for therapy with a psychologist.

An example of **a 'can't-do-anything-about it' problem:** *'I'm worried my son might have a car accident.'* If you know he's a dangerous driver, you could possibly encourage him to take a Driving Skills course. Or you could recommend he drive slower and more carefully and let him know that you worry about his speeding.

But once you've said that there's nothing more you can do. (Give advice once only, don't keep repeating it if it is not followed!) Life is uncertain. Enjoy the present moment as best you can and imagine your son reaching a happy, healthy old age.

- **Step Four**: If there are any 'can't-do-anything-about-it' worries on the list, stop thinking about them. An example: *'I worry that I or someone I love may contract a life-threatening illness.'*

Remember that what you're thinking about strongly influences how you feel, so thinking about your worries increases your feelings of anxiety and unhappiness.

Worrying about them is totally ineffective as a way of stopping such potential problems from happening.

Worrying about things over which you have no control and can't fix makes you feel bad without delivering any benefits. Is that really the best use of your life?

For two weeks, or longer if you choose, repeat steps one, two, three and four each day, working on that day's worry list.

In my experience, most clients who are reasonably conscientious about keeping a Worry Diary quickly come to recognise how much time they waste, and how they undermine their confidence and happiness by worrying. They also successfully stop worrying about the things they can't change.

In the words of one client, "My diary used to be full every day. Now I don't have anything to write in it. Because I've stopped worrying."

As Sara Edelman observed: *'Worry does not give you control unless you're problem-solving.'*

Don't Ruminate

A dead giveaway that you're letting yourself be hijacked by anxiety is when you find yourself ruminating. You're ruminating when you keep thinking about a problem or issue in your life.

It goes around and around in your head. It's like being caught in a washing machine of emotion. You don't resolve the issue. You just get more and more worked up about it, like a dog chewing a bone.

Ruminating conjures up more negative thoughts. It becomes a cycle. It seems to be associated with anxiety, PTSD and C-PTSD, binge eating and drinking, depression, paranoia, and other mental disorders.

As suggested earlier, you can significantly reduce the intensity and frequency of anxiety by:

- Catching yourself when you're worrying about something specific, then choosing to think of anything but that (ideally something that is pleasurable or happiness producing). Plan to improve the situation and take action if possible.
- Stopping yourself if you find yourself worrying about something over which you have no control.
- Not letting yourself time-share by going through the motions of whatever you're doing while simultaneously thinking of other things or worrying about your problems.

> Remember that worrying doesn't solve the problem. It merely saps your energy. Bring your full attention to whatever it is you're doing, and you will begin to thrive.

This may sound easier said than done. Like any new habit, it takes practice, practice, practice, before the new habit supersedes the old. However, this exercise has been very effective in helping many of the people with whom I've worked to break, or at least limit, their tendency to worry.

> *'When we walk like we are rushing, we print anxiety and sorrow on the earth. We have to walk in a way that we only print peace and serenity on the earth. Be aware of the contact between your feet and the earth. Walk as if you are kissing the earth with your feet.'* - Thich Nhat Hanh

Applying tips and strategies to manage your anxiety is really worth doing, not only because you will reap the benefit of feeling so much happier. Remember the old adage, 'no man is an island'? Not letting yourself cohabit your life with worry will benefit others in your life. It will also be part of your contribution to a calm, loving and peaceful earth.

Practice relaxation

There are many breathing and meditation practices to calm your mind and allow you to feel more present, grounded, and at peace. The one below is very specific and easily done with the aim of disrupting anxious feelings.

Breathe in, hold, breathe out

When I meet a new client who's anxious, I ask them to follow this simple breathing practice. I recommend they use it whenever their anxiety starts to build. It's remarkably helpful in soothing anxiety. Perhaps you'd like to do it now?

1. Breathe in 2 3 4

2. Hold 2 3 4 5
3. Breathe out 2 3 4 5 6

- Repeat this set ten times, making sure to breathe deeply, right down into your diaphragm.
- Notice how much calmer you feel as you do this.
- The longer out-than in-breath activates the parasympathetic nervous system and has a calming effect.
- I suggest you practise this set of ten breaths three times a day, so that you become familiar with it as a relaxation practice. Becoming familiar with this sequence as one of your options or habits will make this breathing a natural response when you aren't feeling calm and resourceful.
- Do four or five sets whenever you sense your anxiety is increasing.

Invitation to Be a Regular Meditator

Because meditation and mindfulness have a proven track record in relieving anxiety and depression, I cannot leave this chapter without:

- Drawing attention to groundbreaking findings of neuroscience, and,
- Providing guidelines for a few of the basic practices, to encourage you, if you don't yet meditate, to introduce this into your daily routine.

Every workshop and personal development training I've ever attended has recommended meditation. You may be like I was when I was encouraged to meditate daily. I would do an inner eye roll. I might try for a week or two, feel I wasn't doing it well enough, then have a few particularly busy days and find meditation had slipped off – and stayed off - my to-do list.

I have since become a daily meditator. And I've discovered that you aren't failing if your mind wanders. Even as an experienced meditator, I still find thoughts arise while I'm meditating. Nowadays, I merely notice them, then bring my mind back to concentrating on whatever practice I'm doing, whether it be following my breath or repeating a mantra.

The benefits I experience are many and varied. I now find I'm less likely to be reactive when something happens that I don't like. I seem to be more easy-going and have more emotional resilience.

More often than not, I now express myself from a wiser part of me, which helps me slow down and think before I speak. As a result, I feel more at peace and my relationships have improved. My intuition is stronger. I 'hear' my quiet inner guidance more easily and I choose to follow that guidance, rather than ignore or go against it. And that always works out well!

The Proven Benefits of Meditation and Mindfulness

As early as the 2nd century BC, Patanjali, the Indian yogi and sage of Yoga Sutra fame, taught students to cultivate focused attention through regular meditation. His promise was that this would enhance their mental powers and emotional health.

It turns out that Patanjali was right. Over the past couple of decades, major universities like Harvard and the Universities of California and Wisconsin have looked at the effects of meditation on the brain via neuroscience study after neuroscience study.

Results confirm that twenty minutes of daily meditation profoundly influences your experience of the world by actually remodelling the physical structure of your brain. If that weren't enough, the science also finds that meditation bestows many health benefits on committed meditators.

A study published in 2009 in the journal *NeuroImage* used magnetic resonance imaging (MRI) to identify visible differences between the brains of meditators and non-meditators.

This work was the brainchild of Eileen Luders when she was at the Department of Neurology at the University of California, Los Angeles School of Medicine.

She found experienced meditators have more grey matter in the regions of the brain that govern attention, emotional regulation and mental flexibility.

Brain scans revealed that when meditators concentrate on one thing, like counting the breath or gazing at an object, this activates regions of the brain critical for controlling attention, resulting in improved concentration.

Similarly, the brains of meditators who focus on feelings of love and compassion develop in such a way that they spontaneously feel more connected to others.

The Clinically Applied Affective Neuroscience project conducted by Phillipe Goldin at the Department of Psychology at Stanford University used fMRI (or functional MRI) to demonstrate benefits of mindfulness meditation among people with anxiety and depression.

At the end of a mindfulness course in stress reduction (typically an eight-week course) people with anxiety claimed they worried less, their self-esteem had improved, and they put themselves down less.

Similar research with people with serious depression found that when they practised meditation, not only did their depression lift, but they were also less likely to relapse.

The key to the change was that **meditation reinforces positive emotions**, teaching participants to handle distressing thoughts and emotions without being overpowered by them.

As a result, they were able to observe their negative thoughts without becoming anxious. In other words, one of the benefits was that meditation **changed the way their brains responded to negative thoughts**.

Other studies established that twenty to thirty minutes of daily meditation strengthened the immune system, reduced blood pressure and reduced the tendency to feel anger, which improves survival after heart surgery. It also accelerated healing of other conditions, for example, the skin condition psoriasis.

Meditation even has an official medical stamp of approval. In Australia it's a Medicare-approved treatment for anxiety and depression.

Types of Meditation

Mindfulness meditation entails becoming aware of the present moment. You do this by paying attention to sounds, your breath, sensations in your body, or your feelings – and observing, without judgement and without trying to change what you notice.

If you haven't yet established a meditation practice for yourself, below are a few simple options. You can choose different practices from day to day or find one you like and stick with it. Or you can become an adventurer, searching out the many beautiful and powerful free meditations offered on YouTube® and on different websites and apps like *Calm* or *Insight Timer*.

Repetition is the key that unlocks the benefits. Five to ten minutes a day is better than an hour's meditation once a week.

Exercise: Mindfulness of the Breath Meditation (1)

The intention of a mindful breathing meditation is to remain continuously aware of your breathing, without forgetting it or letting yourself be distracted. If you find your thoughts have wandered, simply bring your attention back to your breath and continue, without guilt, judgement, shame or blame.

Sit in a comfortable position, erect posture, well balanced. Your vertebrae are stacked one on top of the other. Your chin is tucked in slightly towards your throat. Your hands, palms up, rest on your knees. Aim for a daily 20 minutes or longer. That said, it is better to commit to 10 minutes daily than an hour once a week.

Breathe calmly and naturally. Concentrate all your attention on the coming and going of your breath.

- Notice the coolness of the air as it passes the back of your throat.
- Notice how your ribs and abdomen expand as your breath enters your lungs and diaphragm.
- Notice the air leaving, as your diaphragm and ribs deflate.
- Notice the air is warm as it leaves your nostrils.
- Notice the moment when the air is suspended between the out-breath and the next in-breath.

Notice these points with the same focused concentration again on the next cycle of breathing, and the next, and the next...

Repeat this breath after breath, taking care to remain relaxed, and bringing your attention back if it wanders.

Exercise: Mindfulness of the Breath Meditation (2)

Sit in a comfortable position, erect posture, and well balanced. Your vertebrae are stacked one on top of the other. Your chin is tucked in slightly towards your throat. Your hands, palms up, rest on your knees.

- Breathe in, counting 1, 2, 3, 4, 5. As you do so, imagine you are drawing the left side of a square in your mind's eye. Choose a colour for the line.
- Now draw across the top of the square, using a different colour and holding your breath as you count 1, 2, 3, 4, 5.
- Using another colour, draw downwards as you release your breath and count 5.
- Using a fourth colour, draw the bottom line, again holding your breath and count 5.

Keep repeating the above steps.

Simple though it is, this practice bestows many benefits. It lowers your blood pressure. It improves your concentration. It removes waste gases and brings fresh oxygen into your blood. Plus, you receive the other benefits of regular meditation noted earlier.

Exercise: Body Sensation Meditation

I invite you to take a few minutes to try this simple body awareness practice and notice how calming it is. Special acknowledgement to Peter Levine for this *'Felt Sense Exercise.'* This is something you can do anytime you need to calm yourself and slip out of your mind and into your body.

Felt Sense Exercise:

- Sit or lie in a comfortable location where you can be sure you won't be disturbed and where you can focus. Slowly, at your own pace, move through this relaxation exercise.

- Savour each step. You could record these instructions and use that as a guide.
- Feel the way your body makes contact with the surface that is supporting you.
- Sense your skin and notice the way your clothes feel. Are they warm? Soft?
- Now, slowly sense underneath your skin. Start at the crown of your head. What sensations are there at the top of your head? Do they feel tingly, do they feel comfortable? Now sense under your scalp and face. What are the sensations under the skin of your scalp and face?
- Move down slowly ...through your neck ...your shoulders.... your chest... your back. In each part of your body, what do you sense under your skin?
- Your arms... hands... fingers?
- Slowly, down your torso... your legs... feet and... toes.
- Now gently remembering these sensations, how do you know that you feel comfortable? What physical sensations contribute to an overall feeling of comfort?
- Does becoming more aware of these sensations make you feel more or less comfortable? Does this change over time?
- Sit for a moment and enjoy the felt sense of feeling comfortable.

Challenge Your Thinking - The Power of Cognitive Behaviour Therapy (CBT)

Earlier in this chapter, I alluded to the classic clinical therapy approach to anxiety, known as **Cognitive Behaviour Therapy (CBT)**.

It was developed out of the recognition that our cognitive style, the way we think, plays a big role in determining whether worries morph into anxiety disorders, and whether sadness and distress morph into depression. People who habitually think in unhelpful or pessimistic ways are more likely to experience upsetting emotions and moods, and more likely to develop full-blown anxiety and depression.

Note that this does not suggest you stop having deep compassion for the inequality of different people's circumstances.

For example, living with a disability, caring for a family member with a disability, having a partner who battles alcoholism, or living below the poverty line, obviously makes it much tougher to remain positive.

The danger with what we allow ourselves to think, however, whatever our circumstances, is that once we're in a negative feedback loop, things can go from bad to worse.

Left unchecked, a negative mindset can cause immense pain, damage, and hopelessness. Quite simply, our mind can be our saviour or our persecutor.

CBT teaches people how to challenge their pessimistic, critical and destructive thoughts. Its *raison d'etre* is that people prone to depression and anxiety often display 'reasoning errors' or faulty/limited/unhelpful thinking, such as:

- **Black-and-white thinking** – seeing things in black and white with no middle ground.
- **Situations are either good or bad**; your performance is either good or bad.
- **Over-generalizing** – coming to sweeping negative conclusions that go far beyond the current situation, e.g. *'I always screw up; bad things always happen to me.'*
- **Filtering** by focusing on **one negative detail** instead of seeing the whole picture.
- **Catastrophising**: Predicting catastrophe by expecting the worst things to happen in the future without considering other more likely or less negative possibilities.
- **Mind-reading,** where you assume you know what other people are thinking. *'She was obviously disappointed in me and doesn't like me.'* In reality, this may or may not be the case.
- **Comparison:** Assessing our own performance or worth by comparing it with the behaviour and achievements of others.

Earlier in this book in Chapter Nine, we talked about reframing beliefs to liberate yourself from your old stories and dismantle your false identities. This reframing demonstrates how freeing and helpful it can be to:

- Get in touch with what you actually do believe,
- Challenge or reframe your limiting or unhelpful beliefs,
- Be resourceful and do something altruistic to make a difference, like volunteer, or contribute to a refugee fund, after which you can relax, satisfied that you've done something to create change,
- Embrace new, empowered and optimistic beliefs.

Challenge a tendency to catastrophise

It is particularly important to challenge catastrophic/worst-case-scenario thinking. To test reality, take yourself through a series of questions such as:

- What are the objective facts? Ask yourself: *"Is this really true?"*
- What are my subjective perceptions?
- Is there any evidence that does not support my perception?
- What would a calm, rational friend/person think if they were in this situation?
- Are my worrying thoughts based on facts or feelings? Have my feelings ever turned out to be wrong in the past?
- How much control do I have in this situation?
- Am I worrying about something over which I have no control?
- Realistically, what is the worst thing that can happen?
- What is the best thing that can happen?
- What is most likely to happen?

If you're ready to challenge your beliefs, the organisation Beyond Blue and books like *Change Your Thinking* by Sarah Edelman, provide professional, comprehensive CBT guidelines for challenging beliefs. In today's world, if you want to learn more, the internet and the world is your oyster.

Medication

I would encourage you, dear reader, to believe that by putting into practice the strategies and tips such as those described earlier in this chapter, you can manage your anxiety on your own. You can reach a point where you worry less, go with the flow, and trust more.

However, if your anxiety persists and continues to undermine your pleasure in life, see a psychologist, or consider asking a doctor for assessment and possible prescription of an anti-anxiolytic drug. This can be helpful and give you greater peace of mind.

A True Story of Recovery & Redemption

I include the following story to encourage you to believe in the power of the tips and techniques described earlier to stop anxiety in its tracks.

In just six therapeutic sessions Luke went from severe social anxiety to happiness and a feeling of freedom. I hope his story increases your belief in the possibility of turning problems around and making your hopes and dreams come true.

Anxiety and low self-esteem: a case study

It's always something of a surprise to me when a good-looking, fit young person unfolds a tale of low self-esteem and self-doubt. I find myself thinking *'If you look that good, aren't you popular, and don't doors open for you?'* The answer is: *'No, not necessarily so.'*

It's not so much how others see you. Rather, it's how you see yourself that determines your confidence, the way you approach people and the way you react when others approach you. If you have an inner voice that keeps up a destructive monologue of how inadequate you are, that you're stupid or boring or that you'll say the wrong thing, it makes it very hard to shine socially.

Luke was a case in point. Tall, well-built, well-spoken and good looking, he came to see me on the recommendation of his lawyer to receive 'some counselling' and get a Court Report to support him in his hearing on an assault charge scheduled some six months hence. He came with a Mental Health Plan from a GP, a diagnosis of severe anxiety, moderate depression, severe stress and a history of ADHD, anxiety and panic attacks, which had started during his high school years and continued to this day.

Luke's way of dealing with social anxiety was to drink. After a few drinks, he relaxed and started enjoying himself. Trouble was, when he drank too much, he could become aggressive. This is exactly what had happened four months earlier, one night when he was out on a pub crawl with a group of new friends.

The Assault – from Clark Kent to Superman

Luke had been charged with assault in an incident at a nightclub where the rest of his group were admitted, while he was refused entry and told to go to the back of the queue. When he was refused again, his friend Jack started hassling the bouncer, who threatened Jack, at which Luke (who'd been drinking) leapt to his friend's defence.

He hoped that the therapy would help him manage his social anxiety.

> "It leads me to drink when I'm socially anxious. My alcohol consumption is not addictive, but if I get drunk and if someone is angry towards me, I react very quickly. It's the opposite of when I haven't been drinking."

It was as though, under any provocation, drink turned him from mild-mannered reporter Clark Kent into Superman, leaping to the defence of his weaker friends.

Luke's Remorse and Commitment to Personal Development and Change

> *'Recovery from any disease (or mental illness) is dependent on willingness to explore new ways of looking at oneself and life.'* - Dr David Hawkins

Even before visiting me for help with management of his mental illness, Luke had started taking steps to deal with his anxiety and the effects of drinking.

At our first session, he told me that he was reading Eckhardt Tolle's *'The Power of Now',* doing daily affirmations, and practising meditation. He had already taken the important step of managing and minimising his drinking: he had stopped drinking over the four months since the assault.

He was also receptive to the idea of attending Alcoholics Anonymous (AA), and he raised the possibility of a rehab facility should he need further help.

He claimed he'd learnt from the mistakes he made at the nightclub, which had resulted in the assault and the assault charge, and he bitterly regretted that behaviour.

A History of Mental Illness

Luke described the agony of:

> "...worrying that I'll be awkward and stiff and people will notice. Or I'll say something stupid, especially with people I don't know, and they will think I'm weird. I get all anxious. When I drink, I don't have those thoughts. I feel more confident. The alcohol blocks out those negative thoughts. Or occasionally I take a Valium if I can't drink. I want to stop taking that too. It wrecks the anti-depressant."

He recalled a stage in high school where:

> "I was really outgoing, confident, a bit wild, really popular. I had heaps of friends. Then in Year Nine, I started getting really bad anxiety and had a panic attack in class. I think I had underlying anxiety which came to the surface at that time. I sort of drifted. My parents had it too. I just became more aware of it then. One overthinks too much and thinks negative things and is anxious. When I'm drunk, I feel like I'm back to the early me at high school. So far, drinking has been the only way I can feel that. Now I want to try something new."

His first memory of social anxiety dated back to early childhood. He and his sister lived a socially deprived life with their depressed single mother. He remembered feeling overwhelmed and embarrassed being confronted with people he barely knew when his father took him to the occasional large family gathering. His shyness triggered his father's disapproval.

Luke's Relationship with his Mother

Luke was brought up by his single mother after his father – an alcoholic in denial – left when he was three.

> "I have a memory of a few nights before dad left. I remember me and my sister coming out of our rooms and my sister telling them to stop arguing. Mum said dad had always been an alcoholic. Always at the pub. Never helped with anything. Never wanted to look after us. Also, he had an affair with the woman who became his second wife and subsequently left him."

Luke remembers being close with his mother when his father left. He and his mother and sister moved cities shortly after his parents separated because his mother was accepted into art school. The move destabilised his mother, who was bipolar. She became extremely depressed and suicidal.

> "For about a year she'd get us to school, she'd make dinner, but in between, she'd go back to bed. She'd let us run around; she'd let us watch TV. If we went into her room, or made heaps of noise and stressed her out, she'd start crying and say she wanted to kill herself."

This was followed by a better time. His mother went onto medication and finished her degree with first class honours. Luke felt close to her through that time but describes a socially isolated lifestyle.

Then in his early teens his mother came off medication and had a series of abusive boyfriends who introduced her to morphine and other drugs. Her substance abuse drove him to move out into a share house and later to travel in Europe.

Luke's Relationship with his Father

As a child, Luke spent every second weekend and holidays with his father. Throughout primary school, visits to his father were fun.

> "We always had fun. We went on holiday. He'd run around and be an idiot and we'd have fun. He owned a pub and lived in a flat above it. We were pretty close, but he'd started jumping on me, picking on me, because I was shy. Around high school our relationship turned to shit because I didn't turn out the way he wanted. Especially because he'd wanted me to play rugby. Because my mum is a bit antisocial and shy, we didn't have people around. At mum's it was just me, Mum and my sister and a couple of mates. That was my whole life.
>
> At the pub, dad wanted me to shake hands with people in the pub. If I'd lived with him, it would have been more second nature. Dad would shame me. When I was already uncomfortable, he'd say 'Oh yeah, don't be too loud, Luke!' It made me resent him a bit and I still do. It's hard for me to feel safe with him. I always feel angry. I put a lot of my confidence issues down to him, although I don't think he knew he was hurting me."

Therapy Turned Around Luke's Anxiety

Luke was very responsive to anxiety therapy. By the sixth therapy session, he was feeling much less anxious and more confident. He attributed this to managing his inner critic and keeping a Worry Diary.

> "I'm finding I'm more confident with people at work. It's subtle, but I've noticed it's the way I feel — and when I feel good, I act better. More confident and not anti-social because of thinking about stupid things in my head. I'm more outwardly focused. I've read that stuff you gave me about the inner critic, so I'm conscious about it. I'm attending AA. Most days now, I don't have anything to put in the Worry Diary. I now know it's not true when I'm thinking bad stuff about myself."

Key Points in The Court Report

As his psychologist, I was asked to write a Court Report to support the case to be argued by his solicitor. My report included much of his history covered above, to give the judge a feel for the person before him in the dock.

It also specified the improvements in Luke's mental health and that he no longer drank alcohol. The report went on to state that:

- *It is my professional opinion that Luke has responded very well to therapy. He is hopeful that limiting his drinking and continuing therapy by putting into practice the techniques, strategies and skills he is learning will continue to bring about further improvements in his confidence and his ability to look after himself in a respectful and empowered way.*
- *As his psychologist, I am fearful that a custodial sentence would undo the gains he has made in his mental health. The influence of a prison culture and likely damage to a young man prone to depression and anxiety concerns me greatly. Loss of his job, and interruption of his stable relationship with his girlfriend, would undermine his chances of recovery and maintenance of a healthy lifestyle.*
- *His attitude, his remorse, his lifestyle changes and progress in managing his anxiety suggest that Luke is unlikely to reoffend.*
- *He has used alcohol on only two occasions since I first saw him. One was the occasion when he met his new girlfriend's family, the other a music festival. I am encouraged by the fact that on both occasions he was able to stop at a couple of drinks.*

I concluded by making the following plea on his behalf:

- *I believe Luke's family of origin experiences warrant compassion and empathy. His remorse and desire to change stand much in his favour, and I hope that the Court will show leniency towards him.*

The Best Possible Outcome — A Non-Custodial Sentence

When I saw Luke the day before his court appearance, I ran him through a process of visualising and scripting (putting it in writing) the best possible outcome he could ask for, with the intention that it be 'for the greatest good of all concerned.'

I received an exhilarated text message from him later the next day, that he had received a non-custodial sentence with a 12-month good behaviour bond. His lawyer emailed me to say that without the court report, Luke would have gone to jail. The judge's opening stated that he was "...sick of alcohol-fuelled youth violence! I'm sending you to jail."

After the solicitor tabled the court report and pleaded for a non-custodial sentence, lo and behold, the lightest possible sentence came to pass. And it was exactly what Luke had visualised and asked for in his script.

Time would tell whether Luke would use this opportunity for a new start wisely and have the commitment and courage to continue his personal development journey and live up to his promises. The ball was in his court.

Luke's Update — Six Months Later

Luke touched base with me six months after his court appearance. He was working hard in his day job, and close to completing a TAFE course, which would lead to a better career.

> "It means a lot to me that I've almost finished my TAFE course. Next year I'll enrol for a Certificate IV. Since leaving college I've started a lot of things, but never finished anything. This time is different. I've scripted that I will finish."

When I emailed a draft asking him to sign a consent form for the use of his story in this book, the signed consent came back with the following handwritten note:

> 'To Wendy,
> At our last session, you asked how I had changed since first attending

appointments with you. I realise you probably wanted to know to include bits in your book and I didn't give you a very full answer. The truth is I was borderline suicidal when I went and put myself on a Mental Health Care Plan (to see a psychologist).

I had extreme anxiety and depression and was very negatively focused. I was desperate to always have friends around me and I felt horrible being alone. I was constantly worrying about other people's opinions of me and was putting myself in situations I didn't like, just to fit in. I was constantly stressing about my dad, my court case and other peoples' problems, and leaving no time for my own self help.

Now, none of that is true. I'm not lonely. I've made friends through the gym. I've been dating a few girls, but I'm in no rush. I won't settle for the first girl, like I used to, just to make me feel better. Anyway, a girlfriend isn't in the script for this year.

You taught me a lot of great techniques and gave me some great advice. You really put things into perspective for me and I started to focus and work on myself every day.

Fast forward to today, and I am probably the most genuinely happy and carefree I've been since college (eight years ago.) I'm now strong and independent and love myself and my own company. My depression is non-existent, and my anxiety level has improved dramatically, to the point where I halved my dose of Effexor over a month and am now coming off it altogether!!

I've scripted a great year ahead. Very grateful for your help and best wishes with your book and future,

Luke'

How Might a Worrier's Values and Script Look?

The following possibilities and guidelines could inspire you to imagine how your life might improve if you currently identify as 'a worrier.'

Values: Let's start with the values/ *What's important to you?* exercise, along the lines of the 'Clarify your Dream' process in Chapter Four.

In response to the question below, my hypothetical worrier came up with these life values:

"What's important to you about the way you live your life? To help you focus on the positive, imagine that while you are asleep tonight, a miracle happens, and you wake up a person who no longer worries. What would you be feeling, seeing, hearing and telling yourself about every area of your life? After the miracle, how would your intimate relationship, family, work, emotional, and other aspects of life look?"

- ***Waking up in the morning:*** *When I open my eyes in the morning, I feel a pleasant anticipation of what lies ahead today. I look forward to getting out of bed and starting my day - so different from the pre-miracle me!*
- ***I feel calm and happy. I'm quick to smile and laugh:*** *Life seems easy. It feels as though life is on my side nowadays. I smile and laugh a lot more than I used to. Other people notice that I smile more, that I look relaxed and at ease, and that feels great to me!*
- ***I'm resilient. I get over issues quickly and well:*** *I sail through things that happen. I feel good when they go well, I make a plan to get the best outcome when obstacles show up. I feel like a confident person. I believe that interpreting what happens in a more positive light is one of the benefits of my meditation practice. I have the tools and strategies I need to manage my mood and my reactions in a constructive, enlightened way. I also have a backstop in place, that if I can't shake a feeling that things aren't going well, I'll see my psychologist.*
- ***If I find I'm ruminating or worrying, I check whether this is something over which I have any control:*** *If it's not, I stop thinking about it and focus on something that makes me happy. If I'm feeling bad, I tap into my inner supporter and call out my inner critic. I also check in with my inner child, so she feels heard, and the wise adult in me has compassion for her and soothes her. It works like magic, to calm me.*
- ***I'm patient, loving and approving of Allan and the kids; I stay in the present moment:*** *I really took that guidance to heart. When I'm with the kids, or with Allan, I*

keep making sure I'm giving them my full attention. I catch myself if I find I'm thinking about something else, like a work issue, and I focus on what they're saying and doing, telling myself I'll get back to the work issue when it's appropriate. I feel more connected with them, and our communication and patience with each other is getting better and better.

- ***I give Allan space when he's stressed, confident in the security that we're a solid, committed couple:*** *Being conscious of how I'm feeling and what I'm thinking helps me soothe myself: I look at my limiting beliefs, I reframe them, I challenge my inner critic. At the same time, I've become more assertive, and I ask for what I want. Because I'm able to tell Allan what's happening for me, in a respectful, rather than a blaming way, he's listening to me, rather than going silent and withdrawing. And he's more responsive and makes more effort to please me, rather than ignoring my needs and requests. I feel really grateful that's happening.*

- ***I'm happy in my relationship:*** *I intentionally show warmth and affection to Allan. I cherish him and our relationship. I remind myself about what I like and love about him, and I take my attention away from what is less appealing. That makes me feel much more appreciative and positive about him. It's paying off handsomely. He's noticed how much nicer I'm being, and he's being nice to me. We're now more like we were when we first got together, enjoying each other's company, looking forward to seeing each other at the end of the day. He feels like my best friend again.*

- ***I look after my emotional and spiritual health:*** *I meditate and exercise daily, no excuses. I minimise watching the news. Not having my attention hijacked by the dramas in the news makes me feel the world is a good place. It's been a welcome surprise, how regular meditation has grounded me and made me feel more comfortable with myself in my world. I miss it if I can't meditate for a day or two. It's become an important part of my life. And I find not having the problems of the world thrust at me every day on the news helps me feel calmer and more optimistic.*

. . .

Script: And now the script written by our hypothetical anxiety sufferer:

31 January 2026

1) I'm definitely not the same person I was a year ago. As I started living my values, behaving like the person I described after the miracle happened, I shifted into becoming the new me.

2) I've had a happy year. My relationships with Allan and the kids transformed. We're all more co-operative, caring, considerate, affectionate, patient and loving. Even the kids are learning to ask for what they want, rather than yell or play up when they're unhappy. We no longer do win-lose, do it my way or else!

3) With Allan and me, it's now more like how we were when we were courting. Throughout the year, I have made a point of thinking of what I love about him, what I love about having a partner, what I'm grateful for. That brought in its wake an automatic upgrade of my behaviour, my reactions to him, my feelings and body language. Allan and I now have the bigger picture in mind. We're making a point of applying recommendations on the list of 'winning Relational Therapy strategies', like cherishing each other and the relationship, like doing what will be best for the marriage, rather than needing to win the argument. We are following the coaching 'Who's right? Who's wrong? Who cares?' We have been motivated to be supportive of each other, to make each other happy, rather than dwell on and complain about what we don't like. We've changed the way we raise problems – we've moved from attack: 'I'm right' to 'This is how I feel. This is what I'd like you to do instead.' We're not defensive. We say 'Sorry' and really mean it when we're wrong or have done something hurtful or inconsiderate. This alone sowed the seeds for respect and co-operation, and those seeds are now blooming. We've become best friends again.

4) Over the year, I finally ditched the habit of ruminating. If I found myself doing that, I immediately reminded myself that if I'm worrying about something over which I have no control, that's totally counterproductive. No gain, only pain – so no benefit in doing it. That worked. At the start of the year, there were days when I had to do that ten, fifteen times. *The price of freedom is eternal vigilance!* But here I am at the end of the year, and I've become a low-worry-me.

5) Meditating and exercising have helped me release stress and tension. For the most part, I've been feeling calm and optimistic. And I'm fitter!

6) Deep sea diving was on my bucket list, but I never had the courage to do it. As my anxiety faded, I decided it was time to take the plunge and arrange a diving experience. I booked into a scuba diving course. Allan looked after the kids, and I had a wonderful time. After my initial nervousness, I relaxed and loved the undersea world I'd entered. Another dimension. Pushing myself outside my comfort zone has done wonders for my self- respect and confidence. The whole thing was exciting, exhilarating, uplifting and fun! Can't wait to do another dive trek in a year or two!

7) Work has been satisfying and rewarding. I got the promotion I applied for, with a 50% increase in salary. My newfound calm and quiet confidence has transformed my work life as well.

8) As the year drew to a close, I could see how much happier I was in every area of my life. Not only was I no longer anxious. I was also so much more confident and effective in dealing with life's inevitable ups and downs in a philosophical way - whether problems at work, at home with the kids, with my extended family, and most importantly, with Allan. I see them as things I can handle, and I keep them in perspective.

9) I feel so grateful that I've become a genuinely happy person. I have come to realise that the ability to be that was always there within me. I'm simply using the strengths I always had, applying what I've learned and consciously managing my reactions and mood to be the capable, self-loving, caring person I deserve to be. I now believe in the power of possibility, in the power of choice, and what I choose to focus on. I'm looking forward to the future with confidence, humility, excitement, gratitude and optimism. So much more to learn, so many new worlds to conquer.

10) I choose this or something even better for the greatest good of all concerned.

14

SHIFT DEPRESSION
YOU ARE SO POWERFUL!

In his book *'Conversations with God'* Neale Donald Walsch explains that we create our own dreams as well as our own nightmares. We create our dreams when we are driven by love; we create our nightmares when we are driven by fear.

> *'Fear clings to us and clutches all we have, love gives all that we have away. Fear holds close, love lets go. Fear rankles, love soothes. Fear attacks, love amends.'* - Neale Donald Walsch

We have a choice. In every moment, we can choose **love** or **fear**. Don't think, when you're not setting goals, or imagining a bright future, that nothing you're thinking or doing is influencing your future.
You can't help but influence your future, because what you think and feel in this moment, how you respond and behave in this moment, directly influences what happens in the next moment.
If you wake up like a bear with a sore head, fed up, depressed, dreading the coming day, you've already guaranteed you won't make the most of the day. Your body language (scowl, drooping shoulders, shifty gaze) will make others feel ill at ease as they encounter you.
Contrast that with a day where you wake up feeling good, looking

forward to the day ahead. Or contrast a person who wakes up enthusiastic to be going to work, really grateful for his or her job (smiling face, jaunty body language, shoulders back, steady gaze).

How do you think the people she/he encounters will react? Try the experiment yourself on two different days. It's pretty certain that people will be friendlier to, and more comfortable with, the joyful person/this version of you than with the grouchy version.

Managing Depression

Unhappiness and depression often go hand in hand. Depression is an absence of joy. My approach to helping those who are depressed is often transformational. It is based on my belief that we all have the ability to change our lives for the better.

In this style of transformational therapy, a key emphasis is on helping depressed clients become conscious, rather than remain unconscious, of what they are thinking and feeling. When I work with clients with a diagnosis of depression, I introduce much of what is covered earlier in this book, plus other work as appropriate. The order of these processes varies according to what is going on for each individual.

If you're battling depression, apart from seeing your own psychologist, or a psychiatrist if your depression is extremely severe, I invite you also to take yourself on the transformational journey and follow the recommendations and steps described in this book, which I summarise briefly below.

How to Shift Depression

Read the ScriptWriting process, as described in **Part One** of this book. Write your script, place a crystal-clear vision of yourself living the relationship, career and life you'd love in your future, to allow your dreams to become your reality.

Then commit to working through **Part Two** of this book wherein you'll discover how you view the world – whether primarily with pessimism, resentment, blame and fear, or optimism, generosity, forgiveness and love.

Following the guidelines in **Chapter Nine** will help you identify the limiting beliefs which have held you back and show you how to reframe them.

I invite you to experience how you can choose what you focus your attention on and choose what you think. You can keep imagining your life going well, rather than dwelling on obstacles and problems.

This shift is designed to liberate you from living your old story, repeating the disappointments of the past. It frees you to create and embody a new, happier, more fulfilling story, to craft a new identity; to live a new version of **you**.

Depression and anxiety are likely to be accompanied by a strong inner critic. They also accompany a tendency to ruminate by going over problems again and again. If this is true for you, these are habits which have been holding you hostage.

Chapter Twelve shows you how to separate from and challenge your inner critic. It's much more fun to install an inner supporter. This chapter advises against ruminating and worrying about things over which you have no control. It gives you tips and strategies for doing this and recommends you make a commitment to meditate daily.

Chapter Ten introduced you to your inner child. It offers you a great technique to enter into a dialogue with them, so you can better understand their fears and terrors. This allows the Wise Adult in you to re-parent your inner child. It encourages Wise Adult you to start making the decisions, rather than letting your Adaptive Child, the child in adult clothing, run things for you.

We live in a web of quantum entanglement. Our own web is connected to those of significant others. **Chapter Eleven** suggests some ways of increasing the sweetness in your relationships.

In addition to these techniques and practices, therapy for depression may well include processes and modalities not covered here, including antidepressants, physical and lifestyle health management (e.g. healthy diet, exercise, management of insomnia) and treatment for substance abuse.

Additional treatments and support are necessary for those deeply wounded by trauma, CPTSD and PTSD, substance addictions, and other devastating challenges. Building somatic recalibration in your nervous system helps your body to feel safe, decreasing the primitive 'reptilian'/or limbic brain's influence on your behaviour.

Your personal development and your healing journey are ongoing. As you peel one layer of the onion, you'll encounter the layer beneath. Peel that off and find the layer below that one. **The only way forward is forward.**

You may make improvements in some areas, then find other issues which need to be worked on. Life has its ups and downs. It's sometimes two steps forward, one step back. You won't necessarily get there in one step, but I encourage you to keep going. **I encourage you to be committed to becoming the best version of you that you can be.**

There are many obvious benefits to shifting the thinking and behaviours which have locked depression in place. Not least of these benefits is that, as you observe your power to influence what shows up in your life, you can also use this power to change and soften your attitudes to the past, letting go of the intensity of past wrongs and betrayals perpetrated against and by you.

This is part of this book's core mission: **It can help you transform your past.** It can give you future **courage** and **generosity** to embody and fully honour your new story and the role of your fellow actors in your new story (your partner, your children, your parents, your boss).

You can literally deconstruct your past, your interpretations of '*I did, he did, she did,*' and awaken and return to your heart's love on this journey of transformation.

I'm still on the personal development journey I embarked on in the 1990s. I still attend personal development workshops, learn new skills, hone those skills, and make changes in my behaviour patterns. I still meditate. I still write scripts.

In fact, if you are reading this book, it means that my dream, my script for publishing this book, and for reaching and hopefully inspiring fellow human beings to recognise that this is a skill they too can use to create and live their dreams, has come true!

What is Depression and How Can You Recognise its Causes?

Depression is common. Recent statistics reveal that 10% of women and 6% of men state they've had a major depressive episode in the past year – figures that are similar for the US and Australia. And about double this percentage will experience an episode of major depression at some stage of their lives. Until the age of 15, depression affects girls and boys equally, then the rate for girls increases.

According to *The Diagnostic and Statistical Manual of Mental Disorders (DSM-V)*, the mental health professional's manual, at least five of the following symptoms experienced over a two-week period (including at least one of the first two on the list) indicate major depression:

- Depressed mood for much of the day
- Reduced interest in pleasurable activity
- Changes in appetite or weight
- Changes in sleep patterns
- Lack of energy
- Feelings of guilt or worthlessness
- Agitation or slowing down of physical movements
- Inability to concentrate or make decisions
- Recurrent thoughts of death or suicide.

Depression isn't caused by any one thing. It results from a combination of factors, including:

- **Biology**: for example, disturbances in functioning of neurotransmitters
- **History:** for example, family history of conflict, alcoholism, early parental loss or neglect
- **Psychological factors:** personality style, low self-esteem, excessive self-criticism
- **Environmental factors:** stressful events such as job demands, health problems, financial difficulties
- **Social factors:** loneliness; lack of support networks; relationship problems.

Depression caused mainly by biological factors (melancholic depression) accounts for around 10% of cases, whereas the majority of depression is non-melancholic, and is triggered by adverse life events such as a deeply unhappy marriage, breakup of a relationship, serious illness, bereavement, physical disability, job loss, business failure, loss of reputation, a court case and/or social isolation. In this mysterious game of life, there are, unfortunately, lots of things that can cause depression.

Phillip: One of the Faces of Depression

> "I don't feel well at all. That's why I've come to see you. I'm on the edge. I don't know why. Snappy. I lose my temper and I'm drinking. It used to be a glass of wine with dinner. Now it's a bottle. My behaviour is becoming worse. I'm doing what I don't like. It's making my family and friends very uncomfortable. I know it's wrong. Even at work, I find it difficult to focus, to get motivated. I'm not a procrastinator generally. If anything, I tend to be proactive. But not now. I feel so stressed, I feel like I've e got a headache a lot of the time…I realise I'm at a stage where I need professional help. I didn't think I could do it on my own."

Phillip (not his real name), a professional man in his early 40s, presented with severe depression, which had been troubling him for 8 to 12 months.

His DASS (Depression, Anxiety, and Stress Scale) test scores confirmed he was suffering from extremely severe depression, extremely severe anxiety, and extremely severe stress.

His inspirational story shows how, in his case, only six one-hour sessions spread over four months helped him change many things and return to feeling relaxed and enjoying life.

Phillip decided that if this stuff worked, it was going to work for him, because he would give it everything he had. He didn't make excuses to justify his bad behaviour. He accepted responsibility for it and did his best to change it. He didn't just try to make changes; he made them.

His articulate and thoughtful verbatim quotations over the following pages demonstrate what he put into practice, and how dramatically that turned his depression around. His story offers a general guide to help others wishing to make a similar transformation, from depressed and anxious to relaxed and enjoying life.

However, note that this is not a one-size-fits-all solution. I understand your circumstances may well be different or harder to improve than Phillip's. That said, if you are dealing with depression, and you do some or, better still, most of what he describes, how you see and live your life will most likely feel better. If you are still struggling or feel you need help, do not hesitate to seek out individual, personalised support and therapy.

Family of Origin Experiences and Trauma Contribute to Depression

Phillip's history, especially his relatively recent history, predisposed him to depressive episodes. His father died soon after Phillip reached his teens. His stepfather entered his life a couple of years later. He was hard on Phillip, difficult to get on with, and Phillip was sent to boarding school.

Spending most of his time at boarding school, and in the absence of a father's protection and guidance, Phillip's go-to position when he encountered problems was withdrawing and licking his wounds, rather than getting help or talking about his unhappiness.

His last three years had delivered one traumatic event after another: "Little things kept piling up." These included an unsatisfactory career move, the loss of his driver's licence, his mother's death, then witnessing a head-on collision where two people died in front of him and no one else stopped to help.

It's no surprise that this experience of "one thing after another" triggered non-melancholic depression in Phillip. It would be difficult for any of us to shrug off such a series of not-so-small disasters.

However, such adverse events don't occur in a vacuum. The way we interpret them, and how long we hold onto the resultant sadness, is profoundly influenced by our personality and thinking (cognitive) style.

Enter Learned Optimism

In *'Learned Optimism,'* Martin Seligman's seminal book of the 1990s, he divided people into two groups – the primarily **optimistic** versus the primarily **pessimistic**.

His extensive research, not only with individuals but also with groups such as football teams and companies, found that when adversity hit, those who were primarily optimistic and confident, with good self-esteem, reacted very differently from those who were primarily pessimistic, self-critical and lacking in confidence.

When something goes wrong, e.g. you lose your job, the company loses a major customer, the football team loses one match after the other, it's normal and natural to feel upset or concerned. However, optimists bounce back relatively soon and start feeling at least somewhat better, because they see the problem as:

- **Temporary**: *'I've lost my job, but I'll find another one.'*
- **Specific**: *'I've lost my job, but thank heavens my relationship is strong, I've got great kids, and I've got savings to see us through.'*
- **External to themselves**: *'It's because the company is shedding certain divisions, not because there's anything wrong with me.'*

Conversely, pessimists move from sadness and worry into long term grief and fear because they see the same problem as:

- **Permanent**: *'Things are bad now and they'll always be bad.'* AKA "forever thinking"
- **Pervasive**: *'It's not only my job that's a problem. Everything in my life sucks. My marriage is rocky, my kids are a pain, and I don't have enough savings!'*
- **Personal**: *'There's really something wrong with me. Things always go wrong for me.'*

The good news is that **optimism can be learned.** This is important because, as Martin Seligman's research found, optimists have happier relationships, are healthier and live longer. The key message is that we need to learn to challenge our thinking if it's primarily pessimistic.

Changing Our Thinking

After our first session, I emailed Phillip notes on depression and anxiety and recommended he read *Learned Optimism*. This provided psycho-education and guidance to change the way he thought and felt.

From the word go, Phillip was trusting, grateful and conscientious. He said that he found it helpful to see that what he had been doing and thinking was keeping his depression and anxiety alive. More importantly, he started making changes to relieve them.

On his second visit two weeks later, he reported that he was consciously looking at the positives. "I'm not spending too much time thinking about things. I'm trying not to think about the things that bother me." Phillip said that in these two short weeks, his mood seemed to be much more positive.

> "While there are still not as many laughs as there used to be, I'm controlling my anger much better. Little things used to upset me. For example, my son's school clothes lying about would have tipped me off in the past and I would have lost it. I don't do that now. I'm very happy that I'm reacting that way. It was a small thing, but it was almost like a pat on the back."

When I asked him what else was better since I first saw him (reinforcing in his mind that some things were better) he commented that he thought his wife had noticed that he was a lot more positive.

> "The mood of the house has improved. We're all smiling more. We're talking at the dinner table. Not 100%, but a move in the right direction."

Phillip then admitted his relationship with his wife had cooled over the last few years and their social life had all but died.

> "My wife and I used to kiss each other every morning. Then we became so busy, we just rushed off. It's terrible. Going back to where we used to be, doing the nice things we used to do, takes a fair amount of effort."

Philip wanted to work on his marriage, so we devoted that session to:

- Identifying losing strategies common in marriages which are

deteriorating — **the Don'ts** to be avoided, like venting your anger or going sullen and silent and withdrawing.
- Coaching on how to rebuild fondness, trust, love, romance — **the Do's** to be practised, like *'Ask for what you want, rather than complain about what you don't like. Learn how to cherish your partner and your relationship.'*

Again, I emailed Philip notes, to remind him of what we had covered, and what he could do differently from now on. Over the next two weeks he put considerable effort into reviving affection and emotional intimacy with his wife.

Moreover, following my recommendation that he practise meditation and mindfulness, he and his wife enrolled in an eight-week meditation course. He also followed the recommendation to contact old friends to invite them to dinner or meet for a coffee.

Living Our Values – The Compass for Our Life

The next step in therapy was helping Phillip identify his relationship **values**: we established *'What's important to you in your intimate relationship?'* as detailed in Chapter Four.

Whenever I've helped a client get in touch with what's really important to him or her in their relationship, those relationship values have always been positive and beautiful. It's not that we don't know what a good relationship looks like. It's that we often behave in ways that undermine the loving, respectful, considerate and caring relationship we say we want.

Mental rehearsal is very powerful in influencing upcoming events in your life. Just as sports coaches of elite athletes get them to imagine themselves winning the game, I used the NLP (Neuro-Linguistic Programming) process where I simply read his own values back to him.

I then asked him to picture his future self in the relationship where he knew all of this was present. I asked him to turn up the volume on the feeling of rightness and joy at being happy with his wife again. He then placed this 'mind's eye photo' of himself into his future, took some deep breaths, and blew vitality into it.

He also wrote a script for the year he really wanted, with a particular emphasis on how good he was feeling and how his relationships had transformed.

To say that Phillip was surprised and delighted at the way his marriage improved is an understatement. At the next session, he described how sweetness and joy had come back.

> "Our hellos and goodbyes are more affectionate, emotional. We say, 'How was your day?' We're interested in what's going on in each other's day again. We used to do that. We stopped. Now we're doing it again. It's very important to me. It makes me feel I'm connecting with people again."

By the fourth session Phillip said he was feeling much happier.

> "I'm doing the right thing. The whole mindfulness thing you sent me has made such a difference. Now I focus on the simple thing I'm doing, one moment at a time. I don't feel as busy, or overwhelmed. I don't feel like I need to be doing things all the time. It's a mental state you move into. After you climb this mountain, there's another mountain.
>
> Now I enjoy the climb. I value what I'm doing. I'm present climbing this mountain, not just going through the motions. And I'm no longer drinking – no more second bottle of wine at dinner. I keep telling myself this will become a habit – my natural way of doing things.
>
> I'm writing down three things I'm grateful for, every day. I was not enjoying my life. I could see people around me were not enjoying me. Changing that had to be a deliberate act, to do little things, like watching plenty of comedies.
>
> I'm deliberately thinking positively, making a choice to have a good day, meeting friends for coffee, showing affection and admiration for my wife. We've had some people over whom we used to have dinner with. Refreshing to see them again, enjoyable chit chat. Life's absolutely more enjoyable for me. I don't recognise myself at all as I was living in a way which was causing me a lot of stress."

And this is what Philip did with the recommendation to ask for what he wanted, rather than complain about what he dislikes:

"I'm feeling more relaxed. I can see the positive results of working on things. I do the cooking, but I've asked my family 'Can you help with the dishes? Then the workload is shared.' Both my son and my wife are helping. It's good for me and my family that they know why I was stressed and angry. There's still a long way to go, but instead of being stuck and unhappy, I'm definitely heading in the right direction."

Taking Time-Outs

True to form, having made the decision he was going to implement every strategy he had learned to improve his behaviour, Philip also followed the recommendation to take Time-Outs when he felt he was about to lose it.

Time-Outs are an agreement you make, a contract you take out with yourself, and with your partner, that you will deliberately take at least 20 minutes to 'cool down' and regain composure when you're triggered, or where an argument is escalating. This allows you to stop, to breathe and to think, *'How do I want to behave here? What will be the best thing I can do for us and for the relationship?'*

When you're reacting with self-righteous indignation, defending yourself for all you're worth, when you want your partner to admit she was wrong, your anger is guaranteed to fuel hers and things are likely to get uglier and uglier.

You may recall from Chapter Eleven that couples therapy guru Terry Real asks: *'Who's right? Who's wrong? Who cares?'*

In other words, **rather than having the satisfaction of being proved right,** whatever the cost to the relationship and the goodwill between you and your partner, **you choose to do what will best nurture the relationship.**

Time-Outs move us from our primitive limbic brain knee-jerk where we experience the black-and-white reaction of the child in grown-up clothing within, to the possibility of a more conscious or considered reaction. This is the wise, flexible and considered reaction of the functional adult using the prefrontal cortex or executive brain.

As Philip said, "When I yelled at my family, it made me feel a lot worse. Now I'm trying not to let little things get to me. It's hard. Occasionally, when I see something that's not right and the anger is building,

Create Abundant Possibilities

I decide I need a bit of time out. I decide I need to do a bit of weeding. That gives me space, it shifts my consciousness and allows me to regain my composure. When I come back inside, I can be reasonable instead of expressing my fury."

Reflecting on What Could Have Given You a Better Outcome

As the therapy progressed, Phillip also acknowledged how beneficial he had found it each night to briefly reflect on what had not gone well that day. Then, in his mind's eye, he re-ran the event, imagining himself saying or doing something that would have worked out better. He also set his intentions for the next day by briefly picturing it as a good day. At the second last session, he reported:

"I'm generally very comfortable, very relaxed. I continue with a little diary at night. I just spend 10 minutes where I look at what was good and bad today; at what I could have done to improve that outcome. Then I think about how I'd like tomorrow to be. I like that. It's working. Perhaps it allows me to reflect and tell myself there are a lot of things I can manage by handling them better in the future, just doing something differently than I did today. It's making me more resourceful, more confident. There was a time when I felt overwhelmed. I couldn't control things. It's been empowering. For example, last week, in the middle of what I was doing, my son came in wanting to tell me something important to him. I told him I didn't have time.

That night, as I ran through what had happened, I thought I could have handled that better. I could have put aside what I was doing and listened to him. Next day I made a point of telling him that and apologising to him. He really appreciated it. I find it's almost like daily therapy. It's the most productive thing I could have taken on board. I notice that as things get better, they get better still. Not just with immediate family, but also when you deal with people in a more positive way, they respond in a more pleasant way. I say, 'That's fine. It's not a problem,' and I notice, in the back of my mind, I like that the person noticed I reacted that way. I like that I didn't get angry, that it's not something to get angry about. I remember you said conscious living means if you're doing something that's giving you an outcome you don't like, do anything but that. To get a different outcome, you have to do something different."

What Phillip Got from Therapy

Phillip's last words to me were what every therapist loves to hear:

"This has changed my life. I can't begin to describe how terrible I'd feel when I woke up in the morning 'Oh, another day!' Now I get up early. I jump out of bed and the day hums along.

My relationship with my wife is so much more pleasant. It's almost like it was at the start. I'll continue to work on it because I see the improvement. I had stopped doing things I really enjoyed. You tend to forget that little things do matter. The things you enjoy tend to go on the back burner. I think if I hadn't sought help, things would have got much worse, and who knows? Often things don't turn out the way you had hoped. It still stresses me out when that happens, but now, instead of blaming myself, I move on with the next best option. I personally cannot believe the transformation in the way I view things now. I liked to be in control before. I think I must have upset my friends because they'd stopped including me. I feel good that they've started including me again.

The meditation course teaches that every moment presents an opportunity to reflect and choose. Nothing has changed, but everything has changed. It's a choice I make that I will not look at things in a negative way. Everything has a positive side. Just looking at life in a different way has made such a huge difference."

I'd have to say that Phillip was a model client. He followed every piece of coaching. He put into practice all of the recommendations I gave him about how to manage depression and anxiety and how to rebuild and nurture his relationships.

For example, after I suggested he join a meditation group, the next session he'd enrolled. He then went on to attend each of the fortnightly meditation classes.

Quite simply, he put his all into implementing the strategies and recommendations. The good news is, as Phillip's story shows, therapy can dramatically improve your mental health, your marriage, your well-being, the way you live your life. It can improve your children's lives and their future as well!

Does every client get such good results? Truth be told, the level of improvement varies.

Some clients don't bother to make the changes suggested, or make them half-heartedly and inconsistently, or make them only short-term and then return to their former patterns. Those clients are unlikely to see much change.

Substance addictions need treatment in their own right. Because trauma and neglect in childhood cast such a long shadow before them, some clients need to do trauma work to help build their sense of safety, trust, and wholeness.

A severely dysfunctional marriage, say, with a partner having an affair, and/or suffering from an untreated mental illness, and/or addiction, or a partner who isn't willing to make any changes and be accountable, may require more couples therapy than Phillip's marriage did.

It is nonetheless encouraging to see a relationship improve if only one partner starts doing the things that nurture, rather than things that damage the relationship.

A Hypothetical Script for Someone Who's Depressed

In a similar vein to the hypothetical script for someone suffering anxiety, I offer this hypothetical or sample script which could be written by someone who is depressed. The intention, if you're depressed, is to give you ideas for a script you might write to signal the universe (and yourself) you're ready to dump your old story of who you are and how life is. In writing your script, make sure you take the stance that you've made really worthwhile changes, and you're reacting to and interpreting life in an optimistic way.

> *30 April 2026*
>
> *1) Last year, four months into therapy, I put pen to paper and wrote this script describing the life I had longed to lead. I had already learned about the power of my thoughts, how they act like a tuning fork and draw what I believe to be true to me, like a self-fulfilling prophecy. I had gone*

through the exercises of identifying and reframing my limiting beliefs, I'd worked on integrating the Deeper Truths of the strengths and gifts underlying my core limited identity pattern. I'd visualised myself in a happy, loving relationship, as well as being valued and happy at work. I'd upgraded my communication and relationship skills. My depression had lifted. This is my script for the new me, for the life of my dreams:

2) I am deeply grateful for the way my thinking has changed over the last year. Instead of waking up filled with dread and reluctant to get up and face another day, I now wake with a lightness and enthusiasm about what lies ahead. I am so much more cheerful. I see the good in myself and in things that happen. I have dropped my old tendency to expect the worst. I got better and better, as the year went by, in cutting myself lots of slack, and showing myself and others compassion and care when I ran into problems. I seem so much more capable of being resilient and turning things around. I loved the nightly exercise of revisiting something which didn't turn out the way I had hoped that day, then imagining what I could have done or said which would have given me a better outcome. It's a bit like rehearsing what happened in reverse, after it's already happened. Realising that I could come up with ways of handling things better than I had done in the actual moment of stress gave me more respect for my resourcefulness. And I've found less seems to be going wrong!

3) When I started meditating, I felt I wasn't very good at it. However, I came to love it because, as the weeks went by, it gave me a sense of inner peace and a quiet mind.

4) I have been conscientious about going to the gym, walking, and attending a yoga class every week. I am a lot fitter and stronger now than I was at the start of this year. I was also motivated to eat a healthier diet, because I wanted to look after my body. I have been nurturing the belief that I deserve to treat myself with love and care, and whenever I felt tempted to eat junk food, I reminded myself I owe myself better treatment. I've been treating myself the way I want other people to treat me- as if I matter!

5) I cannot believe the extent of the improvement in my relationship with Sienna. It is now rare for us to argue, which is a big improvement. We have definitely succeeded in turning around bad habits that had crept in year by year. We now work on behaving like wise adults rather than getting stuck in the dysfunction of our inner children. 'I'm sorry' comes easily now to both of us and we have accommodated each other's needs much more than we've been defensive and uncooperative. We revived our old ritual of hugging and kissing 'Goodbye' before leaving the house, 'Hello' when we come home. Another practice we committed to was making time to catch up on what was going on in each other's life. We've made a point of genuinely listening and being interested in each other's headlines of the day. The feeling of caring, connection and fondness has returned, big time. Now we can't believe how we could have let that slip. We've become more emotionally intimate, and found it's the precursor of physical intimacy, so our sex life's regained some of its former energy and passion.

6) In the therapy, I identified and saw where my feelings of not being good enough professionally came from, and how the voice of my inner critic had fuelled my self-doubt. I metaphorically cleared the toxic thoughts and weeds in my mind and imagined doors swinging open for me. I've visualised myself being acknowledged and valued at work. It's almost ridiculous how quickly things improved. The last six months have been the best of my working life. I have enjoyed work and felt more comfortable with my colleagues. As my depression lifted, my concentration improved, and I felt more energised. Another bonus was that I've been more efficient and relaxed in accomplishing what I need to do. I feel confident next year will be even better, because I'll have the trust and enthusiasm to write an even more powerful script for the year to come.

7) As I managed my depression, and realised how I'd been isolating myself, I consciously followed a plan of contacting old friends, and my social life looked up again. I saw the value of fun and entertainment again. I recognise that I have choices in everything I do, and in everything I believe and think, and I intend to use my choices well.

8) As I look back on what has turned around for me this year, I feel deeply grateful that I now understand and have learned the skills to manage my thoughts, my behaviour and my intentions. I intend to aim for the stars. I have learned that I, like everyone else I share this planet with, deserve to be happy. This is now embedded in my psyche. I believe that's the key to maintaining good mental and physical health.

9) I choose this or something even better for the greatest good of all concerned.

If you are depressed, and you choose to do even parts of what this script suggests, I guarantee some of your depression will lift. As one thing improves, so will another. How can it be other than that?

Choose with Love

The hero of this book is ScriptWriting. Script yourself not just a good future. Script yourself a GREAT future. If that future is the possibility you imagine, you dramatically increase the odds of that possibility becoming a probability.

Make no mistake. You are making powerful choices, moment by moment. You either do this consciously, being aware you are creating your future, or you do it unconsciously and reactively, without due consideration that you are in fact influencing what you experience. You can't not do so.

Author and philosopher Aldous Huxley famously said, *'Experience is not what happens to you; it's what you do with what happens to you.'*

The theme of this book is the incredible power of the very words you use, your thoughts, your expectations and your behaviour in determining what you experience and attract into your life. If what has been showing up for you is what you don't like, the key to changing that is to change what you believe and how you behave.

The stories in this book are of people like you who have overcome their limitations and literally changed their life from one of struggle to one of grace. I hope you found their stories both encouraging and inspirational. That said, like me, they haven't arrived at a permanent destination of paradise. We're on the path. Change and movement are inevitable.

A resourceful and optimistic way of interpreting events and wise choices of what actions to take will help them, and me, continue to live with grace in the face of the inevitable ups and downs of life.

You may need to dig deep and get help to identify the sabotage programs that lurk in your shadow and your unconscious mind. You may need therapy and life coaching to help you release trauma, and conditioning, to actualise your potential. This book shows you several ways in which you can do that. It places you firmly on the path of transformation. It also recommends other books and workshops to continue the progression.

Reacting with resignation, as though this is your fate, denies you the empowerment of learning new skills and choosing to use your power to maximise the happiness and satisfaction in your life. Thinking and behaving with love, generosity, gratitude, trust, and faith that you deserve to be happy, and life can be good, will open doors to love, abundance and wellbeing. Conversely, thinking and behaving with fear, greed, resentment, doubt, disillusionment and distrust will attract more of that into your life.

Choose wisely. No wo(man) is an island. Your thinking and choices interconnect and intertwine around mine and contribute to our shared reality.

What of Your Future?

As we say farewell, I hope you feel inspired to script the future that will make you truly, deeply, wildly happy. Script the future you dream of, the future your inner child would love to be a part of. **You deserve to be happy.**

If you are running old stories about what is wrong, if you keep alive and revisit unhappy memories, if you let your beliefs limit what is possible, I invite you to follow the steps in this book, and commit to taking its transformational journey. This will change your perception not only of your present and future, but also of your past.

My dream, my longing for you, is that you'll look back on times of struggle and disappointment in your life and think, *"If only I'd known then what I know now. My past would have looked different. But you know what? I'm so glad I released those saboteurs I needed to let go of. I'm so grateful I now have the understanding and the tools to live a life I love."*

I invite you to script a beautiful, promising future for yourself, for your neighbours, for all life on Planet Earth. Together, let us script a wonderful future, a glorious next phase of evolution for our beautiful planet, for the greatest good of all concerned.

I would love to hear from you, to learn how these practices change your life.

WENDY MCARA

I leave you with my love and blessings that you experience your full measure of love, abundance and wellbeing.

∼

EPILOGUE

This is a book about aligning with abundant possibility and manifesting your dreams: individual possibility, collective possibility, planetary possibility.

I have sat with this gift for decades; teaching individuals and small groups how to fulfil their dreams. Not until now, in the huge crisis and widespread anxiety during and following the pandemic, on top of other global changes, have I felt compelled to share it widely, via this book.

No one can doubt that change is upon us. Once-certain and predictable systems and structures have been shown to be illusory and fragile as the global economy, political systems, climate variations and our daily lives and lifestyles totter and crumble into dust, making way for new ways of living and being.

We are being forced to choose anew, as old choices fade away – choosing anew as individuals, as communities, as nations. Be acutely aware of your profound responsibility for what you create, given that this thought and this moment, gives birth to the next thought and the next moment and then what occurs as a result. Join with me, dear reader, and choose with love in your heart, conscious that your thoughts and intentions carry consequences for you and our shared world.

My dream and heart-felt intention is that you and I be part of creating what helps us transition into a different future of spiritually evolved humans. We are here to create and bring to life generous, generative solutions for the new Earth. This is the dawning of a golden era of purity of intent and expanded spiritual evolution. The ball is well and truly in our court.

No more blaming, no more judgement, no more defensiveness.

Collectively, our power is huge. Let's use it wisely, with love rather than fear. Please choose for the greatest good of all concerned!

RESOURCES

Recommended Books, Workshops & Trainings

In today's world, we have the resources of the universe at our fingertips. We've all become adept at tapping into the information we'd like to find with the mere act of typing in a keyword.

This is a list of the authors, the books and the workshops I've quoted, in the order in which they appear in the book.

They, of course, provide leads to other inspirational resources, should you want to delve deeper and deeper into topics I've touched on.

Mahni Dugan
Future Pace Workshops
A suite of workshops, primarily NLP based, which opened the doors to personal growth for me in the 1990s.

Neale Donald Walsh
Conversations with God
Neale Donald Walsch's God book series has been translated into 37 languages and influenced millions of people world-wide. I have loved and used his teachings in my life.

Rhonda Byrne
The Secret
Rhonda Byrne created and produced the worldwide book and film phenomenon, *The Secret*. It featured many of the thought leaders and teachers of manifestation and the Law of Attraction. Its success catapulted her onto Time Magazine's 100 Most Successful People in the World in 2007.

Alex Chen
https://www.weeklywisdomblog.com
Alex Chen writes about how manifestation works through quantum physics. He details the work of quantum physicists, which demonstrates how physical matter arises from non-physical wave energy.

Dr Joe Dispenza
Breaking the Habit of Being Yourself, © 2012 Hay House LLC, Carisbad, CA.
With a background in chemistry and neuroscience, Dr Joe Dispenza has reached thousands of people in 24 countries. His talks, workshops and books teach how to reprogram your thinking through scientifically proven neurophysiological principles.

Resources

Dr Clare Zammit
Claire Zammit set up and drives her brilliantly successful online transformational learning enterprises, Evolving Wisdom, and Feminine Power Academy. Her Feminine Power courses and Life Coach trainings are, in my view, the holy grail. You can do no better than to enrol. It will transform and upgrade your life.

Terrence Real
The New Rules of Marriage and
Us: Getting Past You & Me to Build a More Loving Relationship
Terry Real is a New York Times bestselling author. I see his state-of-the-art Relational Life Therapy as the most effective model of couple therapy available today. His highly professional Relational Life Institute now provides training to hundreds of therapists.

Dr John Gottman
The Seven Principles for Making Marriage Work
John Gottman is renowned for his extensive research to identify key differences in ways of dealing with problems and differences of opinion in the communication styles of people who end up divorced – whom he dubs 'Relationship Disasters'- versus those who stay happily married – his so-called 'Relationship Masters.'

Amoraea
The Beloved Within
Amoraea is a psychologist and spiritual teacher. He offers extraordinary online workshops for international audiences. I recently attended *'The Beloved Within'* and I can't recommend it highly enough.

Marianne Williamson
A Return to Love
Marianne Williamson is one of the great spiritual teachers of our times.

Jane Monica-Jones
The Billionaire Buddha
Jane is a psychotherapist, author and workshop presenter who specialises in helping people with issues around money and financial security shift self-sabotaging thinking and patterns and change their financial future.

Tim Carter
Journey into The Light
In his heartfelt book, filled with gentle wisdom and guidance, Tim Carter invites and shows you how to awaken and reconnect with your essential nature. This book introduces you to your inner child. It teaches how to access your own inner guidance and find meaning and purpose in your life.

Richard Wiseman
The Luck Factor
A funny and entertaining lecturer, Professor Wiseman talks about *'quirkology, the use of*

scientific methods to study the more curious aspects of everyday life'. In his book and his Luck School, he teaches *'four simple principles that will change your luck and your life'.*

Dr Jean Houston
Quantum Powers Online Workshop
The Possible Human
A prodigiously prolific author and spiritual teacher, Jean Houston has a formidable reputation and has coached and co-authored books with some of the most famous people on the planet.
Her work on manifestation offers a giant leap in using the principles taught in this book for those committed to this journey of learning to co-create with the universe.

Eckhart Tolle
The Power of Now
Self-help and spiritual teacher, best-selling author and presenter on world stages, Eckhart Tolle assures us that the constant and often negative dialogue in our heads is separate from who we really are.
His teaching is to focus on the power of Presence, the awakened state of consciousness.

Dr Stephen B. Karpman
A Game Free Life
Psychiatrist Stephen Karpman is the originator of the Karpman Drama Triangle.
His social model of human interaction contributes to the understanding and healing of dysfunctional relationships.

Dr Jennice Vilhauer
Think Forward to Thrive
Dr Jennice Vilhauer is an expert in cognitive therapy, and consultant to Fortune 100 companies. Her research, therapy and 'Mindset Retraining' are designed to shift unhelpful thinking, to help people regain emotional wellbeing and thrive.

Cheryl Richardson
The Art of Extreme Self Care - 12 Practical and Inspiring Ways to Love Yourself More
This book provides twelve months of guidance and actionable practices to increase self love.

Dr Sarah Edelman
Change Your Thinking
Sarah Edelman's Cognitive Behavior Therapy (CBT) book is a classic clinical psychologist's practical guide to help people who suffer from anxiety and depression manage their negative emotions.

Terri Cole
Boundary Boss
Boundary Boss is loaded with great guidance and tips from renowned psychotherapist,

Resources

Terri Cole. It shows over-functioning, over-delivering people-pleasers who ignore their own needs how to set clear boundaries so that they can live the life they deserve.

Eleanor Payson
The Wizard of Oz and Other Narcissists
This is an evidence-based delineation of the world of entrapment and disempowerment created by narcissistic people for the victims that fall under their sway. Payson makes skilful use of case studies which demonstrate the dynamics set in place in relationships with narcissists and provides a brilliant outline of this world.

Dr David Hawkins
The Map of Consciousness Explained - The Proven Energy Scale to Activate Your Ultimate Potential
As a practising psychiatrist, Dr David Hawkins married clinical and scientific experience with mysticism. His exploration and teaching of consciousness research was devoted to the spiritual evolution of mankind.

Martin Seligman
Learned Optimism
Martin Seligman is known as the father of the science of positive psychology. His best sellers *Learned Optimism* and *Authentic Happiness* offer a wealth of encouragement and provide simple, easily applied techniques to enhance optimism and increase happiness.

Dr Peter Levine
Trauma-Proofing Your Kids
A therapist, a prolific author of many books and a trainer of therapists, Peter Levine has been a leader in the field of the healing of psychological trauma via Somatic Experiencing Therapy.

To learn more go to: https://www.wendymcara.com.au/.

ACKNOWLEDGEMENTS

I owe a huge debt of gratitude to the many wonderful therapists, authors, workshop presenters, mentors and healers who taught me what I needed to learn, to change things I needed to change, to become a better partner, better mother, better person, better life coach and therapist.

I'm still learning, always aiming for a higher level of consciousness, a greater level of expertise. It is all these teachers working through me, who have wrought the wonderful changes and provided the techniques described in this book.

I wish to make special mention of, and give grateful thanks to the late Mahni Dugan, who introduced me to ScriptWriting, belief reframing and NLP processes.

I also honour my dear friend and mentor, Belinda Pate McDonald, without whom this book would not have been written. Her fingerprints are all over the book. Her insights and vision guided the structure, the toolkit was her idea, and she has provided encouragement and invaluable support at all stages of the birth, gestation and delivery.

Dominique Wolf Amanzi is another who has helped shape my life path, and I am deeply grateful for her help and inspiration.

Many teachers, trainers and therapists have preceded me. I stand on their shoulders and have stitched together my eclectic approach from what I have learned from them.

I thank my lovely editor, Lisa Murray of *'Creative Alchemy'*, for her wise and transformational guidance. She helped me see my book and my writing through new eyes, to help it fulfil its destiny.

I thank Meri France Harli of *Meri France Publishing* for her wonderful support and guidance as she walked me through the publishing journey with professionalism, enthusiasm and encouragement. She made publishing a simple and enjoyable experience for me.

For the beautiful cover, which is my book's face to the world, I would like to thank the wonderful designer, Georgia Wilson.

I single out Terry Real for special thanks and acknowledgment, for his brilliant work as a passionate leader in current couples therapy. I love the way his relational approach to working with couples takes on the dysfunction we have inherited from the patriarchy and offers a way back from individualistic 'you' versus 'me' to the 'us' of the couple. I love the role modelling for healthy non-violent relating he provides for the next generations because I believe parental relationships and families are the nursery for social and cultural norms. It is in ourselves as individuals, and in our intimate relationships and families that the healing needs to start.

I am also indebted to Claire Zammit for her inspirational work identifying and transforming the core identity blocks that hold us back. Participating in her '*Feminine Power*' workshop, I felt I had discovered the holy grail. My life coaching is now informed by her Feminine Power coaching model.

My thanks to Peter, my husband, for typing the first draft, for his professional editing and suggestions, and for his belief in me. His unfailing admiration and unconditional love are the wind beneath my wings.

To those who have read and provided feedback on my manuscript, great gratitude – my daughter, Gina Bloom; and friends and colleagues, John Edmonds and Dr Anna Banning.

Thanks to Carol Davis for help with the title, and Michael Davis for encouraging me to write.

Special thanks, great gratitude and love go to my reviewers for the beautiful mirror they hold up to my book: Paula Fenwick, David Kerr, Julie-Anne Geddes, Jane Monica-Jones, Jann Walsh, Wanda McGill, Leisa McMahon, Lena Nordholm, Tim Carter, Jan Hatch, Carol Davis, and Meri France Harli.

The clients who have helped me observe what works and who have done the hard yards of applying what I have shared are heroes of this book. My prayer is that their stories and successes encourage many to keep travelling their journey and shoot for the stars. Each of us has a choice in each moment. As more and more of us recognise how powerful our thoughts and conscious intentions are in manifesting the world we share, our collective power is capable of shifting us from fear to love, from a troubled world to an enlightened, uplifted, spiritually evolved humanity.

    I hope you enjoyed my book. If you did, I would greatly appreciate if you'd kindly give it a 5-star rating and post a review on Amazon.

In gratitude and love,

Wendy

www.ingramcontent.com/pod-product-compliance
Lightning Source LLC
Chambersburg PA
CBHW062155080426
42734CB00010B/1700